Ethics in Marketing

Understanding and appreciating the ethical dilemmas associated with business is an important dimension of marketing strategy. Increasingly, matters of corporate social responsibility are part of marketing's domain.

Ethics in Marketing contains 20 cases that deal with a variety of ethical issues such as questionable selling practices, exploitive advertising, counterfeiting, product safety, apparent bribery and channel conflict that companies face across the world. A hallmark of this book is its international dimension along with high-profile case studies that represent situations in European, North American, Chinese, Indian, and South American companies. Well known multinationals like Caterpillar, Coca Cola, Cadbury and Facebook are featured. The two introductory chapters cover initial and advanced perspectives on ethical and socially responsible marketing in order to provide students with the necessary theoretical foundation to engage in ethical reasoning. A decision-making model is also presented for use in the case analyses.

This unique case-book provides students with a global perspective on ethics in marketing and can be used in a free standing course on marketing ethics or marketing and society or as a supplement to the readings for other marketing classes.

Patrick E. Murphy is Professor of Marketing at the University of Notre Dame, USA. His research on marketing ethics has been published in *Journal of Marketing, Journal of Business Ethics, Journal of Macromarketing, Journal of Public Policy & Marketing* and *European Journal of Marketing.*

Gene R. Laczniak is Professor of Marketing at Marquette University, USA. His research and commentary on marketing and society issues has been published in *Journal of Public Policy & Marketing, Long Range Planning, Journalism Quarterly* and the *Journal of Macromarketing.*

Andrea Prothero is Associate Professor in Marketing at University College Dublin, Ireland. Her research on societal and sustainability issues has been published in *Journal of Public Policy & Marketing, Journal of Macromarketing, Consumption, Markets* and *Culture and European Journal of Marketing.*

Ethics in Marketing

International cases and perspectives

**Written and edited by
Patrick E. Murphy,
Gene R. Laczniak and
Andrea Prothero**

 Routledge
Taylor & Francis Group

LONDON AND NEW YORK

First published 2012
by Routledge
2 Park Square, Milton Park, Abingdon, Oxon OX14 4RN

Simultaneously published in the USA and Canada
by Routledge
711 Third Avenue, New York, NY 10017

Routledge is an imprint of the Taylor & Francis Group, an informa business

British Library Cataloguing in Publication Data
A catalogue record for this book is available from the British Library

Library of Congress Cataloging in Publication Data
Murphy, Patrick E., 1948-
   Ethics in marketing : international cases / Patrick E. Murphy, Gene R. Laczniak
   and Andrea Prothero.
      p. cm.
   Includes bibliographical references and index.
   1. Marketing—Moral and ethical aspects. 2. Marketing—Case studies.
I. Laczniak, Eugene R. II. Prothero, Andrea. III. Title.
   HF5415.M8348 2012
   174'.4—dc23   2011032118

ISBN: 978-0-415-78351-4 (hbk)
ISBN: 978-0-415-78352-1 (pbk)
ISBN: 978-0-203-13268-5 (ebk)

Typeset in Times New Roman
by Cenveo Publisher Services

Printed and bound by CPI Group (UK) Ltd, Croydon, CR0 4YY

Contents

Figures, tables, and boxes

Figures

Tables

Boxes

Case contributors

Jacob Bagha

Jared Benson

Karin Besenbaeck

Lori Lepp Corbett

Geert Demuijnck

Marie Derdzinski

Ethan Fairy

Stephanie Fernandez

Rachel Fisher

Katie Hesemann

Raymond F. Keyes

Barbora Kocanova

Gene R. Laczniak

Ryan Mack

Urvashi Mathur

Rachel Mellard

Brendan D. Murphy

Patrick E. Murphy

Nyla Obaid

Andrea Prothero

Marie-Theres Riegler

Nicholas J.C. Santos

Jennifer Sawayda

Alicja Spaulding

Barbara Stottinger

Mark Vander Heiden

Veronika Vosykova

Matt Yepez

Preface

The overriding purpose for assembling this book of cases is to foster discussion about ethical and socially responsible behavior in marketing. When trust in business is at an all-time low, as it is at the time of this writing, all stakeholders in the business system need to take some remedial action. We envision this text as contributing to the rebuilding of trust by helping students recognize the higher-order obligations of marketing as well as by providing a forum to discuss critical issues and incidents that raise questions about ethics in marketing.

We see this book as being flexible enough to serve many purposes. For example, it could be one of two or three featured books in a "marketing ethics" or "marketing and society" class. Or it could easily be used as a supplementary text, helping to cover ethical issues, in almost any marketing course. This casebook includes enough variety that it will allow instructors to select and combine short cases and/or longer cases, as befits their class needs and preferred pedagogical approach.

We also view this book as attempting to accomplish several specific objectives. First, we want to raise the ethical awareness and recognition of students and managers. A writer in a famous business ethics article observed, "Real moral dilemmas are ambiguous, and many of us hike right through them, unaware that they exist." At a minimum, heightened awareness and recognition of ethical issues in the practice of marketing is essential. Second, we identify core ethical concepts and, in so doing, contribute to the baseline "ethical knowledge" (see Chapters 1 and 2) that managers of marketing ought to possess. Third, we hope that the students and managers who use this book will improve their ethical judgment—that is, their moral reasoning skills and their ethical decision-making should be enhanced. Finally, we hope to stimulate a willingness to undertake ethical leadership on the part of our readers. Enhancing the capacity to play a central role in doing business *ethically* is our aspiration for the next generation of marketing managers and business leaders.

We believe that the goal of business organizations is not purely bottom-line driven. Instead, as stewards of the economic resources of society, organizations and their managers, also have a responsibility to contribute to the well-being of the broader community as they discharge their duties. Without diminishing the latest theoretical knowledge in the study of marketing, we believe marketing practice is self-actualized only when marketing strategy and tactics are tempered with a concern for ethics—that is, conducted with integrity, fairness, and justice in the marketplace.

This book is divided into three parts, and a few words about each are warranted. Some students and marketing practitioners think that cases and situations in ethics can be discussed without a theoretical context. They believe their opinion is as good as the next person's.

We disagree. Hence, Chapters 1 and 2 contain material on seven basic perspectives for ethical and socially responsible marketing. These foundational and advanced perspectives can be used as touchstones to help evaluate whether the discussion of the case situations remains "ethics focused." The cases that appear in Parts 2 and 3 can best be analyzed using the concepts introduced in the initial two chapters. We would particularly draw your attention to Box 1.1, which describes the professional code of ethical norms and values for marketers, promulgated by the American Marketing Association. It is our hope that these ethical perspectives will be used extensively by marketing students, managers, and executives in their reflections about ethical questions flowing from marketing practice.

Chapter 3 contains a single case—L'Oreal—and includes a discussion of two possible approaches to examining the cases in the remainder of the book. One approach is to follow the seven-step process for analyzing any ethical problem or situation as discussed in Chapter 2 of the text. The second approach is to answer the questions that are posed at the end of each case. Regardless of which approach is followed, it is imperative that the subsequent cases should be analyzed in a systematic fashion. The final resolution of this particular case is discussed in the "Rest of the Story" section.

Parts 2 and 3 both feature 10 cases. Each case deals with one or more ethical situations that marketing practitioners may face. The cases in these Parts are of two types. Some deal with well-known companies such as eBay, Coca-cola, Facebook, Cadbury, and Caterpillar. However, several cases are from less well-known companies or are "disguised" situations where the names of the company and/or participants have been changed. Some academics resist the use of disguised cases because of the wealth of documented business records that presently exists. Nonetheless, ethics cases are often a special situation. When it comes to the possibly unethical and illegal activity that is alleged *but not proven* in "ethics cases," it is sometimes necessary to provide a veil of anonymity because of the ultimate truth of exactly what happened is in dispute. Importantly, the situations described in these "disguised cases" were all drawn from recent, real-world events that occurred in a particular firm or firms in the industry at focus. Part 2 presents shorter cases that allow for discussion in a more compressed time period. The cases in Part 3 are more complex and would almost certainly require a longer class period devoted to their discussion and analysis.

It is our hope that these initial chapters and cases will stimulate meaningful and enlightening discussion about ethics in marketing. While this textbook alone cannot reduce the number of ethical challenges that marketing managers will face, it should make each reader better prepared to cope with and respond to such dilemmas. We have great admiration for the many highly ethical and hardworking marketing managers throughout the world whose reputation is tarnished by the unethical actions of a minority of their peers. We are optimistic that the next generation of marketing executives will be even better prepared to take the "high road" in their professional lives.

In closing, we encourage our marketing students to always do good work, to be well, and ever seek to maintain their personal integrity since it is a prized and irreplaceable possession.

Acknowledgments

A book of any type requires the efforts of a large number of people. This one is no different. Many individuals contributed to various aspects of this text—the case writers, our university support staff, and the entire Routledge team.

We particularly want to recognize the authors of the cases that appear in Parts 2 and 3. Several of our marketing and ethics academic colleagues have contributed cases that we hope will make for stimulating discussion. They are Geert Demuijnk of EDHEC in France, the late Raymond Keyes of Boston College, Barbara Stottinger of Vienna University of Economics and Business, Nicholas Santos of Santa Clara University, and Jennifer Sawanda of the University of New Mexico. Several of Professor Laczniak's and Murphy's former undergraduate and MBA students at Marquette, Notre Dame and Vienna University of Economics and Business have also authored cases that appear in this book. They are recognized in the credits associated with the individual cases. To all our case authors, we offer a heart-felt thank you.

As academics who have been teaching ethics for a long period, we would like to thank our respective past students, who over the years, have contributed to interesting and lively debates about all things ethical. Their participation in class discussions, has kept alive and strengthened our own interests in this important field of inquiry. And we look forward to jointly deliberating on the new cases in this book with our future students.

The process of assembling this material, editing some of it, and putting it in a usable format was a challenge. Two individuals at the University of Notre Dame especially assisted in this endeavor. Stephanie Piszczor, a former marketing student, did extensive editing on several of the cases and also assisted in organizing the permissions to reprint the cases. Deb Coch, administrative assistant for the ethics faculty, ably reformatted and assembled various information and materials and put it into final form. We are indebted to Steph and Deb for their fine work. In the book's final stages, Andrea Caldwell, Mick Hammock, Erin Hoekstra and Krissy Kalinauskas were very helpful.

At Routledge, our first editor was Terry Clague, who encouraged us to undertake this project. After he moved to another position within the company, Amy Laurens was also supportive of our project. Finally, Alexander Krause and Stewart Pether helped us in bringing the book to completion. To all at Routledge, thanks a lot.

Despite the substantial efforts of these individuals, errors still will occur. We take full responsibility for them (as we well should given this is an ethics book!).

Patrick E. Murphy
Gene R. Laczniak
Andrea Prothero

Part 1
Background

1 Foundational perspectives for ethical and socially responsible marketing decisions

The ethical scandals plaguing business in the twenty-first century have largely been linked to the professions of accounting and finance. The worldwide economic recession of 2008–9, and its lingering after effects, have been blamed on convoluted financial instruments and aggressive banking practices. The subprime mortgages aspect of this crisis was seen to be more of a financial failing than a marketing one. However, classic marketing principles such as segmentation, targeting, and positioning were used by banks and other financial institutions to locate and sell mortgages to a mostly unsuspecting target group, who were then assured that there would not be major ramifications of taking out high-risk mortgages. Both the overselling of these mortgages and the "packaging" of them with other securities led to a deepening of the financial reversals seen not only in the US and Europe, but throughout the world. We contend that these financial managers were using and misusing marketing techniques to achieve short-term financial gains. As we discuss in this chapter, inappropriate application of marketing strategies and short range thinking often leads not only to ethical problems but financial reversals as well.

In the same vein, the much discussed Enron and WorldCom fiascos of the early years of the 2000s were attributed to financial improprieties and inadequate accounting controls. However, what is often not commonly known about Enron was that in its final years, it was a self-described "trading company" which made future bets on not only oil, gas and electricity but even the weather. These trades involved classic selling manipulations with an emphasis on high-pressure tactics that are often associated with unethical marketing practices. In the post-technology bust period of the early 2000s, numerous companies restated their earlier reported earnings downward, suggesting that overly aggressive accounting practices were at focus. Yet, since so many restatements involved reported sales revenues, it becomes apparent that chief marketing officers (CMOs) were partially complicit as well.

Ethics has personal, organizational and societal implications. Since the shady activities occurring in these organizations were undertaken by individuals, personal ethics are called into question. The corporate culture in these businesses encouraged and often supported unethical actions. Thus, organizational ethics is pertinent to good marketing practice. The societal implications are also relevant in that the economies of the US, Europe, and most of the developed world teetered on the brink of collapse and have yet to fully recover, due to the activities of a relatively few, powerful business firms. The inter-connectedness of the worldwide economy and virtually instantaneous communication about misdeeds through the Internet makes a commitment to ethics a growing marketing imperative as we move forward through the second decade of the new century.

Recent experiences with well-known firms have shown that a commitment to ethics and values over time does not insulate corporations from major criticism if they do not respond quickly and transparently to problems. Two companies that were often held in high regard from an ethical marketing perspective suffered major setbacks in 2009–10. Toyota, long known for product quality and ethical practices, encountered a series of mechanical malfunctions. Beyond the safety and product design flaws, many saw this "crisis" as exacerbated by Toyota's insular culture and its desire to be the largest car company in the world. They fell prey to the "bigger is better" philosophy that plagued many large US firms over the years and compromised product quality in this quest. Johnson & Johnson, the large US multinational with subsidiaries such as Janssen Pharmaceuticals and McNeil Consumer Healthcare, also experienced numerous product recalls, product contamination, and declining product quality in several plants. The firm long known for its Credo (see www.jnj.com/connect/about-jnj/jnj-credo/) and its exemplary handling of the Tylenol tragedies in the 1980s actually hired an outside agency to quietly buy up faulty products on the shelves rather than undertaking a public recall.[1] The moral of these two sad instances—from companies previously proclaimed as moral exemplars—is that managers must be vigilant in all organizations to make certain to take the ethical high ground so that quality and communication issues do not turn into public relations nightmares.

With the brief tour of twenty-first-century ethical failings of marketing as our backdrop, this chapter begins with a definition of marketing ethics that serves as the foundation for all that follows. The core of our message is organized around seven "basic perspectives" for ethical and socially responsible marketing. Each of these normative approaches is explained and discussed in some depth. In order to make this material digestible, this chapter examines the first four perspectives and the second chapter focuses on the final three normative recommendations.

Ethical marketing defined

In an earlier book on this topic, we indicated that *ethics* deals with the morality of human conduct. We went on to say that:

> *Marketing ethics* is the systematic study of how moral standards are applied to marketing decisions, behaviors, and institutions.[2]

The fact that marketing ethics, like legal and medical ethics, is an *applied* field is an important aspect of the definition. Marketing decisions pertain to a host of specific issues like selling cigarettes to teenagers, violence-themed products, pricing at a level that gouges unsuspecting consumers, advertising that manipulates viewers, and so on. The behavior governed by ethical principles involves all personnel involved in marketing—top management, the CMO, sales, distribution, customer service, advertising and public relations. Finally, marketing ethics issues arise in institutions of several types: SMEs (small- and medium-size enterprises), MNCs (multinational corporations) and NFPs (non-profit organizations).

Our approach here is similar, but subtly different, because we take primarily a *normative*, prescriptive approach. Therefore, our definition emphasizes the ideals toward which marketing and marketers should aspire:

> *Ethical marketing* refers to practices that emphasize transparent, trustworthy, and responsible personal and/or organizational marketing policies and actions that exhibit integrity as well as fairness to consumers and other stakeholders.

Because ethics often deals with subjective moral choices, the question becomes *what* moral standards ought to be applied to *which* ethical questions in marketing. For example, is it proper for an advertising copywriter to use a blatant (but legal) sexual stereotyping, which might involve the objectification of women, when the agency has demonstrated that such appeals sell more of a client's cosmetics products? Cynics claim issues like these tend to generate much disagreement and, thus, illustrate the futility of dealing with the "always subjective" ethics area. However, as we shall repeatedly show in the following pages, in many industries and in many situations, there is more consensus about what is accepted by the majority of stakeholders as ethically "proper" than casual observers suspect.

The two aspects of ethics

We see ethics, or the study of moral choice, as having two dimensions. First, ethics, via its foundation in moral philosophy, provides models and frameworks for handling ethical situations, that is, various approaches to ethical reasoning. Typically such models help to describe the behavior of marketers in facing ethical situations. For instance, ethics leads us to consider whether one might judge the moral appropriateness of marketing decisions based on the *consequences* for various stakeholders or on the basis of the *intentions* held by the decision-maker when a particular action is selected. Often, differing approaches lead us to similar conclusions about the "ethicalness" of a specific activity. Unfortunately, different approaches sometimes lead to divergent conclusions. We set out to discuss the fundamental approaches to analyzing marketing ethics in Chapter 1, and we explain what rationale lies behind the way managers actually deal with ethical problems—an approach sometimes called positive or descriptive ethics.

The second dimension of ethics addresses the question: "What is the 'right' thing to do?" This is the *normative* aspect of marketing ethics. When people say that someone is acting ethically, they usually mean the person is doing what is *morally correct.* The underpinnings for understanding what one *ought to do* come mostly from our individual values. These are shaped by our family, local community, religious training, life experience, and personal feelings about how we should treat other people. A prominent manager once remarked that some of the elusiveness about what constitutes an ethical person could be overcome if the word *trust* were substituted for ethics; that is, ethical marketing managers are *trustworthy* in that they can always be counted on to try to do the right thing. Such managers have developed what the Greek philosopher Aristotle and others have called *practical wisdom*.

It is also correct to observe that ethics is a subject where people cannot say anything of substance without revealing quite a bit about their own values. Throughout this chapter and the next, we will make normative judgments about various marketing practices. While some of our evaluations may cause debate and disagreement, our major purpose is to increase students' and managers' sensitivity to the ethical questions which regularly occur in marketing and to assist them in making more consistently ethical decisions.

Normative approaches to ethical marketing[3]

To this purpose, the set of basic perspectives (BPs) offered below address the broader moral dimensions that should ideally characterize the marketing and society interface even as firms operate as autonomous, economic units. In that sense, the social and ethical commentary of this chapter applies to the practices of *all* marketing organizations even as certain observations may be especially relevant to a particular few companies or industries. Our perspective about marketing ethics here is not mainly concerned with the positive details of "what is"—such as the percentage of marketing firms that have ethics codes or their current policies about misrepresentations in sales rep expense accounts. Rather, it is about the normative "what can be," that is, what marketing organizations *ought to* consider in order to better evaluate and improve their ethical behavior. Our observations here are intended to advocate and establish guidelines for better ethical marketing practice rather than attempting to report what practitioners say such practices presently are.

The discussion below lays out a set of BPs essential for better understanding and improving the ethical role of marketing in and upon society, especially from the managerial standpoint of individual firms. The explicit purpose is to highlight many of the enduring moral questions facing marketers such as:

- What general dimensions do managers need to consider when challenged with issues regarding whether their particular marketing practices are "good" or "bad" for society?
- How can marketing managers begin to assess whether their products are sold, priced, distributed, and serviced in a fashion that can be designated as morally "right" and "fair?"
- What are the fundamental predispositions necessary for rendering judgments about whether various marketing practices, policies, and strategies are "ethical" or "unethical"?
- What do marketing organizations aspiring to operate at the highest ethical level need to address in their companies?

In answering these questions by providing commentaries about them, it is our intention to both suggest the basic elements for improving ethical practice as well as challenge students to consider them in the cases which follow later in the book.

The nature of the essential basic perspectives

The seven BPs are described, explained, and are summarized in Figure 1.1. Together, the perspectives create a figurative and aspirational "star" for the analysis and improvement of marketing ethics. The BPs are both interactive and integrative. Every BP is intended to be helpful taken by itself, but each approach also further informs the other BPs in order to create a "Gestalt" of the elements useful for bettering ethical behavior in marketing. The BPs can aid committed marketers to more clearly evaluate the relationship of their marketing practices to society.

While the individual BPs posed here are not unique, this particular set of recommendations, applied to marketing and linked together in the integrative combination described below, constitute a dynamic, comprehensive, connected perspective that will inform marketing executives committed to ethical decision-making and will help students to better understand the challenges they may face in their future careers. Drawing upon 50 years of relevant study, the BPs are anchored in moral philosophy, business ethics research, corporate social responsibility frameworks, public policy thinking, religious values, legal guidelines, and a modicum of utopian idealism about how marketing practices might be ethically improved from an organizational and societal standpoint. It is with the crucial social perspective in mind that we begin our discourse.

BP1–Societal Benefit: ethical marketing puts people first

The marketing system should always be of service to people. To make this happen, ethically concerned marketers should seek to fully comprehend their societal influence and strive toward

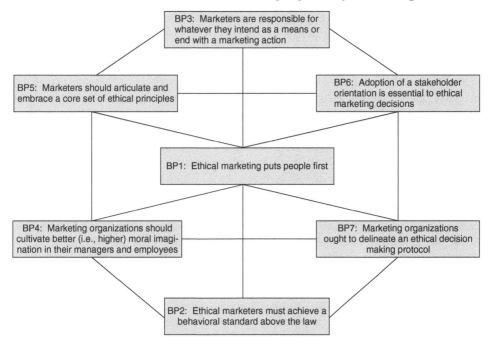

Figure 1.1 A summary of the essential basic perspectives for evaluating and improving marketing
ethics

Source: G. Laczniak and P. Murphy, "Normative perspectives for ethical and socially
responsible marketing," *Journal of Macromarketing*, 26(2), 2006, p. 157.

creating marketing operations that have a perceived and real social benefit. People should
never be treated merely as cogs in the marketing system, whether they are customers,
employees, suppliers, distributors, or another stakeholder. Marketers who ignore public
opinion—the articulated attitudes of the populous—and whose practices overtly or covertly
damage society, place their firms in substantial ethical and financial jeopardy. Managers
ought to begin their deliberations about the ethical impact of marketing activities on society
with this fundamental dictum of "people first" if they hope to prosper in the long run.

There are several reasons for this. First, that marketers should serve people seems a
straightforward observation intuitively consistent with the revered *marketing concept*.
A fundamental tenet underlying principled marketing practice is to subscribe to the marketing concept; that is, to accept the notion that most of marketing planning is driven by the
discovered needs and desires of consumers and to align organizational resources in a manner
that creates sustainable, competitive advantage for the firm in serving these consumers.

Consumer satisfaction however is only a first-order understanding of what ethical
marketing is. A second reason for keeping person-centeredness at focus is that satisfaction
for a particular segment of consumers does not necessarily translate to *net* benefits for
society. Clearly, the satisfaction of *some* consumers sometimes allows for dysfunctional
second-order effects or beyond. Tobacco marketing is the most obvious example. Smokers
willingly pay for this product and are presumably satisfied in the short term. But recent

social history has made clear the horrific long-term effects on individuals and society of this particular product. Another example is aggressively marketing credit cards to college students, who may not be sufficiently mature to handle debt or discerning enough to avoid temptations of the attractive purchases that are easily obtained with readily accessible credit. And another instance of unintended spillover involves alcohol advertising to underage markets. Traffic fatalities, addiction, and large insurance settlements are all societal impacts of such practices. From a societal standpoint, it is from these second-order or even third-order effects of marketing practice that ethical questions often emerge.

According to BP1, the market system should primarily serve people. Thus, this proposition strongly suggests a third reason: that people (especially the consumers in a marketing transaction) should never be viewed as merely a *means* to a profitable *end*. Those familiar with moral philosophy will recognize this decision rule as a marketing oriented version of Immanuel Kant's well-known categorical imperative.[4] Marketing practices violating this "means versus ends" proposition are, at minimum, ethically suspect. Selling and promotional tactics that treat consumers as mostly means rather than ends likely include:

- High-pressure selling tactics such as those in certain sectors of the financial services or real estate industries [e.g., junk bonds peddled by "boiler room" investment firms or various hard sell "time share" condominium presentations];
- Coercion in the channel distribution, such as demands for price concessions, by the channel partner having significant economic leverage [e.g., the dealings of powerful retailers with developing country suppliers or even home country suppliers, such as small, vulnerable family farms];
- "Over the top" psychological approaches, such as the utilization of fear appeals in the sale of hand guns or elective cosmetic surgical procedures;
- The sexual exploitation of gender or ethnic stereotyping (or other demographic exploitation) in magazine, television, and Internet advertising for attention getting purposes;
- Price gouging in times of product shortage, such as natural disasters like the oil spill in the Gulf of Mexico or the tsunami in Japan.

A fourth reason why marketers should place people at the center of their actions is to live true to universally accepted dictums such as the "dignity of the person" that is central to almost all religious traditions. This approach states that each and every person, irrespective of economic and social position, has inherent dignity and should be treated fairly in all roles (e.g., consumer, employee, business partner, or member of the larger society). The examples noted above such as coercive selling, price gouging of disaster victims and advertising exploitation violate the principle of human dignity.

When marketers treat their stakeholders mainly as means, they flunk the test of placing people first. The inability of marketers to adhere to the adage of never treating their consumers (and other stakeholders) as merely a means to an end, if sustained, will usually result in the invocation of the "iron law of social responsibility,"—an exercise by regulators that, from a cost standpoint, is often detrimental to the violating marketer or perhaps all marketers. The *iron law of social responsibility* posits that when entities, such as marketing organizations, have great economic power and do not exhibit proportionate social responsibility, they will have their power proportionately diminished.[5] Usually, the diminishment of business freedom takes the form of additional regulations, adding costs to the average marketing transaction.

BP2–Ethical Expectations for Marketing Must Exceed Legal Requirements: two realms

Ethical marketers must achieve a behavioral standard in excess of the minimum obligations embedded in the law. Typically, the law represents the lowest common denominator of expected behavior for marketing and business practice. Ethical marketing organizations should always strive to exceed the legal minimums of social compliance. Thus, the law and ethics represent two-tiered layers of constraint impeding socially troubling marketing practices. It is worth distinguishing more formally between these two concepts—law and ethics—and their interconnected realms.

- *Marketing law* constitutes the baseline expectations upon marketing by society. It is a black letter set of rules and regulations that are codified over time to address the dynamics of business practice that deals with the marketing function. The formalization of restrictions by law typically lags public opinion. Obvious examples of marketing laws and related regulatory oversight include anti-trust legislation, which modulates competition; the US Federal Trade Commission (FTC) which oversees sales and trading practices in the US; the Advertising Standards Authority which is the UK's independent regulator of advertising across all media; the European Union's Misleading and Comparative Marketing Communications Regulations of 2007; and the US Consumer Product Safety Commission (CPSC), which specifies the safety standards for various products and dictates the removal of potentially harmful products from the US marketplace. Despite the existence of some ill-conceived business laws and regulations, especially in the international arena, when firms intentionally break the law, they are quite likely to be in *ethical* jeopardy as well. Table 1.1 provides a list of illegal marketing practices in most of the developed world.
- *Marketing ethics* encompass the societal and professional standards of right and fair practices that are expected of marketing managers in their oversight of strategy formulation, implementation, and control. The most basic ethical standards are often articulated in professional codes of marketing conduct. The American Marketing Association's (AMA) Statement of Ethics (including explicit discussion of ethical norms and values), is presented in Box 1.1. It represents a useful, duty-based specification of marketer responsibilities that exceed those codified in law. It is illustrative of the expectations incumbent in the practice of marketing not captured by law. While basic theories of ethics do not change over time, the norms and values that are clearly embraced by society, or by a profession at any period in time, are subject to slow shift. For example, in the mid twentieth century, the operation of retail stores on Sundays would have been perceived by many as unethical.

Clearly ethics and the law are connected, but they are not the same. Understandably, many questionable marketing practices are both illegal and unethical. As shown in Table 1.1, illegal and unethical examples would be price fixing as well as "bait and switch" advertising. However, many other marketing techniques and strategies may not be illegal but could raise ethical questions. For example, "ambush marketing"—creating an advertising campaign that mimics competitor promotions for which they have NOT paid sponsorship fees to the major sporting events like the World Cup or Olympic games—is not illegal per se, but generates spirited debate among ethicists and practitioners concerning its inherent fairness. Finally, a few practices are illegal but not necessarily unethical. For instance, providing small "grease

Table 1.1 Illegal marketing practices

Product safety

The European Union (EU) introduced a General Product Safety Directive in 2001 (2001/95/EC) and this was revised in 2004. The Directive aims to protect consumer health and safety within the EU. Member states must enforce the Directive on both the producers and distributors of products. In the US, the Consumer Product Safety Act of 1972 has established the Consumer Product Safety Commission (CPSC), which is charged "to protect the public against unreasonable risks associated with consumer products" and therefore "has the power to establish mandatory product safety requirements." The main difference between the American and the European system is that, in Europe, product safety is regulated mainly by directives and regulations (notably in the Member States by national laws implementing directives or directly by EC regulations).

Product safety

Product safety is used to describe the condition of products when they meet the standards regulated by the United States Consumer Product Safety Commission (CPSC), an independent federal agency founded in the early 1970s that is responsible for protecting "the public against unreasonable risks of injuries and deaths associated with consumer products." Products that are deemed hazardous by the CPSC because their use can be associated with an unreasonable risk of serious injury, illness, or death can be recalled or banned from the market. A number of products such as automobiles, over the counter and prescription drugs, and firearms are known to be potentially unsafe.

Product counterfeiting

The practice of selling a product that is a close imitation of a genuine product of superior quality and/or performance, usually for a reduced price. This practice harms the producer of the genuine product as well as consumers who are often unaware that they are purchasing a knock-off item. The World Customs Organization estimates that over $500 billion is lost annually. Virtually any product can be counterfeited from watches to DVDs and a host of designer clothing and accessory products. Both the US and Europe have strict anti-counterfeiting laws but much of the developing world have a much more relaxed attitude toward this practice.

Price fixing and collusion

Deals made by direct competitors to create monopolistic advantages for themselves by secretly agreeing to charge identical (usually elevated) prices for their products are illegal. This behavior is difficult to prove because competitive markets can naturally result in similar prices and some firms determine their pricing strategies by following a price leader. However, long-standing statutes in the US and Europe prohibit these actions. One of the most recent cases involved the price-fixing strategies of British Airways and Virgin Atlantic, who colluded in their ticket surcharges following an increase in oil prices. Virgin was spared legal action by anti-competition authorities after blowing the whistle on BA who was fined $300 million in the US and £121.5 million in the UK. Even though the fine only applied to BA we can argue that the actions of both companies were both illegal and unethical. The major regulators of antitrust activities in the US are the Justice Department and Federal Trade Commission. The Competition Commissioner is the chief antitrust enforcer in the EU.

Continued

Table 1.1 Cont'd

Predatory pricing

A strategy in which a firm incurs a loss for a short period of time by pricing its products below their cost so that its (usually smaller) competitors struggle to compete with its low prices and are eventually forced out of business. Major statutes in the US and Europe prohibit this type of behavior. In 2003 France Télécom owned company, Wanadoo, was fined €10.35m by the European Commission as a result of its predatory pricing policy for its broadband services, and the European Court of Justice dismissed the appeal by the company in 2009.

Coercion in the channel

This action involves forcing another person or organization within the marketing channel to act in a certain way through some form of pressure, such as threats, intimidation, or rewards. While coercion is difficult to prove in court, most governments in the developed world frown on this practice and bring occasional litigation to curb it. Companies like Walmart and Carrefour, because of their size, are often accused of coercing members in their channel.

Deceptive advertising

Advertising that is deliberately aimed at misleading consumers through either a false representation of product features, an omission of information on the product's flaws, or deceitful practices used to influence consumers' decisions to buy or use the product. Examples are misleading price claims and defective products without adequate disclosures. Deceptive advertising is regulated by the FTC in the US, and the Advertising Standards Authority (ASA) in the UK. In the UK in 2009 the baby milk company Nutricia was forced to remove its magazine ads for follow-on milk, as a result of misleading claims in relation to a child's immune system. In 2010 the ASA also forced the company to remove its television ads for follow-on milk, this time as a result of misleading claims in relation to a child's daily intake of iron.

Bribery in the channel

This activity involves influencing the actions of another person (usually someone in a position of authority or influence) by implying, offering, or giving them items of value, such as money or gifts. Major companies such as Siemens in Europe and buyers of tomato paste in the US have been indicted for bribery in recent years. Historically, bribery of government officials has been a recurring theme especially in the developing world. The Foreign Corrupt Practices Act was passed in the US in the 1970s to address bribery.

Bait and switch advertising

This is considered a type of deceptive advertising by the Federal Trade Commission (FTC). Bait and switch advertising occurs when a company has advertised a product but has no intention of selling the item to consumers. Usually, the company lures consumers into the store by advertising a cheaper product (the bait) and then tries to sell them a more expensive product once they are inside (the switch). The growth of the Internet has brought more accusations of bait and switch for items offered exclusively online or by bricks and mortar retailers who use the net to advertise their products. Like many of the other practices discussed here, it is often difficult to prove beyond a shadow of a doubt that bait and switch has occurred.

Misleading online advertising

Misleading advertising can also be in the form of on-line communication strategies. In 2011, for example, the Irish airline company Aer Lingus was found to be misleading consumers by the ASA for Ireland as a result of a direct email advertisement distributed to the company's subscribers. The email highlighted special offer prices on air tickets between Ireland and Britain which complainants argued were misleading. In the UK in May 2011 the ASA upheld a complaint against Cassava Enterprises (Gibraltar Ltd.), the owners of the 888 Casino company, following a Facebook banner ad campaign, which was deemed to trivialize gambling addiction.

Sources of information for this table come from L. Oswald, *The Law of Marketing*, Cincinnati, OH: West Publishing, second ed., 2010, Wikipedia and other Internet sites. Thanks to Stephanie Piszczor for her assistance in preparing this table.

Box 1.1 American Marketing Association Statement of Ethics

- AMA Statement of Ethics (revised 2008)

Ethical norms and values for marketers
Preamble

The American Marketing Association commits itself to promoting the highest standard of professional ethical norms and values for its members (practitioners, academics and students). Norms are established standards of conduct that are expected and maintained by society and/or professional organizations. Values represent the collective conception of what communities find desirable, important and morally proper. Values also serve as the criteria for evaluating our own personal actions and the actions of others. As marketers, we recognize that we not only serve our organizations but also act as stewards of society in creating, facilitating, and executing the transactions that are part of the greater economy. In this role, marketers are expected to embrace the highest professional ethical norms and the ethical values implied by our responsibility toward multiple stakeholders (e.g., customers, employees, investors, peers, channel members, regulators, and the host community).

Ethical norms

As marketers, we must:

- Do no harm. This means consciously avoiding harmful actions or omissions by embodying high ethical standards and adhering to all applicable laws and regulations in the choices we make.
- Foster trust in the marketing system. This means striving for good faith and fair dealing so as to contribute toward the efficacy of the exchange process as well as avoiding deception in product design, pricing, communication, and delivery of distribution.
- Embrace ethical values. This means building relationships and enhancing consumer confidence in the integrity of marketing by affirming these core values: honesty, responsibility, fairness, respect, transparency, and citizenship.

Ethical values

Honesty—to be forthright in dealings with customers and stakeholders. To this end, we will:

- Strive to be truthful in all situations and at all times.
- Offer products of value that do what we claim in our communications.
- Stand behind our products if they fail to deliver their claimed benefits.
- Honor our explicit and implicit commitments and promises.

Responsibility—to accept the consequences of our marketing decisions and strategies. To this end, we will:

- Strive to serve the needs of customers.
- Avoid using coercion with all stakeholders.
- Acknowledge the social obligations to stakeholders that come with increased marketing and economic power.

- Recognize our special commitments to vulnerable market segments such as children, seniors, the economically impoverished, market illiterates and others who may be substantially disadvantaged.
- Consider environmental stewardship in our decision-making.

Fairness—to balance justly the needs of the buyer with the interests of the seller. To this end, we will:

- Represent products in a clear way in selling, advertising, and other forms of communication; this includes the avoidance of false, misleading, and deceptive promotion.
- Reject manipulations and sales tactics that harm customer trust.
- Refuse to engage in price fixing, predatory pricing, price gouging or "bait-and-switch" tactics.
- Avoid knowing participation in conflicts of interest.
- Seek to protect the private information of customers, employees, and partners.

Respect—to acknowledge the basic human dignity of all stakeholders. To this end, we will:

- Value individual differences and avoid stereotyping customers or depicting demographic groups (e.g., gender, race, sexual orientation) in a negative or dehumanizing way.
- Listen to the needs of customers and make all reasonable efforts to monitor and improve their satisfaction on an ongoing basis.
- Make every effort to understand and respectfully treat buyers, suppliers, intermediaries, and distributors from all cultures.
- Acknowledge the contributions of others, such as consultants, employees and coworkers, to marketing endeavors.
- Treat everyone, including our competitors, as we would wish to be treated.

Transparency—to create a spirit of openness in marketing operations. To this end, we will:

- Strive to communicate clearly with all constituencies.
- Accept constructive criticism from customers and other stakeholders.
- Explain and take appropriate action regarding significant product or service risks, component substitutions or other foreseeable eventualities that could affect customers or their perception of the purchase decision.
- Disclose list prices and terms of financing as well as available price deals and adjustments.

Citizenship—to fulfill the economic, legal, philanthropic, and societal responsibilities that serve stakeholders. To this end, we will:

- Strive to protect the ecological environment in the execution of marketing campaigns.
- Give back to the community through volunteerism and charitable donations.

- Contribute to the overall betterment of marketing and its reputation.
- Urge supply chain members to ensure that trade is fair for all participants, including producers in developing countries.

Implementation

We expect AMA members to be courageous and proactive in leading and/or aiding their organizations in the fulfillment of the explicit and implicit promises made to those stakeholders. We recognize that every industry sector and marketing sub-discipline (e.g., marketing research, e-commerce, Internet selling, direct marketing, and advertising) has its own specific ethical issues that require policies and commentary. An array of such codes can be accessed through links on the AMA website. Consistent with the principle of subsidiarity (solving issues at the level where the expertise resides), we encourage all such groups to develop and/or refine their industry and discipline-specific codes of ethics to supplement these guiding ethical norms and values.

Revision adopted by AMA Board of Directors on 10/24/08. Reprinted with permission.

payments" in certain foreign markets, while technically legislated against in these countries, may constitute a business practice that is both commonplace and widely expected.[6]

Figure 1.2 provides a useful way to envision the relationship of ethics and the law as it often applies to marketing practice. In this instance, the Y, or vertical, axis represents *professional and moral responsibility* and the X, or horizontal axis, represents *baseline societal expectations*. An examination of this figure underscores two basic points:

- *Ethics embodies higher standards than law.* Ethics is typically the leading edge of regulation, thereby implying a higher standard of professional/moral responsibility than law and incorporating wider latitude of societal expectations. In this sense, ethics anticipates the dynamics of societal attitudes and opinions concerning marketplace fairness that eventually may be proscribed and embodied in the law. For instance, numerous ethical questions were raised about telemarketing practices *prior to* the institutionalization of "do not call" lists in various US jurisdictions, and eventually in Federal law. Similarly, sellers of alcoholic beverages and tobacco products were asked to temper their advertising use of cartoon characters and "lovable" animals appealing to children, *before* the enactment of formal regulations restricting such approaches on Kid's TV shows. Thus, for those who claim that the only agreed upon code of morality is the existing law, it should be pointed out that the law is dynamic and that changes to it are often driven by (slowly) shifting ethical and social norms.
- *Ethics assumes more duties than law.* Normally, ethics bestows a greater obligation of moral duty upon marketing managers than merely conforming to the law. The AMA Norms and Values statement (Box 1.1), for example, delineates the basic moral standards expected of marketing professionals by society, but most of these are not institutionalized in laws. The *Integrated Social Contracts Theory* approach to business ethics would characterize such basic hyper norms as creating and constraining a "moral free space" for members of a professional group (i.e., marketers), who then use those

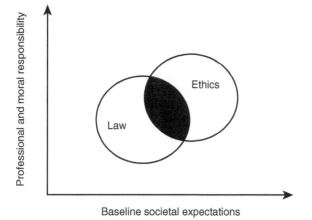

Figure 1.2 The relationship of ethics and law

Source: G. Laczniak and P. Murphy, "Normative perspectives for ethical and socially responsible marketing," *Journal of Macromarketing*, 26 (2), 2006, p. 160.

precepts as a motivating behavioral guide.[7] In contrast, marketing managers who are primarily legal minimalists, and seek to exclusively conform only to the law, will likely exhibit a lower behavioral standard that could jeopardize their company's reputation and subject their organizations to negative consequences if the higher expectations of society perceive such marketers to be lax in their ethical discharge (see BP4).

Marketers, then, must initially abide by the law, but BP2 argues that this is not enough. Those companies that view themselves as ethical marketers aspire to a higher standard. As noted below, some companies and their marketing managers attempt only to meet the letter of the law in the firm's marketing practices. However, as expectations have been raised due to greater media scrutiny, consumer advocate and business watch-dog blogs, we believe that taking a purely legalistic approach to issues confronting marketing is self-defeating. To be successful in the future, it is our position that ethical marketers must embrace decisions that fall in the upper right corner of Figure 1.2.

BP3–Intent, Means and Ends: three essential components of ethical analysis

When formulating marketing campaigns, marketers are responsible for their intent as well as the means and outcomes of a particular marketing action. This essential perspective requires some deliberate explanation. As analysts adjudicate the ethical dimensions of a "questionable" marketing practice, that practice can, and usually should, be divided into three distinct components—the *intent* of the action, the *means* or *method* by which the practice was implemented and the *end* or *outcomes* of the strategy or tactic. The intention is what marketers want to happen; the means is how they carry out the action and the consequences or outcomes are what actually happen. The quality of ethical analysis that is conducted, whether internal or external to the firm is improved by such separate consideration because it allows marketing analysts to sharpen their insight about how a particular marketing situation might be perceived. This approach forces managers to focus not only on the outcomes of their decisions (something that typically has their attention), but also upon the *process* of how they make decisions and why.

From the viewpoint of an "outsider," there is little doubt that the *intent* of a particular marketing action, in terms of its ethical purity, is the most difficult element to judge because it requires evaluating the internal motivation behind a company's particular actions or policy. Since many seller motivations are hidden, the intent behind marketing strategies or tactics can be rationalized ex *post facto* by the decision-maker in a manner that obscures or shields the formulator from responsibility for a dubious marketing strategy. For example, the creators of a TV advertisement that depicts an overweight child as a "pathetic loser" in a competitive contest, or portrays an immigrant man as a "work for food" gardener, might claim that they did not intend such usages to be perceived as social stereotypes that might offend certain audience segments. When receiving unexpected criticism, formulators of debatable marketing tactics commonly claim ignorance of the offense or deny any intended slight, whatever their true and original intention was. Nevertheless, in certain instances, intent can be deduced with reasonable confidence by examining circumstance. For example, when "me too" marketers attempt to closely emulate the colors or trademark of a market-leading brand (an approach frequently practiced in US drug store chains with their private (own) brands), causing consumer confusion in the marketplace, the calculated intent seems to be relatively clear cut and logical. Similarly, if marketers of highly violent video games consistently advertise on TV programs with the largest attainable number of young adolescent boys as audience members (even when following industry guidelines in only promoting these products on programs watched by a majority of adults), the motivation behind such practices seems demonstrably clear. In these instances (i.e., stereotyping in advertising, trademark caricature, willfully targeting a vulnerable market segment), probable marketer intent can shed considerable light upon the likely "ethicalness" of a particular marketing action.

The *means* (or method) of executing a marketing strategy is the second component of a marketing action that requires scrutiny to judge its ethical nature. Obviously, certain practices (e.g., predatory pricing) are explicitly forbidden by law. However, an analysis of the specific method utilized in the execution of a particular marketing strategy can provide useful insight into the ethical propriety of a debated marketing action. For example, highly promoted *product rebates,* which then require multiple purchase documentation (i.e., proof of purchase, UPC code, retail seller verification, etc.) as well as an overly detailed set of conformance steps by consumer in order to successfully execute that redemption, seem by their very method of administration to be ethically questionable. Similarly, TV ads portraying pliant and submissive females easily available to those who drink a particular brand of beer (witness the numerous depictions of "beer bimbos" in some ad campaigns) seem to be a *means* of promotional campaigning that at least raises ethical questions, due to their thematic execution.

The third component to be addressed in assessing the ethicalness of a questioned marketing action is its *outcome*. Because many outcomes have considerable overt visibility associated with them, the consequences of marketing actions are probably the easiest components for outsiders to judge when analyzing the acceptability of particular marketing actions, and should always be considered.

One especially useful framework for judging the ethics of business practices based on this approach was advanced by Thomas Garrett and it provides the theoretical basis for BP3. The straightforward pragmatism of his particular method of analysis—*the proportionality framework*—holds considerable appeal for decision-oriented marketing managers interested in applied ethics.[8] The *principle of proportionality*, adapted from Garrett, combines all the essential elements discussed above into one ethical decision-making rule that encompasses and extends BP3: marketers are responsible for whatever they intend as a means or an end. If both are "good," they may act, accepting a certain (i.e., minor) risk of side effects.

According to Garrett, with regard to side-effect outcomes, marketers should never take actions which result in a direct *major* negative outcome for another stakeholder. For example, a seller who rigs a bidding process in order to secure a supply contract has caused a major negative harm to other stakeholders, that is, competitors who lose a chance at fairly winning the contract; shareholders who forego the opportunities presumptive in a higher-profit margin; society which expects honest and even-handed business practices.

Marketing practices which intentionally cause (or are likely to cause) a major negative outcome for stakeholders affected by the transaction in question are almost always unethical. Sometimes there are unintended side effects from marketing actions that are taken by sellers that also cause major or minor negative outcomes. If these side effects can be designated as *major* negative outcomes and they are intentional, the action must always be subject to careful ethical scrutiny. For example, suppose a sales rep of a pharmaceutical house has been properly providing experimental drugs to a research hospital to be used in scientific studies. In the course of the sales process, suppose further that the sales rep learns that the unapproved drugs are being dispensed to a handful of patients that are not part of the research study. In such an instance, it is probably unethical for the sales rep to go ahead with further drug provisions because the possible (major) side effects of the protocol (while legal in its purported use for experimental treatments) could produce significant negative consequences for other stakeholders (i.e., the patients).

It is true that almost any marketing action can have unintended side effects. For example, some small proportion of an audience watching television might view ads for *Viagra* or other erectile dysfunction products as being offensive. However, such unintended, negative side effects of marketing actions, if minor, are part of the complexities of an advanced marketing system and can be tolerated from an ethical standpoint.

In the last analysis, the proportionality framework described above is still highly judgmental. For example, what constitutes a *major* negative outcome versus a *minor* negative outcome from an ethical standpoint? Which side effects are *intended* versus *unintended*? This entire approach rests upon marketing decision-makers being fairly sophisticated and reflective in their ethical perceptions and moral intuitions. The three-component framework of intention, means, and outcome is not a perfect system for judging the ethics of a particular situation. Yet, when used in combination with other basic perspectives (see BP5 in Chapter 2), it can serve as a helpful, initial analytic, inherently recognizing that marketing decisions are multifaceted and demand evaluation from different process standpoints in order to validate their propriety. The proportionality approach is also particularly useful in helping balance the claims of various stakeholders affected by marketing actions (see BP6 also in Chapter 2) because it asks marketers to articulate a full range of intentions, means, and outcomes.

BP4–Marketing Managers Differ in Moral Imagination and Development: four types

Marketing organizations striving to improve their ethical aptitude should cultivate better (i.e., higher) moral imagination in their managers and employees. It is important to recognize that in most firms the managers making marketing decisions will differ in their ability to evaluate and resolve ethical issues. This is because managers will possess varying levels of moral development. Some marketing executives will have lower ethical sensitivities while others will have the capacity for significant *moral imagination*—that is, the character and ability to morally reason to creative ethical solutions when encountering an ethical question.[9] In other words, managerial quotients of moral sensitivity and capability will not be the same, owing to different life experiences and individual core values as well as their basic human character. This personal state of affairs, that is, the likely differences among managers in their ability to engage in critical ethical evaluations, implies that organizations should seek to understand the nature of these different moral aptitudes and strive to instill an improved ethical reasoning capacity among their managers.

Theoretically, this natural variance among managers is best recognized by Kohlberg's framework of moral development.[10] Business firms have the potential to utilize such models through their organizational and design programs for improved social responsiveness. Similarly, managerial moral styles vary greatly across organizations as well. The importance of a perspective such as Kohlberg's depends upon realizing that, in many instances, a firm's ability to handle ethical issues is only as good as the capability of its managers. Significantly, recognizing managerial differences in moral imagination implies that, given training and experience, managers can enhance their ethical skills. At the most basic level, *inspired directly by Kohlberg,* we posit four broad types of marketing managers.

- *Egoistic or relativistic marketing managers* are the least morally developed and have a strong tendency to resolve moral situations based on their own immediate interests and consequences (the egoistic type) or societal norms to determine what is right and wrong (relativists). Individuals at this stage of moral thinking give strong weighting to the incentives and sanctions that will affect only them. They tend to heavily rely on rules and authority such as the force of law or the likelihood of organizational sanction. The language that characterizes the egoist/relativist managerial approach includes rationalizing phrases such as: "everybody else does it"; "the lawyers haven't told us this is wrong"; "we were only following orders."[11] Such managers respond mostly to organizational rewards and punishments and their personal moral resolve is relatively undeveloped because of their preoccupation with personal or company gain. Managers at this unrefined stage of moral development will include individual egoists who will choose actions that benefit mostly themselves, given this sort of option. The relativists are oftentimes most apparent in an international setting where the manager from a developed country will follow the more lax standards of a lesser developed country. And unfortunately, at the extremes, there may also be some "crooks" in this category— managers who know the actions being taken are clearly wrong, but who will choose to do them anyway because of the probable personal or company payoffs involved. Surely, the pirate CEOs and CFOs that raided Enron and WorldCom in the US and Parmalat in Europe, as well as various global banking executives in the more recent financial scandals are of this corrupt category of manager.[12]
- *Legalist Marketing Managers* are the second type. They overtly espouse that the law is their guide in adjudicating the propriety of any marketing action. Legalists often perceive business as a game, with profits as the only winning criterion and all tactics not expressly prohibited by law as "in play" regardless of consequences. These sorts of

managers believe that as long as they do not transgress the rules of the game as set by law, they have the legal right to shape marketing strategy without reference to anything but its profit impact. This "law equals morality" approach certainly simplifies the challenge of ethical reasoning for such managers. It appears that in recent years, the legalist group has been growing. For instance, an increasing number of MBA grads, who take a primarily financial and narrow (minimalist) perspective toward their management responsibilities, seem to find it safe to espouse such positions.

- *Moral strivers,* our third type, are those marketing managers who have progressed in their moral thinking and development to the point where they are capable of considering multiple stakeholders, when adjudicating what constitutes moral propriety. Their "empathy for others" is what distinguishes these moral strivers from egoistic managers since their ethical reasoning often will be tempered by additional factors such as organizational loyalty (e.g., to co-workers and suppliers) as well as other basic duties to society (e.g., written guidelines embodied in industry codes or ones like the AMA's— see Box 1.1). Nevertheless, strivers are still heavily dependent upon company rules and policies in their assessment of moral situations. Some moral striver managers are susceptible to falling back on minimalist expectations and reverting to an egoistic or legalistic approach in the absence of readily available guidance. Other strivers really want to do the right thing but prevailing organizational factors, such as time pressures, demands to meet financial objectives, or an uncertainty about proper moral norms, sometimes lead them to avoid the time-consuming work of ethical reasoning. Put another way, unless provided with some form of codified ethical guidance, strivers lack the *moral imagination* to creatively reason through the more complex ethical problems. This state of affairs helps provide an answer to the often asked organizational question: "Why do seemingly good marketing managers sometimes make very unethical decisions?"

- *Principled marketing managers* (type four) have reached a high level of moral development. Managers who attain this sophisticated state address their ethical problems by regularly applying both prevailing ethical norms and applicable laws to the situation at focus. Principled managers also have substantial moral imagination and therefore are better able to foresee the ethical impacts of their marketing decisions on others; they have developed the moral capacity to incorporate basic rights, industry norms, and legal constraints into their moral calculations; they can creatively apply universal ethical principles–ones they believe all fair-minded managers should follow given a similar set of facts or situations. This category of managers has two commonalities with Maslow's well-known *Hierarchy of Needs*. Being at the self-actualization (highest) stage, these individuals "are strongly ethical, have definite standards, and they do right and do not do wrong."[13] And, like the classic self-actualizers, few managers (unfortunately) reach this stage.

Our executive training and development experience has shown that in a typical marketing organization, the moral development of managers will vary, with the majority of managers being of the "moral striver" type. This view is consistent with opinion polls of executives conducted over the years, where the majority of executives assert that most managers and businesses try to do the right thing almost all of the time. Thus, the most common organizational situation involves morally striving managers who, when facing an ethical question, are guided by relevant laws *along with* the specifically articulated ethical norms of their particular organization and/or industry. In these cases, when ethical values are well defined, striver marketing managers will be in a position to apply company and industry guidelines to the ethical question at hand and reason to an ethical evaluation.

Many such morally striving managers also might be described as "seekers" because they are looking to do the ethical thing but need organizational guidance in order to do so. When faced with difficult ethical questions, some marketing managers, absent the availability or clarity of specific company guidelines, quickly revert back to the position of "egoists" or "legalists" and are constrained only by the limits of law and personal hubris, and thus side-step the challenge of ethical analysis. Strategically, if firms are trying to manage better ethics, they should attempt to articulate, communicate, and reinforce those ethical norms and values considered to be essential for their company and industry sector. This will allow managers who are *strivers* to have available the required ethical guidance and will decrease the tendency of some marketing managers to revert back to legalistic or egoistic thinking.

The task of organizations serious about their ethical operations is to try to minimize the number of egoistic or relativist managers (sadly, the plain crooks may be beyond help with regard to ethical formation) and to move them at least to the striver level of moral thinking via ethics education and training.[14] Given the propensity of egoist managers to respond mainly to rewards and punishments, the organizational challenge here is to significantly reduce their opportunity to capture illicit rewards that might be gained by engaging in unethical actions. Such opportunities are usually minimized through strong internal company compliance programs and a system of corporate governance with many checks and balances.

Principled managers, that is, those who have developed ethical value systems and the capacity for consistently applying them, are, as previously stated, the minority in most organizations. Obviously, cultivating managers to be *moral exemplars* and to always try to pursue what's ethically right in their marketing decisions is the ideal for those firms aspiring to operate at a highest ethical plane. In conformance with BP2, companies must be resolute that merely complying with the law is not sufficient to achieve meritorious corporate citizenship and ethical responsibility. It is often said that virtue is its own reward, but the pragmatic benefit of having principled managers—those who know the core values of the firm and always try to operationalize it in their decisions—is that such leaders can embody needed moral imagination and propel their organizations to the forefront of enlightened social responsibility. Some argue that being a corporate "good guy" leads to greater customer loyalty (e.g., Ben & Jerry's and Lego), greater employee retention (e.g., NML Financial Services) and better access to equity capital (e.g., Green Bay Packers). But whether being the moral exemplar *directly* corresponds with economic reward is the subject of much debate. Good companies do not necessarily do best financially. But, avoiding major ethics scandals certainly seems to mitigate significant corporate punishments and its associated costs.

Commonly, one motivation for principled managers to live out high ethical ideals comes from a cohesive ethical culture. Such an ethical culture may be the result of the values of the company founder or it may come from a long time CEO who expects fair play and honesty in all operations.[15] Corporate cultures that are ethical don't just happen by chance but rather are the result of a premeditated effort by corporations to explore their values, articulate them, and then train all employees in the details and importance of living these company ideals.[16]

Figure 1.3 shows a comparison of the four types of managers across different behavioral drivers. The moral, legal, personal, and societal points of view are explained above in the discussion of BP2 and BP4. The one new driver is "agency" which is basically doing the

The four types of marketing managers (BP4)

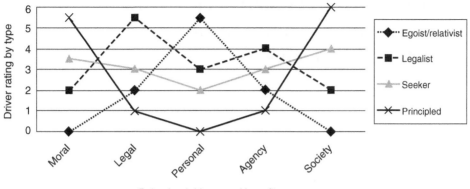

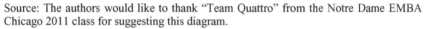

Behavioral drivers and benefits

Figure 1.3 Marketing manager types and behavioral drivers

       Source: The authors would like to thank "Team Quattro" from the Notre Dame EMBA Chicago 2011 class for suggesting this diagram.

bidding of the owners or shareholders. As noted above, the egoists and relativists are strongest on the personal dimension while the legalists place the greatest emphasis on legal followed by the agency perspective. The seekers are in the middle of the diagram on most dimensions and are highest on both the moral and societal areas because they want to do the right thing. The principled managers score higher on both the moral and societal perspectives and are much lower on the other three drivers. That means that they are driven much less by personal or organizational gain and take a strong moral and societal stance in their decision-making.

Conclusion

This chapter has provided an overview of four of our BPs and how they are central to the understanding of ethical marketing. As Figure 1.1 indicates, the BPs are interconnected and, significantly, place *people* at the center of the diagram. Ethical marketing starts with people and the other BPs flow from there. This chapter also puts forward a definition of ethical marketing as well as some core, theoretical perspectives that are useful in examining the individual cases that are included in Parts 2 and 3.

2 Advanced perspectives for ethical and socially responsible marketing decisions

The foundational discussion of the four basic perspectives (BPs) developed in Chapter 1 is essential to constructing the final three normative, ethical perspectives explained in this chapter. It was also important to define and introduce the scope of marketing ethics before examining the more theoretical concepts presented here. We reaffirm that any analysis of business or marketing ethics must begin with a primary focus on persons as was outlined in BP1. Also, understanding that the law only provides minimal guidance for ethical decision-making is another basic proposition (recall BP2) for justifying the comprehensive ethical theories we discuss below. The three components of *intentions*, *means*, and *outcomes* (BP3) are shorthand but important descriptors of the fundamental elements for understanding marketing ethics. Furthermore, the reader should recollect the distinctions between the four types of managers when contemplating possible marketing actions (BP4). Recall how the development of moral imagination among all managers is essential to nurturing an ethical culture. With those four BPs as a groundwork, we now continue our exposition with the major ethical theories that will be most useful in undertaking a thorough analysis of the cases in the subsequent parts of this book.

Additional normative approaches to ethical marketing

BP5–Essential Frameworks for Enlightened Marketing: five theories

Marketers who aspire to operate on a high ethical plane should articulate and embrace a core set of ethical principles. A definitive distillation of *the* essential moral precepts for evaluating marketing practice is as elusive as ranking business schools or creating the perfect product. All marketing firms need to reflect on the core values referenced in their mission statements and then work to derive an appropriate list of sacrosanct ethical guidelines. However, five ethical principles for assessing the propriety of marketing practice are offered here in order to stimulate debate and further the dialogue about enhancing marketing ethics. An honest review and utilization of these normative principles will go far in generating the ethics conversation among managers and/or policy makers necessary to improve on the rectitude of marketing practices.

These principles might be considered a preliminary answer to a question implied by BP4. Specifically, if principled marketing managers with moral imagination are essential to an ethical organization, then what principles might they regularly integrate into their moral reasoning? The approaches discussed below also help address ethical issues concerning the "rightness" or "fairness" of various marketing tactics in the marketplace.

It should be understood that ethical questions about marketing could be raised by employees (e.g., can I inflate my expense account to recover gratuities incurred as part of my business travel?), customers (e.g., is this price fair?), regulators (e.g., should Internet sellers incur the cost of collecting the appropriate state sales tax?), the media (e.g., should marketing press releases require documentation for performance or compliance achievements that are made?), competitors (e.g., should all material product claims contained in advertising be substantiated on the company website?), as well as other stakeholders. Merely raising an "ethical question" does not presuppose a practice is unethical. For example, many questions have been asked about the practice of product "puffery," that is, vigorously exaggerating a product attribute for dramatic effect. As an illustration, stating that a new model sports coupe has an engine that "purrs like a kitten" would be a product puff. Most analysts find most puffing tactics to be ethically defensible even though it usually raises some concerns and questions.

Five ethical theories are presented. The first four cover the major philosophical theories that can be applied to marketing decisions—utilitarianism, duty-based ethics, virtue, and the social contract. The fifth approach—religious models—pertains to the theological underpinnings of ethics that are implicitly used by some marketing managers. Before turning our consideration to these comprehensive theories, we draw your attention to Box 2.1, which lists several moral maxims that are sometimes used by marketers in making ethical decisions. While they are short and pithy, they do provide some initial direction in guiding the ethical assessment of marketing managers—quick fix ethical rules, of a sort.

Consequences-based ethical theories

The first of the five major ethical precepts are consequences oriented theories—sometimes called *teleological*, from the Greek word "telos," meaning end or purpose. That is, a marketing decision is judged as ethical or unethical depending exclusively on its *outcome*. The major category of theory that falls within the consequences approach is utilitarianism.

UTILITARIANISM

Probably the most widely understood and commonly applied ethical theory is *utilitarianism*. In an organizational context, utilitarianism basically states that a decision concerning marketing conduct is proper if and only if that decision produces the *greatest good for the greatest number* of individuals. "Good" is usually defined as the *net benefits* that accrue to those parties affected by the choice. Thus, most utilitarian thinkers hold the position that moral choices must be evaluated by calculating the net benefits of each available alternative action. Importantly, *all* of the stakeholders affected by the decision should be given their just consideration. As mentioned above, teleological theories deal with outcomes or end goals. The often-stated declaration, "the end justifies the means," is one classic implication of utilitarian thinking.

Several formulations of utilitarianism exist. Their differences go back to the original writers on the topic, nineteenth-century British philosophers and economists Jeremy Bentham and John Stuart Mill.[1] One major school of thought, *act utilitarianism,* focuses on the *action* which has been taken, analyzing it along the lines of whether the selected action produces more good than bad consequences. For example, Facebook seems to be operating by the principle that it will revise its privacy policy if enough significant criticism arises. The company has revised its privacy policy and expanded it several times in recent years because the impact of not doing so would likely have resulted in dissatisfaction with the site. The managers of the firm appear to be making these decisions depending on the perceived

Box 2.1 Moral maxims for marketing

Several maxims which might aid a marketer facing an ethical dilemma are the following:

The Golden Rule: Act in a way that you would hope others would act toward *you.*

The Professional Ethic: Take only actions which would be viewed as proper by an objective panel of your professional colleagues. (The American Marketing Association Ethical Norms and Values for Marketers presented in Box 1.1 is an example of a professional code.)

The TV/Newspaper Test: A manager should always ask, "Would I feel comfortable explaining this action on TV or on the front page of the local newspaper to the general public?" (This test is sometimes referred to as *The Wall Street Journal* or *Financial Times* Test.)

When in Doubt, Don't: If a manager him or herself feels uneasy in his/her mind, heart or gut about a decision, there is probably reason to question it. We advise our students that if the decision does not seem right it should be postponed. The individual should probably seek guidance from a trusted person before proceeding with the decision.

Slippery Slope: This maxim suggests that companies must be careful not to engage in debatable practices that may serve as a precedent for undertaking other even more questionable strategies later. For example, there could be good reason for a sales manager to push sales "up the channel" toward the end of a fiscal quarter so that a hard working group of sales reps achieve their bonuses. However, such tactics may lead to an increasing acceptance by management that it is okay to be "fast and loose" with inventory figures (i.e., the slippery slope). (Although this maxim does occur in marketing, we see the recent scandals that plagued several financial firms and the accounting profession as classic illustrations of the slippery slope.)

Mother/Founder on Your Shoulder: Would your mother or the company founder be comfortable with the ethical decision being made? Could you explain it to them in common sense terms they would understand?

Never Knowingly Do Harm: This asserts that a manager would not consciously make or sell a product not deemed to be safe. Certain observers call this the "silver rule" because it does not hold marketers to as high a standard as the Golden Rule does.

Examine How Results are Achieved: This statement focuses on the means rather than the ends in the selling of products (recall BP3). If attention is devoted to ethically accomplishing results, they are likely to be justly achieved.

Ethics is Others: This comment implies that ethical individuals will always consider others in making decisions. It goes against the egoistic conception of individuals that always place themselves first (Henry Shea, University of St. Thomas, 2009).

negative consequences of not taking some action. This is a representative application of act utilitarianism.

A second formulation, *rule utilitarianism,* looks at whether the option or choice conforms to a *rule* that attempts to maximize the overall utility. Some have criticized act utilitarianism on the grounds that it often gives the wrong ethical answer when evaluating individual actions. To use an example from banking that has occurred many times in recent years, suppose a banker is considering whether it is right to foreclose on the mortgage of a widow and her children. To consider that decision in isolation, it is fairly easy to show on "act utilitarian" grounds that foreclosure would generate more costs than not foreclosing. However, suppose we had a rule that said that banks should not foreclose whenever the action of foreclosing would cause more harm than not foreclosing. If that *rule* were adopted, then banks would be reluctant to ever lend money. Thus, the rule permitting foreclosure on widows is better for society than a rule which forbids such disclosure. Rule utilitarians, then, focus on the rules for acting rather than on individual actions themselves. For a rule utilitarian a rule is morally correct when it provides more social good than any alternative rule. For act utilitarians rules are just rules of thumb. For rule utilitarians, rules are determinate of right and wrong.

Marketing executives commonly embrace such consequentialist approaches to ethical problems, because they are so compatible with traditional business thinking. Why? Just as this results-based theory seeks to maximize happiness or *the good*, business executives often hope to maximize sales and/or profit, return on investment, and/or share price. If a businessperson draws the broader conclusion that the greatest good is equivalent to the highest profitability then this situation produces the most benefits for society; thus, it is easy to see how these two systems (classical utilitarianism and financial optimization), both oriented to maximizing results, are philosophically compatible.

UTILITARIAN PHILOSOPHY AND MARKETING MANAGEMENT

A strong appeal of the utilitarian approach is its *cost-benefit* character. Marketing managers regularly weigh the pros and cons of alternative economic and managerial actions. This approach to problem solving is a staple of most business schools. Executives appreciate the fact that utilitarians recognize that not everyone will benefit from a particular action. Hence, the emphasis in utilitarianism is upon the *net* utility of the set of outcomes resulting from a decision being considered. Marketing managers, of course, also realize their business decisions must often be placed in the context of a "win-lose" situation. That is, the consequences of a business action are seldom singular; rather they are multiple and may "cut both ways." For instance, in mature markets, the only way to *gain* market share is for at least one competitor to lose share—a zero sum game. Or the only approach to increasing long-term shareholder value is to sacrifice near-term profits (and perhaps management bonuses) in favor of future product or market development expenditures.

Another reason a marketer is so accepting of utilitarian thinking lies in its *flexibility* in response to differing situations. Utilitarianism accommodates complex circumstances more easily than other, more absolute, philosophical approaches. The factors considered in a utilitarian framework can be conveniently varied from the short term to the long term or from financial to partially non-financial criteria. While conflicting stakeholder claims *can* be recognized, managers typically weigh business owner or stockholder goals associated with corporate profitability as more important than the goals of other groups such as employees or the community.

For example, in a situation involving the distribution manager of a grocery chain sending lower quality cuts of meat and vegetables to less profitable stores in disadvantaged neighborhoods, one can see how this approach *might* be defended. The manager rationalizes that as long as the meats and vegetables are above some minimally acceptable quality level, it is in the best financial interest of the supermarket chain to take whatever action it can to enhance overall operations. With respect to units located in the least affluent areas of the city, economic advantage is maximized by systematically discriminating against these less profitable units. Alternatively, management may also calculate (quite reasonably) that the marginal value of the store in a disadvantaged neighborhood can only be maintained by offsetting the impact of higher insurance and security costs and lower sales volume per square foot with other cost-cutting measures. This reasoning may also be combined with recognizing the need to provide higher quality to customers in more affluent areas that may also present the greatest threat from competitors. When compared to the alternative of closing an otherwise unprofitable store (with the external costs of unemployment and less service to that neighborhood), the current practice *may be* the most ethical in a strict utilitarian sense.

LIMITATIONS OF UTILITARIANISM

Consequentialist approaches to ethical reasoning are obviously not without their problems. Perhaps the most evident concern, which applies to almost any formulation of utilitarianism, is the question of who decides what "the greatest good" is. Indeed, usually many opinions exist as to what constitutes the nature of the actual benefits of a particular action. When this is the case, *who is* it that decides which perception of what "good" shall prevail? Is it the CEO, the Vice President of Marketing, the product manager, some set of agreed upon professional norms or customer perceptions? Second, it appears that utilitarianism is a philosophy where ends sometimes may justify otherwise unacceptable means. That is, just because the outcome of a particular action produces a "net good" for a corporation, or, for that matter the whole of society, should that outcome necessitate a major penalty or expense for some parties? Should any product be permitted in the market if it causes a significant and lasting health problem for a minority of users? A common situation is the side effects of many prescription drugs. Those who practice most forms of utilitarianism recognize that, in the ideal, one should not cause great harm to certain others in order to achieve a desirable or noble end. This seems to be partly the point that animal-rights activists stress in advocating a ban on the use of animals in safety testing cosmetics. In fact, one of the greatest simple ethical precepts (mentioned in Box 2.1) is *never knowingly do harm.* But, the definition of what constitutes "a significant harm" and a harm to whom (for instance, animals) is subject to debate.

Finally, those marketing managers who adopt a primarily economic interpretation of utilitarianism must answer whether such an approach is compatible with the concept of justice. The transformation of utilitarian theory into economic utilitarianism is somewhat understandable, in the sense that a business organization is primarily an *economic* enterprise. But simply because an action is economically beneficial does this mean it is just and proper? For instance, since the market demands sexually explicit Internet pornographic material—and pornography is profitable to most of the parties involved in its production and consumption—is it *ethical* to market these products and services? Even though a particular action has produced the greatest economic good for the greatest number, that still does not *prove* that the action is just and proper. Both production and consumption can victimize some participants in both societal and economic terms. Two of your authors have noted that this financial interpretation of utilitarianism is increasingly associated with advanced education in business.

This unspoken ethic of MBA education might best be described as a form of restricted economic utilitarianism. In the absence of other articulated values, MBAs gravitate to using cost-benefit analysis with utility measured in dollars (mostly calculated in the short run since the long term usually cannot be reliably estimated) and oriented toward large shareholders (the primary stakeholder group whose good is being evaluated and maximized).[2]

In short, the utilitarian principle—to act in ways that result in a greatest good for the greatest number—is a popular method of ethical reasoning used by many marketing managers, but it also presents problems in its application under various circumstances.

Duty-based ethical theories

A second category of ethical theories are classified by philosophers as *deontological,* the term coming from the Greek word, *deon,* or "duty." This impressive sounding word basically indicates that actions are best judged as "good," standing alone and without regard to consequences. Thus, the inherent rightness of an act is *not* decided by analyzing and choosing the act that produces the best consequences, but rather according to the premise that certain actions are morally "correct" in and of themselves because they stem from fundamental obligations. Intentions or motivations, and not exclusively the act itself, determine whether a marketing decision is ethical or unethical.

Perhaps the most famous duty-based theory was developed by the German philosopher Immanuel Kant.[3] He contended that moral laws took the form of categorical imperatives—principles which defined behavior appropriate in all situations and that should be followed by all persons as a matter of duty. Kant proposed three formulations of his supreme categorical (i.e., unconditional) imperative as follows:

1. Act only on maxims which you can will to be universal laws of nature. (Universality formulation)
2. Always treat the humanity in a person as an end, and never as a means *merely*. (Human dignity formulation)
3. Act as if you were a member of an ideal kingdom of ends in which you were both subject and sovereign at the same time. (Moral community formulation)

The first formulation argues that there are universal moral standards. For example, could any society universalize customer shoplifting? The answer is no. Similarly, bribery of government officials by marketers is unethical following the first formulation. The second formulation is concerned with treatment of all stakeholders as persons (recall BP1). The application of this principle in marketing is to never treat customers merely as means, manipulating their behavior to attain company goals. One of the controversial areas of marketing that seems to violate this formulation is high profit margin sales to impoverished markets. The third formulation views any marketing organization and their stakeholders as a moral community. Managers, then, should respect the humanity of all workers in the firm and employees should try to achieve common goals and shared ends.[4] For example, would a "big box" retailer consider their vendor selection policies to be "fair" if they were a supplier? In a larger sense, a market, including its network of suppliers, competitors, and customers, constitutes a relevant moral community.

For business, duty-based approaches to ethics have important implications. This theory suggests, among other things, that cost-benefit analysis is inappropriate to the evaluation of some situations. Why? Decisions that produce good corporate outcomes but significantly hurt other stakeholders in the process are not morally acceptable using this line of reasoning. For instance, if marketers have a special obligation to vulnerable consumers, such as the elderly, children, or less educated citizens who are unable to resist manipulative advertising appeals, then they violate that obligation. Also, it suggests that the goal of seeking the maximum *net* consequences of an action may include intermediate steps, which could be judged as morally inappropriate. Why is this so? Because *means* as well as *ends* should be subjected to moral evaluation. Thus, an implication of duty-based theories is that sometimes business executives must take actions, which do *not* produce the best economic consequences. To do otherwise could be ethically wrong. That is, some actions might violate the basic duty to treat everyone fairly. For example, reflection indicates that the customers of the low-income stores, where the poorest cuts of meat and vegetables are sent, have been used merely as a *means* to obtain a satisfactory economic *end*. A similar judgment might be applied to using fear appeals in promoting certain security products (e.g., hand guns or burglar alarms).

Like utilitarianism, duty-based theories are controversial in part because there are many different deontological theories. Various moral philosophers have compiled lists of basic obligations or duties. While the lists overlap, they are not identical. Second, duty-based theories represent the antithesis of modern relativism (i.e., the notion that moral decisions can only be made in the context of particular situations). Hence, they are viewed by some as not being well suited to our complex, multicultural, and global marketplace, because they emphasize the development of *universal* rules. The very nature of such absolute approaches includes certain problems that are inherent in the development of categorical imperatives. Among these are the following:

1. **There are always contingencies that seem to complicate real-world situations.** For example, suppose a sales organization has an absolute rule against the practice of providing gifts to customers. Now suppose, further, it enters a new international market, like Japan, where gift giving is a common and expected practice. Also consider the prospect that success in this market will determine whether the firm can survive. Should the universal rule be violated or changed to accommodate these contingencies? Other examples also might be explored. What about the prospect of dire consequences if one tells the truth? Are duties to customers or employees conditioned by their comparative economic vulnerability?

2. **Universals also do not take into account the ethical character of the formulator of the universal principle.** That is, they do not precisely specify who the formulator of the principle should be. If the morality of the person formulating the principle is flawed, it is possible that the principle itself will be deficient. For example, one might take issue with the universal maxims formulated by egoistic or relativistic managers in BP4 who see business as merely a game, the sole purpose of which is the accumulation of personal wealth.

3. **There may not be a mechanism for resolving conflicts among two absolute moral duties.** Managers clearly have a fiduciary responsibility to their shareholders and a duty of fidelity to their employees. What happens when action requires a trade-off between these duties? Which duty takes precedence? Is one universal more absolute than another? What about the duty to a friend versus loyalty to their job and company?

Contract-based ethical theories

Social contract theory is the third major type of ethical theory. It is based on the most fundamental considerations for maintaining social order and harmony, that is, people must generally agree to abstain from exploiting one another and, to ensure that this does not occur, rules and mechanisms to enforce cooperation are required. For marketers, social contract theory (SCT) has special obligations for relationships among competitors and for transactions with less powerful buyers and sellers, especially those who are dependent on the marketer as either a customer or supplier. By implication, social contract theory demands obedience to laws and adherence to the provisions of business contracts.

SOCIAL CONTRACTS THEORY (SCT)

A *hypothetical social contract* takes into account ethical standards developed by groups through real social contacts and is based on their mutual interest in supportive or, at minimum, benign interaction. In other words, managers both desire and expect that there be basic ethical rules to govern their marketplace transactions. They envision global humanity coming together to work out a rational arrangement for ethics in economic life. Humans at this global "convention" would recognize that moral rationality is bounded in the same way that economic rationality is bounded. Thus, SCT concludes that business communities or groups, including marketing managers, should have "moral free space," because they want to keep their moral options open until they confront the full context and environment of a decision.[5] Though the idea of moral free space recognizes *some degree of relativity*, we are mindful of the importance of the power-responsibility equilibrium (discussed in BP1) where more is expected of large, powerful organizations. Furthermore, there are certain core values—called hypernorms—that remain sacrosanct and these are examined next.

In theory, there may be norms that condone murder as a method of enforcing contracts, or that endorse racial or sexual discrimination. As a consequence, it can be assumed that the vast majority of people would want to restrict the moral free space of communities by requiring that, before any community norms become ethically obligatory, they must be found to be compatible with the most basic of human values. *Hypernorms* (the norms by which all other norms are to be judged) entail principles so fundamental to human existence that we expect them to be reflected in a convergence of religious, philosophical, and cultural beliefs. A list of hypernorms likely includes:

- An obligation to respect the dignity of each human person,
- Core human rights, such as personal freedom, physical security and access to the means of well being-basic healthcare, education and right of property ownership,
- Equity, the fair treatment of similarly situated persons,
- Avoiding unnecessary injury to others, and
- The preservation of the physical environment so that it is *sustainable* for future generations.

The notion that "acceptable standards" of business or industry practice cannot violate hypernorms is one of the basic contributions of this approach. Social Contracts Theory has been applied to the question of international bribery and political corruption and it establishes a means for displaying the ethical relevance of some existing norms in industries, corporations, and other economic communities, even as it limits the acceptable range of such practices. This theory advocates much closer scrutiny of existing ethical beliefs and practices in both micro and macro institutions as dissimilar as the European Community, the Nintendo Corporation, the international magnesium market, and Muslim banks. Because the SCT theory approach clearly suggests that core values of marketplace practice exist and they are universal, there are absolute rules of the business sector that apply across the globe.

RAWLSIAN THEORY

Another contemporary contract-based theory was formulated by the late American Philosopher John Rawls.[6] Rawls proposed two principles of justice, which, like Kant's categorical imperative, are never to be violated. Rawls formulated these rules using a "thought experiment" involving the *veil of ignorance*. Briefly, this experiment supposed how fair-minded individuals would create the rules of morality to be formulated if they did not know their future position in society—that is, when they emerged from this "veil," they might be king or beggar. From this, two principles are derived: the *liberty principle* and the *difference principle.*

> The liberty principle states that each person is to have an equal right to the most extensive basic liberty compatible with a similar liberty for others.
> The difference principle states that social and economic equalities are to be arranged so that they are to the greatest benefit of the least advantaged.

The liberty principle is fairly understandable in light of Western political tradition. It implies that people have inherent rights, such as freedom of speech, to vote, to due process of law, and to own property, and that they have a right to exercise these liberties to the extent that they do not infringe upon the fundamental liberties of others. The controversial health care plan passed by the Obama administration in the US represents a good illustration of the liberty principle, because individuals who had previously been unable to secure health insurance are now protected under the provisions of this bill—that is, they have access to healthcare consistent with that which others already had. (It should be noted that all other developed countries already had provisions for making healthcare a universal right.)

The difference principle is a bit more complicated. Basically, it states actions should not be taken that will further disadvantage those groups in society which are currently the least well-off. In other words, corporate actions should be formulated in such a way that their social and economic effects are not to the detriment of the least advantaged. Over time, it is an egalitarian principle that should make those least well-off, better off. The difference principle also emphasizes that it would be unethical to exploit one group for the benefit of others. For example, if a public relations firm was considering whether to accept a foreign government with a questionable human rights record as a client, the difference principle would suggest the agency should forego that opportunity because the implementation of a public relations campaign could add legitimacy to the (presumably corrupt) ruling foreign government. Furthermore, it might exacerbate the position of a worse-off group, namely, citizens in a country where human rights are systematically violated. More generally, it suggests that marketers have super-ordinate duties to consumers who are illiterate in the workings of the political and economic marketplace.

Virtue-based ethics

A fourth comprehensive theory of ethics is referred to as *virtue ethics.* It has a long tradition and is currently receiving renewed emphasis. In part, virtue ethics is a modern day reaction to the rampant relativism wherein society seems to lack a way of reaching moral agreement about ethical problems. The relativistic approach to morality seems to be based on the strength of persuasive appeals and personal intuitionism, whereby, when interests collide, one opinion is as good as another. It is almost a one-person, one-vote method to establishing what is ethical. Virtue ethics has been resurrected to counteract modern relativism.

What exactly is virtue ethics? Its key criterion is seeking to live a virtuous life. In many ways, it is a renaissance of the Greek ideal suggesting that the guiding purpose of life should be the quest for goodness and virtue. In philosophical circles, the most prominent proponent is Alasdair MacIntyre of the University of Notre Dame (USA). MacIntyre defines virtue as acquired human qualities that enable persons to achieve "the good" in their chosen vocations, that is, the development of personal and professional character.[7]

Virtue ethics differs from the consequences, duty and contract based ethics in that the focus is on the individual and not the decision to be made or the principle to be followed. As such, virtue ethics is fundamentally unique among the theories. Advocates of virtue ethics suggest that one problem with contemporary organizations is that when they do look at situations based on popular ethical perception, they become preoccupied with what the public thinks. Put another way, today's corporations may be entirely too reactive, wondering at times whether their actions will be perceived as "opportunistic," "exploitative," or in "bad taste" by the general public. This may be a misdirected effort that can be rectified through virtue ethics. Thus, organizations should instead focus on questions, such as "What kind of organization *should* we be?" and "What constitutes the ideal ethical firm?" Companies that know what they stand for and then embody these beliefs in a company credo or values statement are following this approach to ethics. In short, the virtue ethics perspective seems to imply that the question of *understanding* virtue precedes the discussion and development of rules of conduct. Once management understands the nature of a virtuous organization, ethical decision rules are much easier to develop.

Followers of this approach find much worth in the writings of ancient Greek philosopher Aristotle.[8] While the essence of virtue ethics cannot easily be captured in a few sentences, there are some key elements that reflect this mode of thinking. First, virtues are essentially good habits. In order to flourish, these habits must be practiced and, the uninitiated managers in the organization must learn these virtues. This point has powerful implications for managers, including the notion that (a) firms can only become virtuous by actually engaging in ethical activities and (b) organizations have to teach managers precisely what the appropriate virtues are. In other words, companies have the responsibility to help foster ethical behavior. Wharton Professor Thomas Donaldson says that, "Aristotle tells us that ethics is more like building a house than it is like physics. You learn to be an ethical manager by managing, not by reading textbooks on philosophy." Professional philosophers sometimes view the practice of business ethics as a theoretical pursuit, continues Donaldson. "It's not. It is an art. It can't be reduced to a science." For an Aristotelian, it's impossible for a company to be too ethical.

A second dimension of virtue ethics is that admirable characteristics are most readily discovered by witnessing and imitating widely acclaimed behavior. Aristotle, while focusing on the individual rather than the organization, listed such virtues as truthfulness, justice, generosity, and self-control as characteristics to which the noble person should aspire. In the theory of virtue, much attention is placed on role models. The insight here is that to be an ethical person is not simply an analytical and rational matter. It takes virtuous people to make right decisions, and virtue is learned by doing. Put another way, the ultimate test and source of ethical conduct is the character of the actor. Aristotle often discussed the lives of obviously good Athenians in order to teach ethics. One learned the right thing to do by observing good people and by doing what they did. Such lessons reinforce the importance of top management serving as role models or mentors and looking to the best practices of admired corporations in the formation of an ethical corporate climate.

Companies that are acclaimed for their ethical corporate culture very often can trace their heritage back to their founder's intent on developing an organization that respected personal dignity and insisted on a humane way of life. Founders of such companies as McDonalds shaped their organization so that they embodied the values and virtues that proved personally rewarding. The way of life in the company was not a result of an abstract code of conduct, but rather statements that were later used to spell out exactly what was at the heart of the existing corporate culture. For example, the top management of Levi Strauss has introduced four guiding values/virtues—empathy, originality, integrity, and courage. (For a complete discussion, visit www.levistrauss.com/about/values-vision.) Significantly, the apparel company Patagonia also opted to retain private ownership and not publically offer their stock as this would detract from their core principles of corporate social responsibility (CSR).

Third, a key to understanding virtue ethics and the discipline it requires is based on the *ethic of the mean.* Applied to virtue ethics, the mean is an optimal *balance* of a quality that one should seek. An excess or deficiency of any of the key virtues can be troublesome, as Aristotle argued.[9] For example, an excess of truthfulness is boastfulness. A deficiency of truthfulness is deception. Both of these outcomes (the excess or the deficiency) are unacceptable. The Swedish language has a word, *lagom*, meaning "not too much, not too little, but just enough." The virtuous marketing manager, then, strives for such a balance among the qualities it takes to be effective. For example, she should not be so directive as to be authoritarian, nor so easy-going as to abdicate her leadership role. Golfers may appreciate the analogy that one's goal in the sport is to stay in the fairway and out of the rough. This, according to virtue ethics, is the way a marketing manager should behave, by not going to extremes.

Obviously, there is disagreement about exactly what characteristics should appear on a list of virtues to which an organization should aspire. Over the years, different philosophers have compiled many different lists. Business executives and professors have enumerated virtues (Table 2.1) that they feel are most important for relationship marketing.[10] Whether or not a particular corporation elects to foster those virtues is another issue.

However, let's assume for a moment that an organization accepts the virtue ethics approach to corporate conduct. In other words, they subscribe to the belief that an organization should be "all that it can be" in an ethical sense. Then, with regard to the various common business practices, one might conclude that (a) the virtuous organization has no need to provide expensive gifts to purchasing agents in order to secure product orders, (b) the virtuous organization should always be truthful; therefore it has no problem with disclosing a change of components as well as updating consumers with regard to the reliability of all their brands; and (c) the virtuous organization will not stoop to fear-generating, emotional appeals to sell its products—emotional manipulation is wrong, thus, most fear appeals would be inappropriate.

One logical objection to the application of virtue ethics in an organizational context is that it would sometimes be very difficult to agree on what, in fact, constitutes "the good." What virtues should an organization emulate and how should those virtues be operationalized in company policy? The contemporary philosopher MacIntyre and other recent proponents of virtue ethics seem to deal with this situation in the following way. First, they recognize a great diversity of virtues exists in society. However, in many cases, particular organizations are self-contained. It is within the context of individual companies that the notion of appropriate virtues should be explored. Second, consistent with Aristotle, they

Table 2.1 Relationship marketing and virtue ethics

Virtue	Definition	Related virtues	Applications to marketing
Integrity	Adherence to a moral code and completeness	Honesty, Moral courage	Conveying accurate and complete information to consumers
Fairness	Marked by equity and free from prejudice or favoritism	Justice	Selling and pricing products at a level commensurate with benefits received
Trust	Faith or confidence in another party	Dependability	Confidence that salespeople or suppliers will fulfill obligations without monitoring
Respect	Giving regard to views of others	Consideration	Altering products to meet cultural needs and refusing to sell unsafe products anywhere
Empathy	Being aware of and sensitive to the needs and concerns of others	Caring	Refraining from selling products to consumers who cannot afford them
Transparency	Making actions clear to others	Openness	Being open with customers and other stakeholders

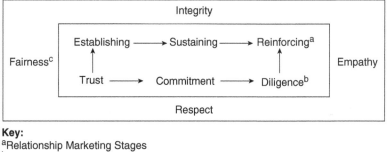

Key:
[a]Relationship Marketing Stages
[b]Key (Foundational) Virtues
[c]Facilitating (Supporting) Virtues
[d]In Communication and Action

Source: Adapted from P. E. Murphy, "Character and Virtue Ethics in International Marketing," *Journal of Business Ethics* (January 1999), 113; and P. Murphy, G. Laczniak and G. Wood, "An Ethical Basis for Relationship Marketing: A Virtue Ethics Perspective," *European Journal of Marketing* (2007), 44.

assume these virtues will be "other directed" (i.e., undertaken for the good of the community rather than in a self-serving manner). Third, this theory assumes people aspire to a higher level of ethics. Unfortunately, we know that this is not always the case. Hence, virtue ethics is sometimes criticized as being far too idealistic.

It is important to note that we find the corporation among the more controlled communities in modern society. Each firm, large or small, has its own *corporate character*, sometimes rooted in religious values (discussed next). It is within the context of corporate culture that a particular company can seek virtues appropriate for that organization. All of this, of course, underscores the importance of developing an ethical corporate culture that facilitates appropriate managerial behavior and is rooted in ethics following from the "shared community" view (3rd formulation of Kant's categorical imperative) discussed above in duty-based ethics.

Religious approaches to marketing ethics

The four ethical schools of thought presented previously are properly characterized as mostly *secular* or *civic*. They are the product of moral reasoning, based on human experience, and can be viewed as applying to and derived from nature as opposed to any religious or sectarian source.

However, it is also relevant to recognize the extent to which religion contributes to the ethical standards observed in the world. Because of the historical importance of trade, both within and between communities, it was natural for people to seek moral guidance from religious sources—and for religious leaders to provide such guidance as representing divine instruction. In particular, Judeo-Christian, Confucian, Jewish, Islamic, and Buddhist religions have ethical precepts at their core. (For a summary of the latter four religious traditions, see Box 2.2.) Although the religious perspective is sometimes expressed as opposing business institutions, many believe that the world's religions have much to offer in terms of ethical guidance to marketers. In recognizing cultural influences over human behavior, regardless of one's own religious heritage, students of marketing (particularly global marketing) are well advised to become familiar with such primary rules and principles from religious sources because they continue to be a dominant force in the development and maintenance of worldwide social norms.

Judeo-Christian religious leaders have often preached that the answers to the majority of moral questions, business-related or otherwise, could be found in the Bible. There has also

---

Box 2.2 Religious models of marketing ethics

Jewish ethical tradition
The Hebrew Torah also offers substantial guidance to marketers.[a] Several Jewish laws are appropriate for the practice of marketing. They are:

Accurate weights and measures
Throughout the Talmudic period, the rabbis appointed market commissioners to inspect measures and weights and to fix prices for basic commodities. These laws are equally applicable today. Wholesalers and retailers must check their scales and cash registers on a regular basis, not just because civil law demands it, but also because Jewish law requires it.

Monetary deception
This concept is based on a verse from the Torah "When you sell anything to your neighbor or buy anything from your neighbor, you shall not deceive one another." Needless to say, these laws are relevant today. It is permissible for a Jew to make a fair profit; it is not permissible to price gouge and rob the customer blind.

Verbal deception
This teaching is based on another Torah verse "Do not deceive one another, but fear your God, for I the Lord am your God." Let us say that Reuven goes into a warehouse outlet in order to buy a computer, but he wants a demonstration before he spends $1000. The warehouse outlet is not equipped for demonstrations. The salesman says to Reuven: "Go to the Apple showroom down the block and ask for a demonstration, then come back here and buy the computer at our low, low price." Reuven complies

and gets a free demonstration plus a discount. When Reuven asks for the demonstration at the Apple store, he has absolutely no intention of purchasing the computer there. He merely wants a free demonstration. The Apple salesman is being deceived. He either loses a real customer while waiting on Reuven, or feels badly when Reuven walks out on him after a half-hour demonstration. This is ona'at devarim, verbal deception.

Stealing a person's mind

We would call it false packaging or false labeling. We are all familiar with this kind of ruse. A wholesaler takes an inferior brand of shirt and puts on Pierre Cardin labels. You buy a box of perfect-looking tomatoes or strawberries, only to discover upon opening the box at home that they were packaged with the bad spots facing down. And we all know how used cars are touched up and polished for the sole purpose of overcharging the customer. Such behavior is clearly forbidden by Jewish law.

Putting a stumbling block before the blind

We would call it "giving someone a bum steer." This law can be readily applied to modern situations: a real estate agent should not dupe a young couple into buying a home with structural faults simply in order to make a fast buck. A stockbroker should not sell his client a bad investment just to collect the commission. A salesman should not convince his customer to buy an expensive item he really has no use for. About such behavior we are warned: "and you shall fear your God, I am the Lord."

Islamic ethical tradition

The Islamic religious tradition has received much closer examination after the tragic events of September 11, 2001. In fact, the mainstream Muslim religious tradition is rich in the moral precepts it espouses. Muslim business executives have followed several axioms of Islamic Ethical Philosophy for centuries. Muslims observe the values of *equity* and *justice*. Among the most prominent are *unity, equilibrium, free will, responsibility*, and *benevolence*.[b] These axioms can be related to marketing ethics in that these are similar to virtues and duties of marketers.

Confucian ethics

The Confucian conception of business ethics is most closely akin to virtue ethics. *Trust*—and *trustworthiness*—are central to the Confucian ethos.[c] An early Confucian philosopher, Mencias, noted three interrelated concepts are central to what virtue is all about. These three notions are *extensions* (t'ui or ta), *attention* (ssu), and *intelligent awareness* (chih). Virtue is actualized by individuals when they learn to extend both knowledge from one situation to other similar ones. From a marketing standpoint, product and advertising managers should learn the appropriate ethical norms in their dealings with advertising agencies and other external consultants. For the attention concept, Mencias pithily commented: "If one attends one gets it; if one does not, one does not." Thus, ethical training depends on the individual perceiving clearly, identifying corresponding actions, and responding only after careful reflection. Finally, intelligent awareness is expressed by the middle way between two extremes: "intelligence should guide our actions, but in harmony with [the] texture of the situation at hand, not in accordance [only] with a set of rules or procedures."[d]

Buddhist ethical imperatives

Trade and industry are viewed as comparatively recent developments in those nations where Buddhism is a prominent religious tradition. Nonetheless, the writings attributed to the Buddha address a number of issues that are relevant to marketers, particularly at the "macro" level.ᵉ Among these are the need to provide for basic needs (in the context of a simple life style); the need for agricultural/rural development (as opposed to concentrating development efforts in urban areas); respect for the preservation of the resources and beauty of nature; encouragement of private enterprise, self reliance, and economic freedom; and the personal and social value of full employment with a living wage (certain business enterprises are also frowned on such as those involving armaments, intoxicating drink, poisons, animal slaughter, gambling, and slavery). There are five Buddhist principles that cannot be broken while working: (1) one cannot cause harm to another, (2) one may not cheat, (3) one may not lie, (4) one cannot promote intoxication, and (5) one cannot engage in sexual exploitation.

Hindu ethics

The Hindu religion also contains directions for spiritual fulfillment. Hindu scripture gives insights into how to balance priorities to attain true success:

Generating wealth (*artha*) is to be pursued within the larger priority of contributing to the well-being of society (*dharma*). Satisfying desires (*Kama*) is to be pursued within the larger priority of spiritual fulfillment (*moksha*). In accord with the wisdom of these spiritual teachings, we can see that business success naturally emphasizes contribution to society and spiritual fulfillment. When traditional measures of business success—shareholder return, market share, industry power, and so on—are subordinate to these higher priorities, wealth can be generated and desires can be satisfied while naturally promoting well-being rather than harm, service rather than greed, and an uplifted spirit rather than unscrupulous competition.ᶠ

A practical example comes from Isaac Tigret, the founder of Hard Rock Café. One of his objectives was to open an "absolutely classless" (aiming at all social classes) restaurant in London. While on a spiritual pilgrimage in India he heard the saying, "Love All, Serve All." To him, it embodied the ultimate goal of life: to love people and to serve from that place. That became the spiritual source of the company culture:

> *All I did was put spirit and business together in that big mixing bowl and add love. I didn't care about anything but people…just cherish them, look after them, and be sensitive to them and their lives.*ᵍ

a See, for example, Meir Tamari, *In the Marketplace: Jewish Business Ethics* (Southfield, MI: Targum Press, 1991); Moses L. Pava, "The substance of Jewish business ethics," *Journal of Business Ethics*, 17:6 (April I, 1998): 603–17; David Vogel, "How green is Judaism? – exploring Jewish environmental ethics," *Business Ethics Quarterly*, 11:2 (April 2001): 349–63; and Hershey H. Friedman, "The impact of Jewish values on marketing and business practices," *Journal of Macromarketing*, 21:1 (June 2001): 74–80.

b M. Saeed, Z. Ahmed, and S.-M. Mukhtar, "International marketing ethics from an Islamic perspective: a value-maximization approach," *Journal of Business Ethics*, 32:2 (2001): 127–42; see also, R. Beekun, *Islamic Business Ethics*, Herndon, VA: International Institute of Islamic Thought, 1997.

c D. Koehn, "Confucian trustworthiness and the practice of business in China," *Business Ethics Quarterly*, 11:3 (2001): 415–29.

d F. Varela, *Ethical know-how: action, wisdom, and cognition*, Stanford, CA: Stanford University Press, 1999.

e V. Wee, "Buddhist approach to economic development," in *Buddhist Perspective in the Face of the Third Millennium,* Proceedings of the Year 2000 Global Conference on Buddhism, Buddhist Fellowship, 2001. See also, Bodhipaksa, "Reinventing the wheel: a Buddhist approach to ethical work," in *Spiritual Goods: Faith Traditions and the Practice of Business*, edited by S. Herman with A. Schaefer Bowling Green, OH: Philosophy Documentation Center, 2001, pp. 33–54.

f "Defining Business Success," in *Put Your Spirituality to Work*, Book 3.5, Spiritual-Based Leaders, www.globaldharma.org.

g Ibid.

been considerable debate about the level of guidance generated by such religious principles. On the one hand, proscriptions like "thou shalt not steal" are unambiguous. On the other hand, many situations the contemporary corporate manager is faced with are exceedingly complex and defy the simple application of biblical precepts. Despite the difficulty of applying religious teachings, often rooted in centuries-old social conventions, to modern marketplace problems, to ignore them would be a serious omission. (We use Catholic Social Thought (CST) as an example of Christian ethical thinking, knowing several prominent (and very compatible) Protestant approaches also exist. Most of these principles are also consistent with the teachings of other major world religions—discussed further in Box 2.2.)

PRINCIPLES OF CATHOLIC SOCIAL THOUGHT (CST)

Starting in the late nineteenth century, in a philosophical response to the challenges posed by the Industrial Revolution, popes and bishops of the Catholic Church began to seek scriptural wisdom as it applied to social issues and to interpret it in light of modern circumstances. One especially notable attempt to inject moral values into the marketplace was the pastoral letter authored by the American Catholic bishops.[11] Within this broader, Catholic social tradition or CST, seven major principles have been advanced that relate directly to marketing ethics. While the Catholic Church, like most large and long lived institutions, has had its share of corruption and "not practicing what it preaches," these principles can be used by both believers and non-believers as a coherent and blended theory of business ethics. The argument has also been made in the marketing literature that all these principles can be derived from non-sectarian sources and that, therefore, they collectively constitute a hybrid ethical framework of independent merit.[12]

Human dignity—The most basic and fundamental instruction of CST flows from the idea that *all* persons have inherent worth regardless of race, color, or creed. Dignity is not "earned" but rather it is always a given right to be accorded to all persons in all circumstances. This principle is used to argue that *"The economy exists for the person, not the person for the economy"*[13] and that an excessive focus on profit maximization can be harmful to authentic personal development because rewards and burdens may not be justly distributed. Following this principle, the exploitation of workers in third-world countries to achieve cost advantage is clearly unethical. Similarly, charging premium credit rates to those least likely to handle their debt load seems to be an unambiguous violation of this principle.

Common good—This principle flows partly from the idea that persons typically live in community and, therefore, social rules should contribute to the benefits of the commonwealth. While CST clearly affirms the right of private property, this teaching provides a foundation for the notion that all persons have the right to secure the basic necessities of life (e.g., food, shelter, available work, as well as access to education and affordable healthcare). Following this principle, a marketing firm would assess the impact of its products on multiple stakeholders. A clear violation would be cigarettes that clearly do harm to consumers, often impact families negatively due to loss of loved ones and also impact society in terms of increased medical costs. The common good always should be a consideration in *outcomes* assessments (see BP3).

Subsidiarity—This is one of the most basic articulations of rights and responsibilities inherent in CST. Specifically, "It is an injustice…to assign to a greater or higher association what lesser and subordinate organizations can do."[14] Commentators on this principle also imply that the concept warns about the dangers of over-regulating business activities and, indeed, such an argument can be sustained. However, the same principle is also used in CST to insure that sufficiently powerful parties (including government) weigh in to offset persistently unfair practices in society. Following the subsidiarity principle means that companies would allow marketing departments, product managers, and salespeople the latitude to make decisions at the lowest feasible level regarding the treatment of customers and other stakeholders.

Preference for the poor and vulnerable—This teaching recalls the admonitions of Scripture to "Love thy neighbor" and "What you do for the least of my brethren, you do for me." Here CST argues that the proper end of economic activity is the progress of the entire community, especially the poor. The centrality of the obligation to help the poor is manifest not only in CST, but also in *every* other major religious doctrine—Jewish, Protestant, Islamic, Hindu, and Buddhist. Finance schemes that target the debt-laden or using fear tactics to sell second-rate products to the elderly surely would violate this principle. Securing market research information over the Internet from unsuspecting children is another clear trespass of this doctrine.

Worker rights—This theme advances the idea that work is central to human growth and that workers help to continue the wonder of creation – the oldest teaching of modern CST, dating back to 1891. A more recent affirmation proclaims: "All people have the right to economic initiative, to productive work, to just wages and benefits, to decent working conditions as well as to organize and join unions or other associations."[15] These writings grant workers the right to organize in unions and contend that past loyalties by workers always need to be recognized by the firm. This principle suggests that managers have a moral obligation to create trusting, nurturing communities in which employees can improve as persons, just as workers should be motivated to provide a productive work for their employer.

Solidarity—This concept recognizes that all people and social groups are united in a brother-hood that seeks common growth and fulfillment, dependent on one another for the support that we require in community. It provides a framework for the idea that "…economic life should be shaped by moral principles" because all persons both seek and want a fair opportunity to attain betterment in their lives.[16] This foundational theme of CST is the basis for advocating responsibilities of rich nations to poor as well as the special ethical obligations of multinational businesses operating in developing countries. This means that international marketers should develop products that are economically affordable and appropriate for customers in less affluent markets.

Stewardship—This precept captures the responsibility of every party—including corporations—to contribute to the care of the earth. It is among the newest in the evolution of CST. It calls for economic actions always to "respect the integrity and cycles of nature" and to fastidiously avoid environmental exploitation.[17] It views the physical environment as a common pool of abundant resources not to be exploited for the benefit of only a few or at the expense of future generations. It connects to the "green ethic" and "sustainability" so prominent in current business strategy discussions. Marketers practicing the stewardship principle would likely develop less environmentally harmful versions of their products, never engage in "greenwashing" (make deceptive environmental claims) and would create reverse channels for the disposal of their products.

BP 6–Embracing the Stakeholder Concept: six precepts

Adoption of a stakeholder orientation (SO) is essential to the advancement and maintenance of ethical marketing decision-making in any organization. The first stakeholder precept has to do with the definition of stakeholders. In its broadest conception, *a stakeholder* is any group or individual who can affect or is affected by the achievement of the organization's objectives.[18] This definition covers both those that influence decisions like employees and marketing managers as well as those impacted by marketing practices such as customers and suppliers.

A second aspect of the stakeholder orientation embodies the notion that the marketing system operates in and for society. Failing the acceptance of a stakeholder approach results in the default position that marketing operations exist mainly to maximize shareholder return, subject only to obeying the law (recall BP2). Taking an ethical perspective means that a broad notion of stakeholder is beneficial both for the company and society which is far-reaching when one considers the impact of multinationals like Unilever, General Electric, or Samsung.

A third major precept is that stakeholders can be classified in three ways (see Figure 2.1 for Southwest Airlines example). The first are primary stakeholders. *Primary* stakeholders have a *continuing and essential interest* because the organization would cease to exist without them. For employees and suppliers, this stake is usually a contractual one. Interestingly, and ethically troublesome as well, in some situations, not all customers are perceived to meet this primary criterion of a continuing interest. In consumer products and retailing sectors, heavy users, brand loyal customers, and "change adverse" customers would easily fit this primary classification. But the emerging area of customer relationship management seems to be typically predicated on the fact that not all customers are primary stakeholders—indeed some (unprofitable) customers are unwanted and better strategy might dictate that they be driven away. In a B2B setting, major customers such as the airlines for Airbus would

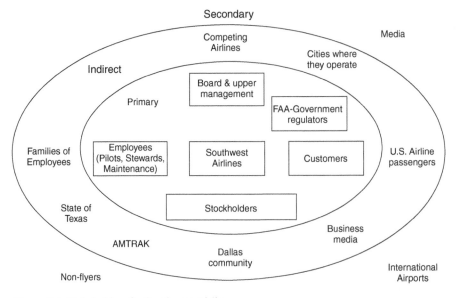

Figure 2.1 Stakeholders for Southwest Airlines

be considered primary. Another stakeholder that can be primary is the local community. Our conception would hold that the community is also a primary stakeholder if the firm or organization is a major employer in an area.

Indirect stakeholders possess an *abiding but more separated interest* in the organization. The distinction here is that the relationship is not as close as in the primary category. The term "indirect" is used in that the interaction with the organization is a more distant one. However, they are not "fringe" stakeholders because these groups have an ongoing concern for the marketing organization and can express it in a number of ways. For instance, their interest and stake is more immediate than the secondary group (defined below) but their support for firm success is not as essential as the relationship with primary stakeholders. Most alumni of private colleges and universities, direct competitors who are members of the same industry associations, families of employees and suppliers to a firm's supplier represent examples of indirect stakeholders. In Figure 2.1, the indirect stakeholders for Southwest Airlines include most of the above groups as well as the community in that this organization is only the tenth largest Dallas-area employer.

Finally, *secondary* stakeholders have a *potential interest* in the firm. Our position is that secondary stakeholders are not always affected or influenced by an organization, but that potential still exists. For instance, foreign governments in locations not served by a marketer are an illustration of this level of stakeholder. The media is often a secondary stakeholder in that their interest is only heightened when the organization's activities are deemed newsworthy. The distinction between *indirect* and *secondary* stakeholders is one that sometimes is not easy to categorize, but trying to do so helps firms to more effectively implement a stakeholder orientation. For example, in the case of advocacy groups, "Stop Wal-Mart" and the local Chambers of Commerce where Wal-Mart has operations would be classified as *indirect* to the world's largest retailer as their focus is on that company while general activist groups like Greenpeace and the AFL-CIO could be considered secondary.

A fourth precept of stakeholders is that marketers must engage stakeholders in a proactive way. Rather than passive individuals or organizations, stakeholders should be viewed as active participants in the marketing process. A number of firms including Nike and General Electric now frequently conduct stakeholder engagement meetings. While these meetings can sometimes be contentious, assembling critics and other interested parties may help a firm develop a more transparent and responsive marketing process. While the outcome of this stakeholder dialogue might be that some parties "agree to disagree," they will do so in a much more informed manner than if no communication had taken place.

The fifth precept of ethical stakeholder marketing is that companies espousing this viewpoint practice a "triple bottom line" (TBL) framework, also known as the People, Profit and Planet perspective. This means that marketers are concerned with not only the economic impact but also the social/ethical and environmental ones as well. In an era where ecological costs are increasingly measured by companies and societies, the TBL perspective is one that we expect will receive greater emphasis in the future. While significant impediments to measurement regarding social and environmental dimensions still exist, the Global Reporting Initiative (www.gri.org) and other international NGOs are examining stakeholder as well as TBL impacts.

The final precept regarding stakeholders is that marketers are thinking more broadly and futuristically about the consumer stakeholder, especially those billions of low income consumers in developing countries becoming more integrated into the global marketplace. Until recently, companies were content to look for other customers similar to the ones they are serving in the developed world. The most progressive MNCs added the global market to their target zones. Now, companies are focusing much more consciously on the "base of the pyramid." In fact, impoverished markets in the BRIC (Brazil, Russia, India and China) countries are receiving a great deal of attention. Firms like Hindustan Lever (Unilever's Indian subsidiary) have been successful in catering to this market and PepsiCo recently bought a major beverage company in Russia to increase its penetration there. From an ethical standpoint, there is a powerful case to be made that such impoverished consumers, due to their relative lack of economic and political power in the global marketplace, deserve special consideration as marketers target and sell to these new segments.[19]

BP7 – Moral Reasoning for Marketing Managers: the seven steps

Marketing organizations striving for exemplary ethical conduct ought to delineate an ethical analysis protocol and train their managers to follow it. The ability of managers to "ethically" reason is the *sine qua non* of organizations seeking to operate on an elevated ethical plane. One such protocol is charted in Figure 2.2. Moral reasoning, of course, presupposes as its first step the ability of managers to be *ethically aware*. Such ethical perceptivity is important because moral questions in marketing cannot be addressed unless they are first recognized. For example, despite numerous accident reports and media discussion, Toyota only belatedly became ethically aware of the gravity of the situation pertaining to its cars in the global marketplace. As discussed in BP4, the ethical aptitude of managers is deeply affected by their personal moral development. In addition, a manager's ethical awareness and imagination is a function of environmental factors such as the corporate culture of the organization, the extent to which explicit values positions have been articulated in a corporate ethics statement, the level of commitment by top executives to company integrity (BP4), as well as the presence of "ethical training opportunities" for a firm's employees.

Assuming that managers have a reasonable degree of moral awareness, ethical reasoning is next operationalized through the application of an ethical protocol, that is, the process that

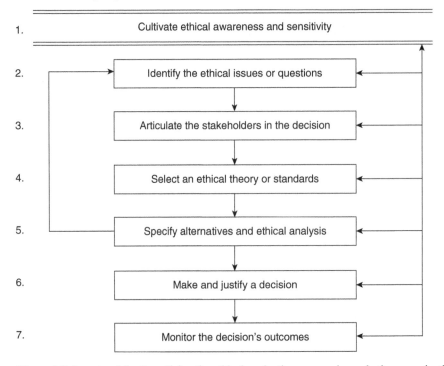

1.   Cultivate ethical awareness and sensitivity

2.   Identify the ethical issues or questions

3.   Articulate the stakeholders in the decision

4.   Select an ethical theory or standards

5.   Specify alternatives and ethical analysis

6.   Make and justify a decision

7.   Monitor the decision's outcomes

Figure 2.2 A protocol for formalizing the ethical evaluation process in marketing organizations

Source: Adapted from G. Laczniak and P. Murphy, "Normative perspectives for ethical and socially responsible marketing," *Journal of Macromarketing*, 26(2), p. 169.

The final, definitive version of this paper has been published in the *Journal of Macromarketing*, Vol. 26(2), December, 2006 by SAGE Publications Ltd./SAGE Publications, Inc., All rights reserved. © [2006].

helps the rendering of an ethical judgment. Our suggested process then unfolds with the *identifying of an ethical issue*. Specification of the ethical issue at focus is necessary for effective moral reasoning as to whether a firm is internally assessing its own marketing programs (i.e., microanalysis) or whether outside parties (for example, public policy makers) are evaluating broader industry practices (i.e., macro analysis). An illustration of ethical microanalysis in framing an issue might be a petroleum services firm that questions whether its proposed advertising campaign depicting a racially diverse workforce should be implemented when, in fact, the racial base of its employee group is rather homogenous. An example of macro analysis in framing an ethical issue might involve a state regulatory agency questioning whether "quick loan" financial service outlets might be judged as "unfair" in a U.S. economy where the annual prime rate has been hovering around 4% but such organizations' *monthly* interest charge might approach 20%. It should be understood that the formulation of an ethical question does not imply that the practice at focus will necessarily be deemed "unethical." For example, the *macro* issue of whether all advertising is inherently "unfair," because it normally presents only positive attributes of a product or service, has been raised many times. The vast majority of analysis finds the practice of adverting as a social institution to be ethically defensible. And advertising regulators are keen to point out how most advertising meets oftentimes strict ethical codes. The Advertising Standards Authority in the UK for example emphasize on their webpage— a) the number of complaints they receive is less than 1% of the total ads seen in a year; b) over 97% of ads meet the standards laid down in ethical codes; c) 99.7% of alcohol related ads and 99% of video gaming ads meet regulatory requirements. But clearly, the beginning of an ethical reasoning process is the specification of the ethical question(s) to be evaluated.

The third step in ethical analysis involves the *articulation of stakeholders* affected by a particular marketing practice (see BP6). For example, in the instance of a petrol company ad campaign, the stakeholder evaluations might include the following queries: Is diverse employee representation in the proposed ad campaign misleading to *customers* when the actual employee base is quite homogeneous? Is this campaign deceptive to future or current *shareholders*? Is it disrespectful to current *employees*? Each stakeholder group is a separate constituency with potentially different effects if the campaign is approved. Alternatively, perhaps the advertising campaign simply captures meaningless "puffing" that mostly depicts a corporation that is honestly desirous of being racially inclusive, at least in the ideal. All three levels—primary, indirect and secondary—of stakeholders should be part of this analysis.

The fourth step in the ethical reasoning process involves the *selection of an ethical theory*. Some number of ethical theories or perspectives (or perhaps just one) should be chosen for application to the ethical issue at focus. Possible standards would include but are not limited to those already discussed. In the case of the short term loan financial services industry, perhaps the initial evaluation standard selected will be minimalist—a *legal* one (i.e., are any existing laws being violated by the industries lending practices?); or alternatively, a *utilitarian* standard might be applied (i.e., are the high rates of interest being charged by these short term loan providers, embodying a high client cost, offset by the benefit to a segment of consumers who otherwise would not have fast access to credit?); or perhaps a *justice* standard is invoked (i.e., is a vulnerable market segment being exploited merely for company profit?). One or more of the five major types of ethical theories discussed in BP5 may be relevant.

Specifying alternatives and conducting an ethical analysis comes next in our protocol. It involves developing viable courses of action and applying the ethical standards to what- ever questions have been framed (above) both regarding the ethical issue at focus as well as to foreseeable outcomes upon stakeholder groups. The quality of this analysis, as noted previously, is likely to be influenced by the moral thinking of the manager/evaluator as well as the particular ethical standard or standards selected for application. Also, the specific stakeholder groups considered will have an important bearing on the process (BP6). The likely sophistication of ethical reasoning provided by different types of managers has already been discussed in BP4. For firms seeking to have a strong ethical posture in the marketplace, such organizations likely would desire principled managers conducting their ethical analysis. This advice is consistent with the dictum that corporations always want seasoned executives with insightful judgments at the head of their organizations. In other words, because "good ethics" should be important to an organization, managers capable of sophisticated ethical reasoning ought to be making the judgments about relevant ethical issues. Therefore, ethically motivated companies should seek to attract and retain morally imaginative executives with practical wisdom in the Aristotelian sense. The engagement of "principled managers" will minimize the possibility of the organization making a costly ethical miscalculation.

In general, we postulate that the greater the number of ethical standards applied to a given situation, the higher the result of discovering an ethical concern. Furthermore, the greater the number of stakeholder groups evaluated, the greater the likelihood of perceiving possible negative outcomes that require further investigation (see again, BP6). Note, it is again imperative to recognize that just because ethical concerns are voiced and/or potential negative outcomes from marketing practices are uncovered, the proposed strategy will not necessarily be judged to be unethical. Minor negative outcomes for some stakeholders, as well as unintended ones, regularly should be expected whenever marketing organizations make complex marketing decisions (recall BP3). Indeed, a negative result for one stakeholder could lead to a positive one for another stakeholder, and it is these dilemmas which make ethical stakeholder analysis so challenging. For instance, consider the hypothetical case of an automobile company deliberating whether it has the ethical responsibility to install side airbags on every vehicle in its product line. A utilitarian analysis, for example, might indicate that the inclusion of side impact airbags will save a few additional lives especially if their autos are involved in collisions with large SUVs. But, the decision to voluntarily install side airbags in all company models would also substantially increase consumer costs, thereby disadvantaging many price sensitive consumers, and perhaps causing them to switch to competitors whose current vehicles (also without side airbags) might afford them an even greater risk of injury.

In the end, despite the many factors, complications, and difficulties in conducting ethical analysis, a *decision* needs to be made about the situation. This is the next to last step of the ethical reasoning process. The generic alternatives available are typically the following: either (a) the particular marketing practice is "acceptable" and allowed to go forward; or (b) the challenged strategy is amended in some fashion to make it ethical; or (c) the practice is abandoned. For instance, in the case of the earlier mentioned petrol firm, assuming that good faith efforts are underway that aggressively seek to hire a more diverse workforce, then the depiction of the multi-racial work group in the ad campaign *might* fall into the realm of "puffing" and be ethically acceptable because the ads depict what the company soon hopes to become. In the situation of the "fast loan" financial services sector, policy makers may decide that the prevailing, compounded, interest rates constitute an exploitation of consumers that is usurious and therefore new industry regulations are required. To use the language of BP1, the "iron law of social responsibility" will be exercised, and the quick loan vendors will now be further legally constrained.

As a final step in the ethical reasoning process, ethical decision makers have the responsibility to *monitor the outcomes of their ethical decisions*. By overseeing what has transpired in the marketplace resulting from an ethics related policy decision, changes then can be made that shape future decision-making protocols. For example, a decision that results in major unanticipated negative consumer experiences (e.g., a growing percentage of consumers perish from side impact auto accidents when driving without side airbags) would necessitate future explorations of similar ethical questions. This situation might involve adjustments such as a greater weighting of an affected stakeholder group, a change in the type of ethical standards applied to the situation or possibly a revisited and deepened ethical analysis. Exactly how this entire calculus of adjusting the decision-making protocol fits together is the realm of *moral imagination*—i.e., creatively applying dynamic ethical reasoning to the peculiarities of a given ethical question in order to constantly improve the depth of an organization's ethical sensitivity and actions.[20]

Ethical lessons from the basic perspective set

When addressed in isolation, the descriptions of the BPs discussed above and in Chapter 1 raise many challenging questions. For example, with regard to BP1, if marketing should strive to serve society, how does one possibly establish society's best interests? With regard to BP2, if ethical marketing requires *more than* conformance to the law, from where does this supplemental guidance derive? Concerning BP4, what values are likely to characterize highly principled marketing managers? If stakeholder orientation of BP6 is to have meaning, how should the necessary trade-off analysis among stakeholder groups be conducted? Within BP7, if an ethical reasoning process is essential to "good" marketing, how does an organization find the managers capable of adhering to this rigorous process of ethical discernment? And so on.

Our point is that many of these questions can be answered by considering the basic perspectives (BPs) as an integrative whole. Philosophers sometimes refer to this process as *moral reflection*. Illustrative of the insights such an exercise might produce are the following observations:

- The "best interests of society" so essential to BP1, can be more systematically taken into account by adopting the stakeholder orientation (SO) described in BP6.
- The ethical reasoning process described in BP7 may be better implemented by seeking to hire or develop the morally principled managers described in BP4.
- The balanced evaluation of stakeholder rights recommended in BP6 can be more pragmatically understood by embracing the tripartite ethics issue evaluation discussed in BP3.
- The benefits accruing to an organization from moral manager "exemplars," implied by BP4, are more fully understood with reference to the ethical precepts, described in BP5.
- The taking into account of conflicting stakeholder's claims discussed as central to the BP7 evaluative process, is simplified by the demarcation of the stakeholder concept addressed in BP6 and the method for breaking down ethical issues dissected in BP3.

The above observations are intended not as a complete listing of the relationship among the essential BPs but rather to illustrate their integrative effects for understanding and improving marketing ethics. The challenge for concerned marketing managers is to work through the network of possible connections among the BPs in the context of the peculiarities and industry-specific issues confronting their own operating environments.

A note concerning marketing in action

In 2007 the American Marketing Association revised its definition of marketing:

> Marketing is the activity, set of institutions, and processes for creating, communicating, delivering, and exchanging offerings that have value for customers, clients, partners, and society at large.[21]

This definition forms the basis for our understanding of marketing today and also encompasses ethical aspects which have been incorporated into the AMA Statement of Ethics (recall Box 1.1). Marketing in practice is very much centered on the premise of creating,

Figure 2.3 The marketing management process
Source: Adapted from P. Kotler and K. Keller, *Marketing Management*, 14th Edition, 2011, Upper Saddle River, NJ: Prentice Hall, Table of contents.

capturing and sustaining value and this concern is reflected in the organizational marketing strategies of the modern day corporation. What the cases in this textbook aim to achieve is a consideration of how ethical issues impact on the marketing strategies and organizational activities of companies (both big and small, profit and not-for profit) as well as society at large. It also allows students to explore examples of good and bad practice and to further consider how the creation of value can be ethically achieved in the future. In the latest edition of *Marketing Management* by Philip Kotler and Kevin Keller[22] the study of marketing has been divided into several major sections (see Figure 2.3), all of which focus on an analysis of the marketplace and an assessment of how to create, capture and sustain value for, as the AMA definition espouses above, "customers, clients, partners, and society at large."

By utilizing the seven Basic Perspectives discussed above and illustrated in Figure 1.1, the cases in the text focus various aspects of marketing management, as depicted in the Kotler and Keller and other major marketing textbooks. As shown in Figure 2.3, there are seven major strategic areas of marketing with three sub-functions under each. The cases that correspond to each of the strategic areas are as follows:

Capturing Marketing Insights—Arctic Desert
Connecting with Customers—Toys from China, TOMS Shoes
Building Strong Brands—Koodo, Honest Tea and Coke, Cadbury
Shaping the Market—Counterfeits on eBay, Another Day in Paradise, Facebook
Delivering Value—Casas Bahia, Tough Decisions, Auchan
Communicating Value—Hunky Dory, PETA, Superior Services
Creating Successful Long Term Growth—Drug Testing in India, Montenegro Electronics,
    Young Pharmacist's Dilemma, Caterpillar

Conclusion

This chapter has provided a comprehensive overview of normative marketing ethics. Each of the three BPs focuses on one aspect of what it means to be an ethical marketer, and, as noted above, many interrelationships exist. Although we have taken a primarily prescriptive point of view, the many illustrations in this chapter and in Chapter 1 also highlight what is actually occurring in the marketplace. All of the BPs, but especially the theories discussed in BP5, can be applied to the cases which follow in the text. It is important that the reader appreciate that marketing ethics draws on individual, corporate, societal, philosophical and religious foundations so that managers will find it easier to take the "higher road" in their decision making. Creating value can be achieved while an organization also adheres to strong ethical principles. We contend that it is companies who are good at both ethics and economic efficiency will be the most successful.

3 Decision model, sample case (L'Oréal), and analysis

This short chapter provides a "bridge" between the first two chapters that focused on the conceptual aspects of ethical marketing and the next two parts that present multiple cases for analysis. The intention of the chapter is to provide students with two approaches that might be utilized in preparing their evaluation of subsequent cases. Your authors have developed a template for case analysis that is firmly rooted in the BPs discussed above. In fact, the model we present uses the seven stages that were presented for BP7. We should add that some instructors will prefer to discuss the questions that are included for every case. We caution students that even if the questions at the end of the case do not seem to have an explicit ethics thrust, the BPs presented in Chapters 1 and 2 should be reviewed before answering the questions.

The balance of the chapter is organized into four areas. First, the decision model for resolving ethical issues is explained as a possible template to analyzing and "solving" the cases from Parts 2 and 3. Next, the L'Oréal case is presented. Its purpose is to serve as an illustration of a case that contains multiple ethical issues. After the case presentation, several questions are posed and are then answered briefly. At that point, we will turn our attention to applying the case analysis worksheet to the case. This helps give student-readers a sense of the type of analysis they might prepare for the other cases. The next section of the chapter includes "The Rest of the Story" since this case has been "resolved." Finally, the chapter concludes with some overall observations on how to consider and examine all the cases in this anthology.

Decision model for resolving ethical issues

 I. Determine the facts—what, who, when, where—and cultivate ethical awareness
(What do we know or need to know, if possible, that will help define the problem? Managers must have the ability to be ethically aware.)
 II. Define the ethical issue in the light of the facts
(Make sure to identify precisely what the ethical issue is. For example, conflict involving rights, question over limits of obligation on safety, responsibility to a certain stakeholder, conflict of interest, and so on are examples of ethical issues.)
III. Stakeholder analysis
(Who are the most important stakeholders? Distinguish between primary—those with a continuing and essential interest, indirect—those with an abiding but more separated interest, and secondary—those with a potential or distant interest. See discussion in Chapter 2.)

IV. Identify major theories or principles that relate to the case
(For example, what ethical theories are most relevant to the case-virtue ethics (integrity, trust, fairness, respect for persons), duties (recall Kant's formulations), consequences—greatest good or costs and benefits or rights/justice? What about contract-based ethics? Do one or more of the principles of CST apply?)
V. Specify the alternatives and conduct an ethical analysis
(Determine if there is one principle/theory or value, or combination, which is so compelling that the proper alternative is clear, for example, correcting a defect that is almost certain to cause loss of life. Identify short and long, positive and negative consequences for the major alternatives. Also, list the major alternative courses of action, including those that represent some form of compromise or point between simply doing or not doing something.)
VI. Make and justify your decision
(Select the alternative that best fits your primary principles or values. How would you argue for your decision when others might disagree with you?)
VII. Monitor the outcomes of your ethical decisions
(What has transpired in the market place as a result of the decision(s) taken? Are further decisions required as a result of the changes occurring in the marketplace?)

L'Oréal—are you worth it?[1]

Marie-Theres Riegler

Several years ago, Garnier, a brand of L'Oréal's beauty division was about to launch a new advertising campaign for the shampoo line Fructis Style. L'Oréal planned to conduct in-store promotions in French supermarkets outside Paris and therefore wanted its recruitment agency Districom (a division of Adecco) to hire hostesses to hand out samples. With the campaign, Garnier hoped to increase its sales as well as the brand awareness among the consumers. Therefore, a business meeting for the next day was set up between the management of Garnier and L'Oréal's marketing team to set all the details of the promotion.

Company information and background

L'Oréal, whose advertising campaigns for years have proclaimed, "because you are worth it," is the world's largest cosmetics and beauty company. The firm was founded in 1907 by a French chemist, and today owns 23 global brands from Maybelline to Helena Rubinstein and the Body Shop. It acquired 674 patents in the year of 2009 alone. L'Oréal employs 64,600 people and has a presence in 130 countries worldwide.[2] In the 1990s, the company struggled with claims over past links to fascism, anti-semitism, and giving jobs to Nazi collaborators after the Second World War. Since then, L'Oréal always stressed its strong commitment to diversity and is proud of the fact that it is currently employing people from 110 different nationalities.

According to the company, "Diversity is a core value for L'Oréal."[3] (See Exhibit 1 for a list of L'Oréal ambitions regarding diversity from the "Our Company" part of the website.) From the wide variety of people who make up its teams to the products developed, diversity has always been a priority for L'Oréal." The ambition of L'Oréal is "to reflect, in its teams and at every level, the diversity of its clients (in terms of nationality, ethnic or social origin, age…), coherently with its employment pools."[4] The company even received the "Diversity Label" handed out by the immigration ministry for good practice in employing ethnic minorities. In 2008, "that image already suffered a battering when L'Oréal executives were forced to deny claims that they had lightened the singer Beyoncé Knowles' skin for a campaign."[5]

Situation/issue

The scheduled meeting took place at L'Oréal's headquarters Tuesday afternoon. After only a short discussion, the team had already agreed on most of the details concerning the Fructis Style promotion. The hired sales-staff would hand out shampoo samples and discuss hairstyling with shoppers. However, opinions widely differed when the question came up "…what type of girls would appeal most to the consumers?" For some employees, it was clear that the women should be attractive, diverse and of different nationalities. They argued that in a multicultural country like France, shoppers could identify with the different backgrounds of the girls. Completely ignoring this argument, the executive of Garnier said explicitly that she wants "hostesses who could express themselves correctly in French" and thus, in her opinion, only French girls could be hired by Districom, its recruitment agency. The marketing manager, Richard, also claimed that ethnic minorities would be "less likely to sell its shampoo in French shops," suggesting that French shoppers were discriminatory.

A couple of hours after the meeting, despite the objection of a few employees, Garnier's executive confidently sent out a FAX instructing headquarters to find an all-white team of sales staff to promote the shampoo in the supermarkets. According to this FAX, women promoting Garnier Fructis style should be 18–22, wear size 38–42 and be "BBR."

Christine Cassan, employee at Districom, the communications firm responsible for Garnier, was surprised to read the fax of L'Oréal because "BBR" (initials for bleu, blanc, rouge—the colors of the French flag) is an expression, recognized in the recruitment world as "a code for white French people born to white French parents"[6] and not those of north African, African, and Asian backgrounds. In fact, Districom had already started the recruitment process for the Fructis Style campaign and Christine had planned to offer L'Oréal a pool of candidates in which around 39% were from ethnic minorities. When Christine tried to talk to a superior of Districom, her own company, the superior said that she "had enough of Christine and her Arabs." Probably because she was afraid of losing L'Oréal as a client, she reluctantly followed the given instructions. When Christine told Marina, a good friend, who has also been involved in the recruitment process about the FAX, she was very outraged claiming that as far as she knows in a normal sample of women recruited for similar sales work, around 40% would be non-white. This is the case in France where there is a high percentage of citizens from ethnic minorities.

Only a short time after their conversation Marina was told by her superior to eliminate candidates with foreign-sounding names or photos showing that the applicant was of Algerian, Tunisian, or African origin, and if one of these girls were to inquire about the position, Marina had to pretend that the list was full.

At the same time two girls from Africa and Asia, who applied for the job and already had a very nice conversation with an employee of the agency the day before, were told that the list was already full and they had decided on another candidate. They were pretty disappointed and could not see what they had done wrong because according to the same employee they both had good chances of getting the job.

Although the deputy managing director of Districom, Thérèse Coulange, had no problems in choosing only white girls for the campaign, claiming that the letters BBR "only
meant that candidates should speak "proper French,"[7] she decided to talk to the manager of
Garnier who stated: "Are you questioning my strategic decision? I have the right to decide
what girls I want for the promotion campaign of my brand and you will get them for me. Do
you have any problem with that? If this is the case, then I have no other choice than choosing
another recruitment agency. Look, I'm interested in increasing the sales and not ruining my
business when hiring the wrong people."

Questions

1. Is L'Oréal's decision/defense justified?
2. What should people working at L'Oréal or the recruitment agency who disagree with
    the instructions do about the exclusion of ethnic minorities?
3. Should the agency run the risk of losing a large client when not following the instructions
    or do they have other possibilities?
4. Do you find any parallels between this policy and the strategy of Abercrombie and Fitch
    for hiring in-store sales people in the US?

Exhibit 1

Diversities are our priority

Our ambitions

*   **Reflect our consumers' diversity of origins within our teams at every level** (in terms
    of nationality, ethnic or social origin, age…), while maintaining our standards of
    excellence in terms of competencies.
*   **Promote gender equity within our teams**: promote the access of women to positions
    of responsibility, facilitate gender equity in functions that are currently over-staffed by
    men or women (marketing, industry), and ensure equal treatment in terms of salary.
*   **Encourage the employment people with disabilities.**
*   **Valorize work experience** in anticipation of a longer work life.
*   **Develop an inclusive managerial culture**, respectful of all.
    Source: www.loreal.com/_en/_ww/html/our-company/our-policy.aspx?

Teaching notes: L'Oréal campaign

Answers to the questions

1. Is L'Oréal's decision/defense justified?
    On ethical grounds it is difficult to justify L'Oréal's decision. It does not follow the
    company's own statements and positions on diversity. Using the major ethical theories,
    the women are being treated as a means to an end (Kant's second formulation
    from Chapter 2). The firm is definitely not practicing virtue ethics. A few might make a
    utilitarian argument that the company economically benefits more from the campaign
    than the women lose. However, the position taken by the firm appears to be much more
    egoistic (watching out only for itself) than utilitarian.

2. What should people working at L'Oréal or the recruitment agency who disagree with the instructions do about the exclusion of ethnic minorities?
    Several of the individuals at the agency did speak up and raised reservations about the campaign. The case does not indicate that any person questioned the decision with the highest levels either in L'Oréal or the agency. This might have been an option that some employees could or should have taken. The most extreme decision would be to resign over the situation. No employees were willing to take that position.

3. Should the agency run the risk of losing a large client when not following the instructions or do they have other possibilities?
    This is a decision that is likely made by the top management of companies. As mentioned above, the upper tier of management at Districom should probably have been informed of the situation. They might have resigned the account even though it would be costly in the short term. A parallel is that some advertising agencies refuse to take cigarette companies as clients because of the known health risks of the product. Management at the agency might have tried to use either persuasion with L'Oréal or the negative implications of being discriminatory. A decision like this one is where managers might consider using moral imagination to come up with a better solution.

4. Do you find any parallels between this policy and the strategy of Abercrombie and Fitch (A&F) for hiring in-store sales people in the US?
    A&F is well known in the US for giving preferential hiring treatment to young, thin and, oddly enough, blond sales associates (both men and women). The company contends that these individuals convey the "young and beautiful" image that the company is trying to convey to its youth audience. Some argue, similar to this case, that the posture they take is a discriminatory one. In both instances, a number of ethical issues raised in the answer to Q1 should be addressed.

Decision model for resolving ethical issues

The facts

L'Oréal, the largest cosmetics and beauty company in the world, has worked hard to make diversity a core value of the company. The company decided to launch a new Fructis shampoo in French supermarkets. L'Oréal hired Districom, a recruitment agency, to find models who are "BBR" (bleu, blanc, rouge—in other words white native-born French girls) to promote the shampoo in the supermarkets. Richard, the marketing manager at Districom, and his employee Christine are tasked with finding the models that L'Oréal executives have requested.

The ethical issue(s)

–   A conflict involving human dignity and discrimination toward certain minorities.
–   A question over whether it is acceptable to hire on physical appearance and ethnic heritage.
–   An issue of whether a smaller firm (and its employees) should resist the pressure of a larger firm (L'Oréal) to undertake unethical activities.

Stakeholder analysis

Primary: L'Oréal, Garnier and Districom, as well as the models in the campaign, are primary stakeholders. More specifically, Richard and Christine and the executive team at L'Oréal all have a direct stake in the campaign.

Indirect: L'Oréal's competitors and customers certainly have an abiding interest in what happens. Also, the supermarkets in which the campaign will take place and competitors of Districom have an indirect stake. Any company that hires women as salespeople would have an indirect interest in the outcome of the L'Oréal case.

Secondary: Women's activist groups, the media, and potential future consumers (e.g., young girls) for the new shampoo are secondarily related by their distant interest in the selection of models for the campaign. It could be further argued that French business and society are secondary stakeholders because the actions perpetuate stereotypes of the French culture.

Identify major principles/theories

Duty-based ethics—L'Oréal is treating the models as merely a means to an end without regard for diversity or adherence to their stated core values. If this behavior were universalized, minorities would have great difficulty getting jobs with any business. Using this theory, one would not want to universalize discrimination.

Utilitarianism—The parameters of the recruitment process were limited to what would bring the most sales, regardless of the consequences of that. However, the utilitarian argument can be broadened to a societal perspective and the negative overall consequences should be considered. As mentioned in the answer to Q1 above, the company is likely taking an egoistic stance rather than a utilitarian one here.

Virtue Ethics—The virtues of diversity and respect are not followed in this case. In fact, all the virtues listed in Table 2.1 including integrity, transparency, and the others were not practiced by L'Oréal or Districom in the case. The Districom employees were definitely not transparent with the minority applicants.

Catholic Social Thought—The recruitment requirements bring into question the principle of human dignity and the inherent worth of all people regardless of race, color, or creed. The principle of the common good is also violated by the actions of both firms. These companies are going directly counter to the principle of the preferential option for the vulnerable by discriminating against them.

Specify alternatives and conduct an ethical analysis

1. ***Stop the Campaign***—This would solve the problems related to discrimination of the models and could avoid damaging L'Oréal's reputation in light of its core diversity principle. However, it would be expensive and time consuming to either create a new campaign or begin the hiring process again without limits on ethnicity. Evaluating this alternative from an ethical theory standpoint would indicate that the major theories of duty-based, virtue and CST would support this position.

2. ***Continue as Planned***—For Districom, they would be following their client's instructions and delivering what was asked of them. L'Oréal would stay on schedule for the campaign and generate the higher sales they were expecting. On the other hand, they would be guilty of discrimination and denying the ethnic models their basic human dignity. As mentioned previously, this is the egoist option. The short-term benefits

might argue for this alternative, but the long-term consequences are likely to be negative.

Make and justify your decision

The decision in this case is clear in light of the applicable ethical principles. The current campaign must be changed and a new one introduced or the parameters for the models be altered. Further underscoring this decision, L'Oréal is in violation of its own core value of diversity in the current campaign. Even in a purely financial sense the current campaign does not hold up if one considers the irreparable damage to reputation and the potential for legal repercussions of going forward.

Monitor your decision

The company did implement the campaign. The consequences were that Christine was fired from Districom and the French anti-racism activist group SOS Racisme produced evidence suggesting that discriminatory practices were used in hiring the models. The group brought suit in French court and it ruled that the policy was illegal under French employment law. (See full discussion below.)

L'Oréal: the rest of the story[1]

Stephanie Piszczor

Although L'Oréal's "because you're worth it" advertisements may be convincing to con-sumers, the French cosmetics giant was unable to convince the French courts that they truly believe that everyone is equally "worth it" when it comes to recruitment. The company was found guilty in 2007 of racial discrimination by the French high court (equivalent to the US Supreme Court) because of its racially selective criteria for hiring a sales staff to sell its shampoo.

The sales staff was hired through the Districom division of Adecco, a temporary recruit-ment agency. The allegation was that a Districom employee sent a FAX to its headquarters requesting hostesses that were between the ages of 18 and 22, wore small size clothes, and were "BBR."[2] This last requirement is a commonly recognized expression in the French recruitment world that stands for the colors of the French flag: "bleu, blanc, and rouge." Specifically, hiring hostesses that were "BBR" meant that they were white French women born to white French parents.[3] Thus, the hiring criteria excluded racial minorities, specifi-cally Black, Arab, and Asian women, that did not fit this profile.

Prior to the FAX, the recruitment agency offered Garnier a pool of candidates in which 39 percent represented ethnic minorities. However, with Garnier's intentions to exclude these candidates in an effort to increase sales, only 5 percent of the hostesses hired for the campaign were black, Asian, or Arab, which suggests that the original ethnic candidates were blocked during the final stages of recruitment.[4] France has a total of 5 million ethnic minority citizens out of a population of 63 million.[5]

This was not the first expression of racial discrimination within the company. L'Oréal had already been accused of lightening singer Beyoncé Knowles's skin for a campaign in prior years.[6] Despite the fact that her skin was noticeably lighter in the advertisements, the company denied these allegations, claiming, "It is categorically untrue that L'Oréal Paris altered Ms. Knowles' features or skin tone in the campaign for Féria hair colour."[7]

With this new case brought against them, the company continued to deny that racial prejudice was present within the company. However, the French high court, La Cour de Cassation, found L'Oréal and its recruitment agency, Addecco, guilty of racial discrimination. In accordance with the ruling of the Paris Appeals Court, both entities were required to pay €30,000 in fines and an additional €30,000 in damages to the SOS Racisme, the anti-racist campaign group which brought the case to court.[8] Although L'Oréal was disappointed in the ruling, the SOS Racisme was pleased that it was able to secure the judgment against the large multinational. "Samuel Thomas, the vice-chairman of SOS Racisme, described the ruling as a 'very great victory'. He said: 'whatever the size of the company, none is able to escape prosecution.'"[9]

It is interesting to note that the €30,000 fine for L'Oréal is small for a firm whose revenue was €17.47 billion in 2009.[10] The greatest damage was to its reputation. However, this case did not receive much publicity outside of Europe. The damage, then, appears to be rather minimal.

Today, looking at L'Oréal's website, it is evident that the company has been persistently trying to reverse the damage done to its image by putting an emphasis on the importance of diversity within the firm. The company claims, "Diversity is a core value for L'Oréal. From the broad variety of people who make up its teams to the products developed, diversity has always been a priority for L'Oréal."[11] The exhibit in the case contained some of this language. Although the statement may be somewhat embellished in light of the prior allegations, the company seems to be moving forward with the hopes of disassociating itself with its past discriminatory policies.

One concluding point is that the behavior of L'Oréal and Addecco was not only unethical but also illegal as judged by the French Courts.

Conclusion and comment

This chapter has outlined the type of case analysis that should be conducted in Parts 2 and 3. The L'Oréal case and its aftermath illustrate that making unethical (and in this instance) illegal decisions can have a number of negative consequences. Part 2, which follows, contains 10 shorter cases while Part 3 also includes 10 longer ones. Some of the cases are about actual companies like Coke, Auchan, and Caterpillar. The information used in writing these cases is based on published or reported secondary sources. A number of the other cases are based on actual companies but the identity of the firm is disguised. For all cases, the following comment applies: this case is "for classroom discussion rather than to illustrate either effective or ineffective handling of an ethical or legal decision." Because not all the relevant facts may be known, the situation should be construed as hypothetical rather than actual. The cases are intended as experiential exercises that allow students an opportunity to apply the ethical concepts from Chapters 1 and 2 and utilize an ethical decision process to analyze and defend their chosen course of action or point of view.

Part 2
Short cases

4 Going along to get along[1]

Raymond F. Keyes

Terry Peters was in a tough situation. His boss was asking him to do something that Terry believed bordered on dishonesty. However, if he refused to go along, he was pretty sure that his position as a sales representative with the Acme Instruments Corporation would be seriously jeopardized. As a new member of the Northeast Medical Instruments team, Terry was just beginning to learn the ropes regarding his responsibilities as a field sales rep calling on hospitals, medical laboratories, and other medical facilities. His job called for regular sales calls on each of his assigned accounts to provide product information and to take orders for new and replacement medical instruments products. Since he was one of five sales representatives in the Northeast region, he, along with his fellow team members, traveled extensively from account to account in a widespread geographic area. Terry's territory covered western Massachusetts, northern New York, and Vermont. It was not unusual for him to be "on the road" for two and sometimes three nights a week. In order to properly cover his accounts, it was important for him to have a dependable, comfortable automobile. It was in the area of reimbursement for the automobile expenses and for other related travel costs that Terry was confronted with his ethical dilemma.

Before coming to work for Acme, Terry had worked as a sales representative for a pharmaceutical firm. Because of the nature of the job, all the salespersons were paid on a straight salary basis with modest end-of-year bonuses for accomplishment of corporate and regional sales objectives. In addition, the sales reps were supplied with leased cars and a fairly liberal reimbursement program for expenses related to sales calls and customer entertainment. While this job provided a good, safe income, it did not offer much of an opportunity for income growth in response to solid sales performance. Therefore, Terry had decided to go to work for Acme because of its excellent product line and its salary/commission sales plan. The salary portion of the plan provided adequate income for basic living expenses, while the commission component provided additional income in direct proportion to individual sales effectiveness and results. Terry favored this approach because he was confident that he could perform well and enjoy increased earnings as he mastered the job and generated increased sales returns for the company.

One significant difference in the new company was in the way they handled automobile and sales expense reimbursements. The company did not provide lease cars but rather gave each new sales rep a $15,000 signing bonus, primarily to cover the down payment on a new car. In addition, an ongoing mileage reimbursement plan was designed to cover gas, repairs and subsequent automobile payments. The logic of this plan was to position the salesperson to buy a car and to pay it off in three years. At the end of that time, the salesperson could buy a new car, using the trade-in value of his existing car to cover the new down payment. The mileage reimbursement would continue as before as the source of funds for the continuing car payments. This plan seemed fair to Terry, and he appreciated the $15,000 signing bonus and the opportunity to purchase and own a car of his own choosing as opposed to using a leased one. It certainly seemed simpler this way for the company and for him.

After he had been on the job for six weeks, Terry's sales supervisor, Ralph Porter, took him aside to discuss a problem that the sales reps on the team were having with the company's expense reimbursement plan, especially in the automobile area. Under the plan, sales reps were paid 40 cents per mile to cover their gasoline costs, upkeep repair of the cars, and ongoing car loan payments. According to Ralph, the 40 cents did not provide an adequate amount to position the sales reps to cover expenses and to position them to replace the cars at the end of three years. The reps had presented their case to company management, but the accountants insisted that the plan was fair, particularly insofar as the reps were allowed to use the cars for their personal use as well as for business purposes. According to Ralph's calculations, the sales reps should receive between 45 and 50 cents per mile in order to generate the necessary funds to cover automobile depreciation and replacement. In the face of management's refusal to increase the mileage rate, Ralph had come up with a simple plan to which his sales team had agreed. Each sales rep would add 100 miles to his or her weekly mileage figures, over and above the amount actually driven. The added miles would provide increased reimbursement, and according to Ralph's calculations, this would make up for the shortfall in the existing company plan. According to Ralph, this was the fair way to solve the problem in the face of the "damned accountants and their niggardly approach." All of the team members had agreed to this strategy, and Ralph presumed that Terry would agree as well. He said that it would look bad if one sales rep's mileage figures were significantly lower than the others in comparable territories. In fact, the sales rep who preceded Terry in the territory had used the 100-mile inflating device before being promoted to larger territory. Ralph pointed out that it would not look good to have Terry turn in mileage numbers that were significantly less than his predecessor's.

In this same meeting, Ralph had some other suggestions concerning expense reimbursements. Company policy allowed sales reps to be reimbursed for reasonable expenses for overnight accommodations and meals. It did not, however, allow for reimbursement of expenses related to entertainment or other non-business out-of-pocket expenses. The accountants reasoned that the sales reps would be paying their own entertainment expenses if they were at home, and so should they do the same when traveling. "The company reimbursement plan is not designed to cover expenses not directly related to the business of doing business." Here again, Ralph believed that the "accountants" were being unrealistic and unfair. He felt that the sales reps should receive some compensation for the inconvenience and hardship of being away from home. "Are they expected to sit in their hotel rooms every evening reading the Bible?"

Ralph went on to explain that at the recent trade show in Chicago, he had advised his reps to build up their expense chits with extra charges for taxis and tips and other phantom expenses to make up for the $75 to $150 that they each spent on their evening out on the town. "How can you get people to work at these trade shows if there isn't some incentive in the form of entertainment and relaxation? You may think that this is simply padding the expense account, but I really believe that it is the fair way to handle things in the face of the unrealistic stance of the company's management."

It is now two weeks after his meeting with Ralph, and Terry is in the process of filling out his monthly expense reimbursement form. He is very uncomfortable with Ralph's plan involving the recording of extra mileage. In addition, he resists the idea that he should make up some business-related expenses to offset some of his non-business ones. However, it is not as easy as simply recording the correct figures. In his role as sales supervisor, Ralph sees every one of the expense forms. He will know that Terry has not built up his mileage or other travel-related expenses. This could create real problems for Terry in that it would be evident that he had acted against the instructions of his supervisor and against the wishes of the other members of the team. His actions would clearly be interpreted as a sign that he believed that they were acting unethically. Clearly, this would not get him off to a very good start in his new job. Ralph is in a position to do Terry genuine harm in his periodic performance evaluations and in his daily interactions with him. The other team reps can hurt Terry as well since the team concept requires that the people work together and assist one another in their various sales endeavors. Terry feels that he is confronted with the problem of "going along to get along" versus adherence to his own moral standards.

Questions

1. What is the ethical problem or dilemma here, and what moral standards are involved?
2. Who will be affected by Terry's action? How will these stakeholders be affected if Terry goes along with Ralph and if he does not go along?
3. What alternatives does Terry have? What are the ethical implications of the alternatives? What are the practical implications of the alternatives?
4. If Terry does go along with Ralph's approach, can he be absolved from responsibility because of Ralph's hold over him as his superior? If Terry goes along, can he claim that he is only following orders?
5. What would you do?

5   Hunky Dory[1]

Andrea Prothero

"It has positioned the brand at the forefront of public consciousness. ....Any slice of attention, anything that creates a buzz, can be worthwhile. The fact that we're talking about it means the campaign has done its job" (Richard Delevan, McConnells Advertising Agency).

In April 2010, Largo Foods, the company behind the Irish brand of potato chips, *Hunky Dory*, launched an outdoor advertising campaign on billboards and bus stops throughout Ireland, designed by the advertising agency *Chemistry*. (For the controversial ads, see www.trendhunter.com/trends/hunky-dory-crisps-irish-rugby-campaign#!/photos/73923/4.) Largo Foods also had a dedicated microsite for the campaign on its webpage. The campaign cost €520,000 and was shot by world famous sports photographer Walter Iooss Jr in Miami, Florida. A number of posters were developed featuring scantily clad women playing rugby, a sport which is currently popular in Ireland. Fuelling the sport's popularity was the country's recent win in 2009 of the Grand Slam for the annual Six Nations competition between England, France, Ireland, Scotland and Wales, something they had only ever achieved once before. The ads featured a number of different Tag Lines such as "Others Haka, We Hunky," "Tackle These" and "Are you Staring at my Crisps?" On each of the posters the same tag line "Proud Sponsors of Irish Rugby" was also featured.

The Advertising Standards Authority for Ireland (ASAI) received over 300 complaints from males and females and a number of different women's support groups, religious organizations, and student bodies. There was huge discussion of the ads in Ireland's broadsheet and popular press, as well as debates on the TV and radio and on various Irish blog sites. As the ads were placed in Northern Ireland, complaints were also made to the UK Advertising Standards Authority based in London. The story was also picked up and debated by the international press.

The Irish Rugby Football Union (IRFU) publically criticized the ads and threatened legal action against Largo Foods with their spokesperson emphasizing: "Rugby is a family sport and we work with all of our existing and real partners to ensure that their advertising campaigns promote that. We monitor the ad campaigns to ensure that they are responsible and reflect family – and Hunky Dorys is not an official sponsor."[2]

Largo Food sponsors Navan rugby club, a very small, relatively unknown provincial team and the IRFU took great exception to the "Proud Sponsors of Irish Rugby" tag-line on each of the ads. As well as being critical of the ads content Padraig Power, the Commercial and Marketing Director for the IRFU emphasized that it also had a negative impact on the official sponsors of Irish rugby.[3]

Although the ads were only on billboards for a relatively short time period they generated a large amount of coverage and discussion: *The Irish Independent* reported there had been a 17% sales volume increase following the campaign.[4] O'Leary Analytics assessed the social media impact of the campaign; highlighting that immediately preceding the campaign there had been no mention of Hunky Dory in various social media outlets, but in the 3 weeks following, there were 291 comments.[5] Further assessment via a "tone and sentiment assessment" of the comments, however, showed that social media commentary was more negative than positive. Various terms used to discuss the ads included "sexist," "exploitation," "horrendous," "offensive," and this, they argued, needed to be considered in conjunction with the significant brand awareness for the product at the time of the campaign. Examples of commentary on *Boards*, that is, a popular Irish blog site, were as follows:[6]

If they pull this advert, I'll be writing to the Advertising Standards Association giving out about "objectifying males" in that stupid perfume ad where the bloke is leaping around half naked or for having men dressed up as women on the Bounty/Plenty adverts!

Don't like it because the ad agency seems to believe that to get me to buy a product all they have to do is cosy up between things I like, like sport and pretty ladies. "That's patronising."

Look at the nice boobs near our product…look at the boobs, next time you see our product you will associate it with boobs. …

Actually, next time I see your product I'll be associating it with arrogant patronising marketeers…and I hate them.

My French wife laughed and just said "They'd be naked in France…" There's food for thought.

I cannot understand why anybody would be offended by these ads. Why is it any different from the ads with scantily clad men in chocolate ads?

The advertising companies know sex sells, and obviously the Hunky Dory company want more men to buy their product and what better way to get them to do that than associate their crisps with boobs?

The catch phrase isn't great but who is going to remember what is written?

I also remember the huge publicity about the Wonderbra ads—didn't some of their billboards have to be taken down because they were causing driving accidents or something?

Actually, it's been suggested by a few advertising analysts that objectifying women (and men) in such a way, reducing them to objects rather than people and making them appear less than human, trivializes those people and their place in society, which in turn can lead to violent crimes against them.

The ASAI emphasized that complaints for the ads covered the following issues:

Most broadly the main complaint centered around the portrayal of women where "the campaign was offensive, exploitative, tasteless, degrading and sexist towards to women, and brought advertising into disrepute."[7]

As the images of the women themselves could not be associated in any way with the product (potato chips) it was argued that the advertisements objectified women, and treated them as sex objects.

A number of women's sporting groups criticized the ads for being demeaning towards women who were active in sports.

The Rape Crisis Network in Ireland were strongly critical of the ads, and emphasized that they were "cynical and unhelpful in terms of building a society that is free from sexual abuse and violence."[8]

The support group RENEW questioned the ethics of Largo Foods by emphasizing that the publicity surrounding the ads led to an increase in sales of the product and also free advertising for the company.

Largo Foods responded to the complaints by emphasizing that during a time of general doom and gloom in the country (at the time of the ads Ireland was experiencing its biggest recessionary period in decades) the ads were meant to be a source of fun and entertainment and the company had not meant to offend anyone. It was also argued that the tone of the ads signified and reflected the general personality of the brand. The company's CEO, Raymond Coyle emphasized: "Everything is so serious and gloomy now.......And we want to inject a little bit of fun into things."[9] The company stressed that they had received significant levels of support for the ads, both via written communication to the company and in discussions on TV and the radio. Thirdly, the company again reiterated the fun nature of the ads and that the campaign represented women playing a sport. Some press reports printed the opinions of a few of the models in the ads, with one 21-year-old model from Belgium stressing how much fun she had had working with a world class photographer, and in playing rugby, and how she personally did not find the ads to be sexist.[10] Finally, in response to one of the more serious complaints that the campaign "condones dangerous behaviour or unsafe practices, provoke violence or anti-social behaviour," the company emphasized that they did not see how their ads could "in any way be deemed to encourage such behaviour."[11] The company also drew attention to other recent campaigns, depicting both men and women, which they considered to be more sexual in their content than the Hunky Dory campaign.

Questions

1. The advertisements were criticized by the general public and various public interest groups on a number of different grounds. What are your opinions of these criticisms and the company response to them?
2. Some commentators argue that Largo Foods deliberately made an ad which would cause controversy as this would lead to increased publicity and free advertising for the company. What are your opinions on the ethics of such actions by organizations? Can you provide examples of other similar cases?
3. Do you think Largo Foods should withdraw the ads? Why or why not?
4. In some of the blog discussions reference is made to the portrayal of men in advertising and how these portrayals tend to receive fewer complaints than the portrayal of women. Why do you think this is the case? Can you provide examples of ads which depict men in an overtly sexual manner or which objectify men in some way?
5. Provide two examples of advertisements which have been withdrawn in your country as a result of gender complaints. How do these cases compare to the Hunky Dory example?
6. How is advertising regulated in your country? In your opinion is self-regulation by an industry body acceptable or should regulation be government led?

6   Tracking down counterfeits on eBay

Whose responsibility is it?[1]

Barbara Stottinger

It was a late afternoon in London, when Chris Littleton, marketing manager for eBay, and Suzanne de Viliers, Louis Vuitton's chief legal advisor, stepped out of the conference venue to grab some sunlight. The Anti-Counterfeiting group, a non-profit trade association, had convened its annual meeting to bring together its members, nearly 200 companies and organizations, for whom counterfeiting is an issue. They are either affected in their business as original brand owners or as advisors.[2]

Over the past few days, Suzanne and Chris had been attending lots of workshops and discussions around a topic that was of major concern to all of them—counterfeiting. The Anti-Counterfeiting Group has come up with a definition that captures the phenomenon: "*product counterfeiting is a crime, a deliberate attempt to deceive consumers by copying and marketing goods bearing well-known trademarks, together with packaging and product configuration, so that they look like they are made by a reputable manufacturer when they are, in fact, inferior illegal copies.*"[3] For the counterfeiter that means piggybacking on someone else's brand and marketing success without major investments, thus high profit margins and comparatively low risk. For the consumer—they get the prestige of the original brand without paying for it!

As producing and selling fake products is illegal, official numbers do not exist, but counterfeiting is said to account for around 7% of world trade worth an estimated $600 billion a year.[4] Louis Vuitton is among the most highlighted brands, when it comes to counterfeits. In 2004, the fakes of LVMH products accounted for 18% of all counterfeits seized by European customs. Some experts even claim that 98% of all Louis Vuitton products available in the global market are fakes.[5] While the damages to the brand and consumer perception is incalculable, Louis Vuitton has to put substantial financial means on the table to fight counterfeiting: in 2003, about € 12 m, five times more than 10 years before,[6] and this amount will have increased even more until now.

The Internet as a global market place has opened up new opportunities for buying and selling fakes. In 2004, the Internet already represented the third largest market for sale and distribution of counterfeits behind China and Italy.[7] With predicted annual growth rates from 20 to 30%, the importance of the Internet as a marketplace for fake goods is likely to increase. The problem is even worsened because of a wider acceptance of online shopping and a growing appetite for designer branded goods.[8]

After days of intense discussion and exchanging ideas, Chris and Suzanne still seemed so engaged in the topic that they continued talking on the hotel patio enjoying a cup of coffee. Suzanne seemed seriously concerned, when she addressed her counterpart: "Chris, we have been working together on this issue for quite some time, and personally, I appreciate your collaborative spirit and drive in our joint fight against counterfeits, but your company, eBay, has too relaxed an attitude in this case, I find. As the major online market place, you must take responsibility and help us fight those individuals or firms that sell fake products to consumers."

"I share your concerns," Chris replied, "but you have to give us credit for all the activities that we do. Take the policy section on replicas, counterfeits and unauthorized copies.[9] It provides detailed information for buyers and sellers on the issue. If you look at these policies, there is really no doubt, what our position is, when it comes to counterfeiting. Plus we make it very clear that if firms or individuals would go against this policy, they have to bear the consequences such as suspension of their accounts, for example.

And just to support my arguments with some facts, Suzanne, we spend over GBP 10 m per year to maintain a safe site, 2000 employees around the world support the fight against counterfeits. In 2007, we removed 2.2 m listings, which allegedly were selling counterfeits.[10] This is not anything!

We also invest in customer education on our website: there is an extensive section on the downsides of counterfeiting. It points out that fake products are simply illegal, they undermine the trust that one has in original brands and it is detrimental to the honest sellers who deal in authentic products. We try very hard to help consumers make an educated choice. They need to realize why buying a fake product is not a peccadillo, but a serious issue. For example, we direct interested customers to www.myauthentics.com to check out the latest news and information on counterfeits. They can also learn how to spot a fake or discuss related issues with like-minded consumers.

To prevent serious damage, we recommend using PayPal for payment, because only then you can reclaim your money under the Buyer Protection scheme, if the handbag, sunglasses, watches or T-shirts you bought on eBay were fakes.[11]

"Chris, I would like to take you up on this last comment," Suzanne interjects. We received a lot of complaints of customers who tried to take action after finding out that their Louis Vuitton handbag purchase on eBay was a fake. Often, these consumers turn to us in anger and fear to help them. So I know of cases, where tricked consumers – in line with what you recommend on your website – contacted the seller first – without much success. Subsequently, they filed a complaint with you. The success was limited. The answer they received was disappointing: as you cap refunds at $ 200 and, in addition, charge a processing fee, this may leave customers with considerable losses."[12]

"Yes, but do not forget that the majority of transactions are below the $ 200.[13] So we are covering most customer transactions that way" Chris argues. Already slightly irritated, he shot back to Suzanne: "Suzanne, I think it is not as simple as that! You cannot put all the blame on us! We are trying hard, but we see little support from luxury goods manufacturers like Louis Vuitton or Tiffany. You guys refused to enter our Verified Rights Owner Program (VeRO).

VeRO was developed as a joint initiative between us and rights owners to rally in the fight against counterfeits. Through this program, you can report potentially infringing listings and have them quickly removed from the site.[14] Just to give you an idea on the figures we are talking about: in 2008 we removed 2.1 million listings that way, the large majority within 12 hours after reporting."

"Chris, nice idea, but I can tell you why we or Tiffany would not join this program.[15] You are basically shifting the responsibility to us as the brand holders. We have to spot counterfeiters on your marketplace and then you would take action." Suzanne replied getting angry.

"But Suzanne, you are demanding too much here! Just consider our business model: we never take possession of goods sold through eBay. We are not experts on clothes, sunglasses, jewelry or your products. How would we be able to detect fake products? We are experts in building a marketplace and bringing buyers and sellers together.[16] We can support you, but you have to do the job!"

"Fair enough, but this does not get us around the question of whose job it is to prevent sales of these items. And you know that! Still it is too easy to buy fake products over your market place." Suzanne counters. "We recently bought a set of our products – the fake version though – with prices ranging from as little as 10% of the retail price to as much as full price. And these were sellers who received mostly positive feedback and who guaranteed the authenticity of the products.[17] Let's also not forget that you earn money from this – what we would call illegal – business with every transaction. This is also why we at Louis Vuitton refused to join VeRO.[18] And you know what: the sellers as well as buyers have become creative. As the German police are very aggressive in tracking down counterfeiters on the Internet, German buyers or sellers bypass eBay's German site to trade on Dutch e-Bay, just as an example[19] So where does our protection get us?"

As the discussion was heating up and arguments on both sides were tossed back and forth, Chris Littleton tried to cool down the situation. "Suzanne, I perfectly understand your point and I see the difficult business challenge that you are facing. Be assured that I will do everything to support your cause. We know each other long enough that you realize what I am saying is sincere. Overall, we may be fighting on a battleground that is not the most important one. We should just not forget that, globally, we have listed about 2.7 billion listings and only 0.15% were identified as potentially counterfeit.[20] So I guess what happens on Canal Street in New York's China Town, on night markets in Asia or on Mediterranean beaches, where you can buy any fake in any quality in open daylight should concern you much more."

"Chris, I do see your point. Of course we are aware of these problems too, but you have to see that with the Internet and mediums such as eBay and other auction sites selling counterfeit products has become easier than ever before. You also know that the courts are on our side. Just recently courts in the US or France ruled that eBay is to be held accountable, as you are profiting from and assisting those who sell counterfeit products."

"True, but courts in Belgium and Germany saw that differently and support our position. We do not own the goods and with our VeRO program to remove infringing items we have gone at great length. Brand owners should police their own brands."

For a moment, Chris and Suzanne were pausing, then looking at each other and starting to smile. "So if even courts are not unanimous in their decision, how would we ever reach an agreement?" Chris smilingly said. "You are right! We are both facing an ongoing battle, where we just have to make sure that the counterfeiters succumb and our customers are protected from such malpractice."

Questions

1. Who do you think needs to take responsibility to trace counterfeiters – eBay or the original rights holders?
2. Do you see an ethical obligation for eBay to track illegal sellers, or is their line of arguments "we just provide a marketplace" correct?

3. In her last comment, Suzanne equates the fight against counterfeits with customer protection. Is it not much more about the original manufacturer's interests than the consumer's, who would get similar benefits at a reasonable price, when buying the fake instead of the original?
4. Why do courts in different countries rule differently? Has this something to do with their ethical stance on the issue? Are there other influencing factors?

7 Casas Bahia[1]

Urvashi Mathur

The company

Casas Bahia is a Brazilian retail chain, specializing in home appliances and furniture. Founded in 1957 by Samuel Klein, it is now Brazil's largest retail chain, with more than 500 stores in 11 states. As of December 2009, a company by the name of Grupo Pao de Acucar now owns the chain.[2] It is also the largest retailer in Latin America based on revenue, and is headquartered in Sao Paulo, Brazil. Samuel Klein began his career selling bath towels, linens and blankets door to door in Sao Caetano do Sul to 200 customers after he escaped from a Nazi concentration camp in his native country, Poland, and fled to Brazil. He made his sales by commuting in a horse-drawn cart, and by 1957 his customer base grew to 5,000. That year Klein purchased a store in Sao Caetano. Since most of his customers were from the northeastern state of Bahia, he named the store Casa Bahia. Bahia is the fourth most populous state in Brazil, after Sao Paulo, Minas Gerais, and Rio de Janeiro. The store sold furniture and clothing to customers and relied largely on installment payments and charged up to 5% monthly interest. He then opened a second store that carried only clothing which was operated by his wife, and changed the name to Casas Bahia.

By 1964, Klein owned three stores. However, he did not have enough capital to maintain the company's growth, despite borrowing money from three different lenders. In 1970, he invested in Financeira Intervest, a consumer-loan company and by the end of the year he generated enough capital to buy out his partner. This provided a turning point in his career, as Casas Bahia was then able to finance itself. By 1983, Klein owned 43 stores in Brazil. One distinguishing feature of his stores was that installment payments were required to be made in person at a store location. Casas Bahia had two million customers in 56 stores (in Bahia and Sao Paulo) towards the end of 1988, and 75% of the 100,000 monthly customers were installment buyers.[3]

1992 proved to be a difficult year for Klein, as sales decreased from $618 million in 1991 to $353 million. This drop in sales was attributed to the hyperinflation of the Brazilian currency, which greatly impacted consumer purchasing power. After closing 15 stores, cutting the number of employees by a third, and eliminating the hyper-inflation through a reform program, sales jumped to $841 million in 1994. By 1996, Casas Bahia was the largest non-food retailer in Brazil, with 250 stores across six states and sales of $2.83 billion. Although sales were high, so were the company's expenses. In an effort to keep up with the financial demands of the business, and a large amount of credit extended to customers, the company at this point had a debt of about $800 million, which was almost as much as its assets. The company opened up its books to be audited and soon made a profit in 1998 after issuing debentures and a six-month promissory note. Despite another slump in the Brazilian economy, by 2000, the company had 340 stores in seven states and 20,000 employees, with total sales of approximately $1.44 billion.[4]

All Casas Bahia locations were monitored heavily by top management and if the standard of attracting at least 100,000 customers was not upheld, the store was closed. For this reason, 30 stores were shut down in 2003, however about another 30 were opened in other locations to attract more people. By 2004, sales were up to $3.08 billion from 400 stores, and all competitors were far behind in comparison. Due to such high growth, Casas Bahia faced financial strains and signed a contract with Brazil's largest bank, Banco Bradesco, in order to allow the bank to directly finance part of the chain and to have additional funds for further expansion. As of 2008, the company owned 513 stores and had sales of approximately $7.97 billion. Although Grupo Pao de Acucar now owns the company, Klein's sons Michael and Saul continue to run the day-to-day operations. Michael is in charge of finance, distribution, and employees. Saul is in charge of marketing, sales and supplies.[5]

Brazilian economy

Brazil has an average growth rate of 5%, and is one of the world's most rapidly growing economies. Based on nominal gross domestic product, it is the eighth largest economy in the world, and on Purchasing Power Parity, the ninth. Over the past two decades, the Brazilian economy has fluctuated dramatically. In the early 1980s, Brazil faced an enormous issue of foreign debt and continued borrowing despite this debt, causing economic decline and hyperinflation. The decade ended with continued increasing inflation, a large public debt, a stagnant economy and multiple failed plans for controlling inflation. The beginning of the 1990s saw the same turmoil and inadequate plans until the stabilization program, Plano Real, was implemented in 1994. The Brazilian Real was then introduced, inflation was decreased significantly and eventually eliminated altogether. With substantial financial support from the International Monetary Fund, Brazil finally saw growth in the new millennium, with 5.7% growth in GDP in 2004 and 4% in 2006. The most recent world financial crisis has caused the growth rate to slow down again.[6]

The three most populous cities in Brazil are Sao Paulo, Rio de Janeiro and Salvador with populations of approximately 11 million, 6 million and 3 million, respectively. Rio de Janeiro is the chosen location for the 2016 summer Olympics, and this event will greatly help the growth of Brazil. As of 2009 estimates, the population of Brazil is approximately 192,272,890, of which more than 80% are considered to be at the bottom of the pyramid. Prahalad's book titled *The Fortune at the Bottom of the Pyramid* defines them as individuals who earn less than US$2 per day. However, members of the bottom of the pyramid (BoP) in Brazil represent 41% of the country's total spending capacity. With regards to home appliances and furniture, those in the Brazilian BoP accomplish 45% percent of total spending.[7]

The consumers

Seventy percent of Casas Bahia customers do not have a consistent/formal income, and their professions are mostly maids, vendors, and construction workers who earn around or less than the minimum wage (approximately US$11 per day) in Brazil. For these consumers, three criteria that are essential to their purchase decisions.[8]

1. Affordability—payment schemes aid in encouraging their purchase decisions.
2. Access—since these consumers work all day, they must have access to the purchase location after work hours, and within their residential or work areas.
3. Availability—buying decisions for this group are not deferred; they decide based on the amount of cash they have at hand.

In a *Wall Street Journal* article "A retailer in Brazil has become rich by courting poor," Miriam Jordan states, "While most mainstream Brazilian retailers shun the poor, the former peddler [Klein] courts them assiduously. Mr. Klein's stripped-down stores are located in some of the most deprived neighborhoods of Sao Paulo and Rio de Janeiro."[9] (For a family-oriented ad for Casa Bahia on YouTube, see: www.youtube.com/user/Casasbahia#p/u/26/_eomTvqCuEI.)

The Casas Bahia retail method

In order to serve this extensive market, Casas Bahia provides payment options through their 800 credit analysts. Since most Casas Bahia customers cannot afford to pay the entire price of a product in one payment, if the product costs more than US$335, the option to finance a purchase based on a positive credit score is possible. Once a positive credit score is submitted, the customer receives a credit limit based on total income, occupation, and expenses. This process takes less than one minute. As the customer regularly pays the installments, this credit limit is increased, providing new incentives for the customer to purchase repeatedly. If the product costs less than US$335, no credit check is required and financing is instantly awarded.

With an average monthly interest rate of 4.13%, installments are required to be paid monthly, in the store.[10] This tactic forces the customer to return to the store and possibly purchase something new, since the installment payment desks are located at the back of the store. More often than not, customers walk through the store, see something new that catches their eye, proceed to pay the installment, and are informed that their credit line has been increased, enticing them to purchase once again. Critics refer to this as exploiting the poor, but the company describes this tactic as a means of maintaining strong customer-store relations.

Salespeople are trained to work with customers to purchase within their budget. If a customer wants a 27-inch television but cannot afford it even with financing, the salesperson in order to prevent from losing the sale altogether will recommend a smaller television as a temporary solution. Additionally, all conversations regarding prices are always conducted while sitting down, as once a customer sits down with a salesperson, they are more engaged and less likely to walk away from the purchase.

Competing stores provide similar options but have not mastered the process like Casas Bahia. This is demonstrated by their 16% default rates in comparison to Casas Bahia's 8.5% default rate. An average of 750,000 customers request financing at Casas Bahia every month.[11]

To stimulate consumer demand, Casas Bahia advertises heavily through television, using emotion, celebrity endorsements, and even real customer testimonials. Klein focused on advertising his brand at an early stage of the chain's development and was the second largest advertiser in Brazil. Today, it holds the number one position as the leader in Brazilian advertising. (For a brief discussion and three videos on Casas Bahia advertising, see www.adbrands.net/br/casasbahia_br.htm.)

Questions

1. Is Casa Bahia treating its customers ethically? Why or why not?
2. How much annual interest is Casa Bahia charging them? Is this right?
3. Using what ethical theory is the Casa Bahia retail method acceptable? How would other ethical theories assess this technique?
4. What is your impression of Casa Bahia advertising? Is it ethical?

8 Toys from China and the new Yum Burger Kids' meal[1]

Marie Derdzinski and Gene R. Laczniak

Jake Tanner is the CMO of Yum Burger, a regional fast food chain looking to expand its menu in order to stay competitive with the other international fast food chains. Yum Burger had been losing market share to international chains like McDonald's for eight straight quarters, and ownership was beginning to put massive pressure on management to right the ship. There was talk amongst Yum Burger top management that if they could not increase profits and/or market share soon, Yum Burger would have to start cutting costs. This meant closing company-owned restaurants, and cutting jobs. One product offering Yum Burger was looking to add to its menu was a kids' meal. Kids' box meals were a part of many fast food menus, such as the classic McDonald's Happy Meal, and oftentimes included a small toy, trinket or puzzle along with the meal. Jake felt strongly that a toy would need to be included to make the meal more attractive to children and bring more families into the restaurant. Tanner tasked Emilie Barnes, his top marketing manager, to launch the kids' meal project, and made her responsible for identifying the toys, the content and promotional themes of the kids' meals. Emilie also had a brand new staff member to help her on key projects, Jane Dowling, age 23, a freshly minted MBA.

Jane was very excited about the opportunity to work on a project that would be highly visible in the organization. She had been at Yum Burger a relatively short time of four months, and was looking to make a professional reputation for herself. She began working on the kids' meal project right away by helping brainstorm themes, identifying possible menu items for inclusion, and scouting for potential toy inserts. Emilie told Jane to concentrate on nailing down the details of locating where the toys should be sourced by working with a list of vendors provided by operations and purchasing. After a few weeks, Jane was ready to present some of her ideas to her supervisor, Emilie, and to get feedback about what she had learned. The marketing team was almost at the point where they needed to decide what toys would be offered with the meal. The work teams had done considerable research and gotten several price quotes from various vendors. Jane and Emilie both knew that they needed to get toys at a relatively low price to maintain a profitable margin and stay in a competitive price range with their kids' meal box. All of the toys in Yum Burger's target price range were made in China. The vendors there were flexible enough to produce a variety of items and consistently presented a price advantage of between 20 and 25% compared with any other domestic or global options. Jane presented these ideas to Emilie who was impressed with her hard work and thoroughness. But Emilie had some other issues that she wanted to think about for a few days before moving forward.

As Emilie was getting ready for work the next Monday morning, the day of her weekly meeting with the Yum Burger top management team that was scheduled to include decisions about the Kids' meal project, she overheard an alarming story on the morning news. "Toxic Metal Cadmium found in children's jewelry made in China" was the headline across the screen. The TV report also went on to mention that many toys produced in China had been regularly finished with lead-based paint, another ingredient possibly toxic to young children. Emilie was suddenly distracted from the other details of her proposal and thought back to the toy options, all of which were sourced from China. Was the rest of her team watching this same newscast? Should she update management on the almost ready-to-go status of the kids' meal project? Or should she postpone her report and take a second look at the toy portion of the kids' meal? She decided to wait a week to make a recommendation to Jake Tanner, as she reluctantly felt that a bit more information was needed.

Emilie remained concerned about the recent news about children's toys from China, but she also did not have a lot of alternatives. She asked Jane Dowling to prepare an analysis to aid in her decision-making and to provide any additional information about going forward. Jane was eager to work on the analysis figuring that she could find a creative solution to Emilie's concerns, but as she started doing her research she came across both positive as well as alarming information.

In preparing her analysis, Jane primarily considered two ethical points of view to inform her decision-making. The first point of view was grounded in a cost/benefit analysis of the situation which would focus on maximizing profits for Yum Burger in the most efficient way possible. An alternative consideration for Jane was to ground her analysis in the AMA Statement of Ethics (see statement in Box 1.1 of Chapter 1). The AMA Statement of Ethics outlines marketing virtues and rules of thumb that consider the role of and impact on other stakeholders involved in a potential decision. When applied, the AMA Statement should give marketers a good measuring stick for ethical action.

Jane prepared a SWOT analysis to help her analyze the situation. In her analysis, Jane saw many of the *strengths* of sourcing the toys from China that were widely touted by Jane's colleagues from business school who had experience working with Chinese firms. Several of them had been to China on business and spoke highly of the economically vibrant country and the hardworking people. She had heard the Chinese were very eager to co-operate with American companies, and therefore were especially accommodating about shipping and responsive to customized orders. Local and regional government agencies in China worked closely with businesses to make sure that favorable tax treatments were shaped for the many different types of products being shipped. Another strength of many Chinese companies was their ability to offer products at very competitive prices. This is precisely what attracted Yum Burger to several toy manufacturers in China in the first place. In addition to the potential cost savings working with Chinese firms offered, Yum Burger also stood to benefit from the quick turnaround offered by the firms with which they were considering doing business. The ability to move their schedule ahead quickly could not be discounted given the looming threat of job losses, and pressure from ownership.

Partnering with a manufacturer in China had some *weaknesses* as well. The quality perception of toys made in China was somewhat low and the public was increasingly concerned with safety after the ongoing reports of lead or cadmium in children's toys and jewelry. Quality and safety perceptions of Chinese goods had become so severe, that the Chinese government had even launched a marketing campaign to combat their image and shift the perception of "Made in China." In fact, the two most appealing Chinese firms that Yum Burger was considering partnering with had both been flagged for repeated violations in the past five years. Both had assured potential partners that they had "rectified any potential issues," but the potential for a public relations backlash if there were any problems that could sink Yum Burger. If Yum Burger was going to do business in China, Jane felt they would have to spend considerable resources to monitor their product quality as they could not risk any incidents of toxic toys—families were, of course, the core target market for Yum Burger. With the amount of monitoring and compliance that would be needed, the toys suddenly did not seem that inexpensive.

The great *opportunity* of this venture for Yum Burger is that if they could build a stable partnership to supply the toys for their kids' meals, this would help solve a major obstacle to the kids' meal idea—how to make it price competitive and profitable. Adding a kids' meal "box" (with toy) would also reinforce the Yum Burger image as a family restaurant and allow them to be more visible in the marketplace. Thus, the key advantage for Yum Burger in sourcing the toys from China is that it would allow for greater profit margins on their kids' meal sales. If they could not source the toys for a reasonable price, then the kids' meal would only cannibalize higher margin menu sales and reduce profits.

One major *threat* in getting their toys from China would involve working with the Chinese central government. Recent news reports had alerted Jane to several issues that could arise from working with that government. The first was the lack of privacy that Yum Burger would have to accept. For security purposes, the Chinese wanted to monitor all ingoing and outgoing international communications from the Shanghai supply office that Yum Burger would likely be setting up. Ever since high profile Google had temporarily pulled out of the Chinese market, it sent the message to other companies that business privacy was not respected in the same manner that American and European firms are accustomed to. The second issue was that the Chinese government did not always regulate industries very strictly; sometimes inspectors were receiving money under the table to ignore violations or other corruption existed, such as the necessity to sometimes pay small bribes. The failure of government oversight was demonstrated in the ongoing issue with severely tainted milk in China. As a 2010 *Wall Street Journal* report suggested, "China's continuing problems with melamine contamination – more than a year after the toxic chemical was discovered to be widespread in baby formula and other dairy products – highlight shortcomings in government efforts to ensure the safety of the nation's food supply, despite stricter regulations" (Fairclough 2010). All of this combined news presented possible threats in the form of how doing business with China could go horribly wrong.

After completing her strengths, weaknesses, opportunities, and threats (SWOT) analysis, Jane only felt more conflicted about the decision to source the toys in China, so she turned to the American Marketing Association (AMA) Statement of Ethics for more insight. As Jane began to review the AMA document, she began to have more and more concerns regarding sourcing their toys from China. Jane had once referenced the AMA code in her MBA studies, but this no longer was a hypothetical case; she suddenly was realizing its potential relevance. Specifically, the AMA code stresses always adhering to ethical values in marketing practice, and some of these values were possibly in conflict with the China initiative. First, regarding the *Responsibility* value, Jane was concerned about the Chinese sourced Yum Burger kids' meal toys because children were a "vulnerable market segment" to which special precautions were owed. Recent incidents regarding lead and cadmium in children's toys did not seem to sufficiently protect this vulnerable market, but instead exposed it to significant risk. Second, the *Responsibility* value also asked marketers to always "consider environmental stewardship in our decision-making." Upon investigation, Jane learned that the toy manufacturers in China that Yum Burger had been thinking about contracting with did not always stress environmental sustainability in their business operations; Jane was concerned that local Chinese ecology was getting secondary treatment compared to low production costs.

Finally, another value of the AMA Code of Ethics that would be difficult to uphold was *Citizenship*. The AMA code asks, "…[the] supply chain member to ensure that trade is fair for all participants, including producers in developing countries." Jane was concerned because Yum Burger could not guarantee that Chinese workers producing these toys were being treated fairly, as Yum Burger did not have access to the intricacies of the supply chain in China.

Jane looked at her analysis of the situation and only felt more conflicted. In sourcing to China there was a huge opportunity to turn a quick profit and turn around Yum Burger's fortunes. This would save jobs, and best serve Yum Burger's shareholders. The flip side of this from the cost/benefit perspective was that negative public opinion, or a public incident of any kind could damage Yum Burger in the long run. Looking at the situation from the perspective of the AMA Code of Ethics was even more troublesome. It seemed that in order to maximize profits, Yum Burger would potentially have to overlook worker rights concerns and potential safety hazards, both of which would not be treating all involved as more than simply means to financial ends. Nevertheless, Jack Zilber, one of the other marketing managers who knew Jane was working on this analysis, stated to her, "China is still a developing country, and it is understandable that manufacturing is not as tightly regulated as it is in developed countries. Every country goes through this developmental cycle. First and foremost, the economy has to grow, and then when they become more prosperous, attention can be paid to niceties such as perfecting employee safety programs and corporate social responsibility."

Jane felt as though she were faced with an impossible choice. Working with Chinese firms seemed like the best economic option to ensure that Yum Burger made the profit that they needed, in the time frame necessary to avoid further economic troubles. This did not come without financial risks, namely the potential consumer backlash that would come with any safety or civil rights failings on the part of their would-be business partners. Also, Jane felt that by sourcing the toys from China, it would be difficult to uphold some of the AMA endorsed ethical values. From a personal standpoint, Jane felt that helping cast doubt on what CMO Jake Tanner saw as his key marketing strategy was not the way she wanted to kick-off her career. She also couldn't help but find herself agreeing, at least somewhat, with Jack Zilber's observation about the realities of the developing world. Could the AMA Code of Ethics be enforced in a nation that simply did not have the means to effectively apply it? As she wrote up her report, she wondered how Emilie, her supervisor, would weigh these factors.

Questions

1. Along with the situation analysis, what should Jane recommend to Emilie concerning the proposed toy contract with Chinese vendors?
2. Are there ethical obstacles that should prohibit Yum Burger from pursuing the Chinese contracts for their kids' meal initiative? What ethical point of view do you think best applies to the decision facing Yum Burger?
3. If Jane decides to focus on an economic cost/benefit point of view, do the potential benefits outweigh the potential costs?

4. Can the AMA Code of Ethics apply in a developing nation? If so, are the potential conflicts with the Code enough to make partnering with a Chinese firm morally wrong?
5. Are there any other ethical points of view that you think could provide Jane and Yum Burger more insight?

Sources consulted in the preparation of this case

Fairclough, G. China Hunts for Tons of Tainted Milk Powder. *The Wall Street Journal.* February 9, 2010: A10.

Feds Probe Cadmium in Kids' Jewelry From China. *The Associated Press. FOXNews.com.* http://www.foxnews.com/us/2010/01/11/feds-probe-cadmium-kids-jewelry-china/ (accessed February 1, 2010).

MacLeod, C. New ad campaign touts 'made in China'. *USA Today.* January 8, 2010: 8A.

Pritchard, J. Disney pendants recalled. *Milwaukee Journal Sentinal.* January 30, 2010: 2A.

Pritchard, J & Donn, J. Walmart pulling jewelry cited in AP cadmium report. *The Associated Press. Yahoonews.com*

http://news.yahoo.com/s/ap/20100112/ap_on_bi_ge/us_cadmium_jewelry (accessed February 1, 2010).

Shell, ER. *Cheap: The High Cost of Discount Culture.* New York: The Penguin Press; 2009.

Tainted milk shows China's food safety challenges. *The Associated Press. msnbc.com.* www.msnbc.com/id/35233791/ns/health-food_safety/ (accessed February 4, 2010).

9   Koodo in the Canadian cell phone market[1]

Nyla Obaid

Unhappy with their phones

Ask any Canadian in early 2008 and they would tell you that they were unhappy with their cell phone plans. It didn't matter which of the three available providers they subscribed to; rumour had it for years that Rogers, Bell Canada and Telus Inc. discussed it with each other to keep their plans and pricing structure similar.

The three main areas of dissatisfaction were:

The "system access fees" charged by all three companies was the biggest complaint by consumers. This was an additional $6.95 per month as well as a 9/11 fee of $0.95/month. Originally, providers claimed this was due to government regulation, but in the face of a class-action lawsuit, they had to tell the truth: the service fees went into maintaining and upgrading their infrastructure. Canada was the only country in the world these fees; in other countries, the cost was included in the monthly plans. In addition, these fees were only mentioned in fine print when signing up for any service, meaning that advertised price structures were accused of "bait and switch" tactics.

The difficulty of obtaining a good phone and plan without signing on to a three-year contract with the provider. If a customer wanted to break contract, a cancellation fee of the greater of $40 per remaining month (up to 400) or $200 was charged by all companies.

The very expensive "unlimited" service offered by phone plans, which capped minutes and text messages for the most part.

As Michael Jannigan of the Public Interest Advocacy Group said with regards to the Canadian cell phone industry, "Everything in terms of sales is geared towards getting the customer. Servicing the customer or keeping the customer happy is definitely secondary priority."[2]

A new player joins…

In the midst of this, somebody obviously realized the customer's unmet needs. In mid-2008, ads for a new cell phone company, Koodo, splashed across subways, billboards, and television channels.[3] Koodo branded itself as a "low-cost" cell phone provider, doing away with the hidden charges and customer inflexibility. To the average customer, they were amazing. They offered exactly what was lacking with the other three:

- Koodo was the first company in Canada to get rid of the system access and 9/11 fees. The costs of maintaining infrastructure is any business's fixed costs and should not be passed on to the customer, they claimed.

- There were no contracts. Customers could take up a plan for as many months as they wanted. *In fact, Koodo directly took shots at the big cell phone players that did this, saying 'fixed-term contracts, excess fees, are so gross and sleazy*[4]*' "in their campaign."*
- Koodo also focused on unlimited plans, at low costs.

As a result, Koodo was a hit with consumers! They offered customers the choice of having high cost cell phone service with hidden "bait and switch" prices, or going with Koodo, which implicitly advocated transparency and kept costs low while focusing only on talk and text.

Koodo became the fresher face of honest, cheap cell phone service. Consumers trusted Koodo because they acted against the Big 3 at all times. The ads loudly denounced standard cell phone services. In addition to the ad about fixed contracts being "sleazy," there were other more indirect jabs at standard cell phone offerings. "Say No to Big Billification," "Loose that Chubby Contract," and "Fat Free Mobility is Here" are a few examples of claims made by the advertisements. *The brand positioning of Koodo was to remind customers that they were the antithesis of the other cell phone providers.*

Win-win situation

Koodo was a success story all around. The company's second quarter results showed that it had gained 176,000 customers in that time period.[5] Surely, similar numbers followed on the financial statements. Customers were also very happy. For the first time, Canadians could choose the low-cost provider, and Koodo definitely created a buzz in the city streets, with many choosing to start a service with them. The J.D. Power Highest Customer Satisfaction Award in the post-paid phone market went to Koodo in 2008.[6]

Behind the scenes of Koodo

What the average customer generally failed to realize was that Koodo was a subsidiary of Telus. It was set up as a separate business unit, but of course, the big budgets for all the marketing was coming from Telus, as was the cheap access to the wireless network.

Koodo went out of its way to separate itself from Telus

Among some of its actions were:

- As aforementioned, Koodo's ad campaigns purposely put down all other cell phone companies, including its parents, Telus. It is as though Koodo purposely identified the reasons for customer dissatisfaction with Telus and then created a new brand to address these issues. The worst example of this is the ad campaign that directly called brands like Telus "sleazy."
- The Telus name was nowhere in any of Koodo's marketing. The color, structure, branding, etc. were very different.
- Koodo sales representatives and promotional agents were instructed to deny or hedge around questions about involvement with Telus. To this day, Koodo reps at the store claim that they are "here to talk about our brand, not Telus" when asked a direct question about whether the parent company is actually Telus.

- A separate public relations firm handled all of Koodo's work than Telus. Of course, in a legal sense, Koodo could not completely separate itself from the parent. In very small *letters* when signing the phone contract, Telus was mentioned as a parent company. And although Telus denied any involvement with Koodo in the media even *up* to a week before the brands' launch, cell phone-related media outlets knew the two were branches of one company. But the problem remained that most average customers were not familiar with this, and Koodo wasn't making it easy for them to get information. When asked, Koodo CEO points out that they weren't "hiding" anything from customers; the information was there for anybody that wanted to find it. A Google search on Koodo, even in 2008 eventually showed that it was related to the parent company. Not to mention, Koodo's competitive advantage was in the fact that it was not Telus. He added, "For us, it's not just being different from Telus, it's about being different from every-body else out there."[7]

- The Telus corporate ethics statement says "We consciously apply high standards of courtesy, professionalism and honesty in our interactions with customers…"[8] Is this behavior of Koodo and Telus honest? Where do the real values of the company lie?

What about Telus?

While this marketing campaign was ethically dubious, what some found even worse was the behavior of Telus after the launch of Koodo. What was surprising here was that the brand marketed as Telus, did nothing.

They continued their regular marketing as is. Doing business as usual, they continued to charge the $8 for system access and 9/11 fee. They did not change any plans to have unlimited offers, and fixed contracts for 3 years still applied to all their customers.

The reasoning behind this was simple. Telus was a huge player in the field, while Koodo was brand new. With most customers stuck in contracts, Koodo could not take them away anyway. For new customers, both Telus and Koodo along with all other major players com-peted just as heavily and yes, some potential customers from Telus would be taken away, but so would Rogers and Bell customers. Considering Telus and Koodo shared the same bottom line, the 1.4% drop for Telus brand revenue was worth it.[9]

This question deserves repeating. Where did the values of Telus Inc. which marketed both the brands lay? *Telus Inc. seems to both, as a corporation, hate system access fees and contracts (with Koodo) and apply them (through Telus).* Is this acting with integrity then, to use customer dissatisfaction as a marketing ploy, and for only one of their brands at that? Koodo's marketing sentiments don't match Telus' business ideas.

The people most affected by this were Telus *customers* themselves. After being loyal for years (often due to the fixed contracts), they did not benefit at all. They had to continue dealing with the Telus fees, while potential new customers could go to Koodo instead. *Telus customers could not switch over to Koodo without paying the substantial "cancellation fees."* Was this fair customer service? In order to maintain the competitive advantage of Koodo, they could not mix it with Telus at all. But was this worth it at the expense of customers losing out on a good deal?

New challenges

It is now mid 2010 and both the Koodo and Telus brands are healthy in the Canadian marketplace. But all is not well for Koodo.

Although their secrecy lasted for a few months, by mid 2009, almost all customers on the market knew that Koodo and Telus were linked together (mainly due to social media).

This resulted in Koodo losing consumer goodwill, and customers now look at it with the same weary eye as for other providers.

Following the success of Koodo, Rogers came up with their low-cost Fido brand and Bell upped their Solo line of products. Neither of these cheaper alternatives have system access fees or contracts. In addition, heavy new competition is coming in as the government has slightly deregulated the field and new players like Wind Mobile, Globe Alive and DAVE wireless are coming in by 2011.[10]

Customer dissatisfaction (and often bad press as a result) continues in this industry. On June 17, 2010 the Better Business Bureau gave an "F" grade to customer service by wireless companies.[11]

Questions

1.   In the face of these challenges, what should Koodo do? How do they (re) position themselves?
2.   What about the Telus brand?
3.   Answer the questions posed on p. 80.

10 PETA[1]

Karin Besenbaeck

About PETA

People for the Ethical Treatment of Animals (PETA) is an American non-profit organization dedicated to establishing and protecting animal rights. Founded in 1980, the organization now has over 2 million advocates and prides itself for being the largest animal-rights organization in the world with affiliates in the United Kingdom, Germany, the Netherlands, France, India, and the Asia-Pacific Region. The corporation is headquartered in Norfolk, Virginia, and generated total revenue of $34.5 million in 2009.[2] PETA has 300 full-time employees and enjoys tax-exempt privileges, obtaining its funds almost exclusively from contributions and donations from its members. The organization seeks to promote a healthy vegan diet and demonstrate how easy it is to shop cruelty-free. PETA's organizational motto is: "Animals are not ours to eat, wear, experiment on, or use for entertainment."

PETA first came to public attention in 1981 during the so-called Silver Spring monkey case which sparked a public controversy on animal use for experimental research. In a bid to make new discoveries in the field of neuroplasticity, the Institute of Behavioral Research in Silver Spring, Maryland, conducted cruel experiments on monkeys without providing them with adequate shelter and veterinary care. PETA initiated a police investigation of the laboratory, resulting in the first arrest and criminal conviction of an animal experimenter in the US on charges of cruelty to animals and an amendment to the Animal Welfare Act in 1985.

After this ground-breaking success, PETA felt encouraged to accelerate its animal protection work even further and soon transformed into an international movement. Ingrid Newkirk, PETA's president and cofounder, states that the organization's four main goals are to combat factory farming, fur farming, animal testing, and animal exploitation in the entertainment industry. PETA propagates and communicates its motto through special events, public education, research, animal rescue, celebrity involvement, Congressional activity, protest campaigns, and consumer boycotts.[3]

PETA's marketing strategy

In terms of media activism, PETA uses a wide range of communication channels to reach different demographics. Even though they predominantly rely on traditional advertising tools such as print ads, web banners, radio and TV advertising, they have recently increased their efforts to create a web presence on social networking sites such as Facebook and Twitter. Interestingly, PETA seems to have neglected its conflict-oriented marketing approach from the 1990s in favor of a more pop-cultural and celebrity-endorsed one.[4] The organization is now well known for its attention-grabbing and sexually explicit media campaigns and its close collaboration with movie stars and supermodels who help PETA promote its cause. In contrast, similar NGOs such as the World Wildlife Fund refrain completely from sex appeal advertising and critics thus argue that PETA adopted an "any PR is good PR" attitude.

Some of PETA's more renowned campaigns even suggest that it is not afraid to push the boundaries of good taste. In February 2003, the organization earned harsh criticism for its "Holocaust on Your Plate" campaign which was designed to promote vegetarianism and attack cruel farming methods. The travelling exhibit consisted of eight 60 square-foot billboards that compared the slaughter of animals to the mass killing of Jews in Nazi concentration camps. PETA took these public displays on an 18-month tour through 85 cities in North America and Europe, garnering much media attention and strong reactions such as boycotts as well as a complete campaign ban in Germany on command of its high court. Even though PETA later apologized and admitted that it was a controversial step, the organization seemed nevertheless convinced that this kind of shock marketing is a good vehicle to get its message across.[5]

Back in 2001, Newkirk stated that PETA's "tactics may be unusual, but there is a reason why PETA has been successful for the past 20 years." Furthermore, she described the group's advertisements as "forceful, persistent, pointed, and attention-grabbing."[6] PETA has made headlines again with its "Go Vegetarian" campaign which used imagery of overweight people. Another one of PETA's most contentious ads is its "I'd Rather Go Naked Than Wear Fur" series, featuring naked or scantily dressed celebrities (for Khloe Kardashian ad see www. mediapeta.com/peta/Images/Main/Sections/MediaCenter/PrintAds/KhloeKardashian NakedFur.pdf). Photos of other celebrities posing for this campaign can be found on the same part of the PETA website.

PETA's pro-vegetarian campaign

In 2009, PETA launched a new marketing campaign in Jacksonville, Florida, to promote vegetarian and vegan diets. The organization used billboards with the text "Save the Whales – Lose the Blubber: Go Vegetarian," featuring an image of an overweight woman in a bikini. While some praised PETA for this comical approach, others were deeply offended and called for the immediate end of the campaign. One of PETA's loudest opponents was the Obesity Action Coalition (OAC), an American non-profit organization representing the interests and rights of people affected by obesity, which found the campaign to be inappropriate and discriminatory. Joseph Nadglowski, OAC President and CEO, expressed his concern about the campaign by stating that it "blatantly stigmatizes the overweight and obese." He argued that no individual should be judged based on size or weight and that PETA does not have the right to promote vegetarianism at the expense of these people.[7]

PETA's campaign seems particularly problematic given the fact that more than 93 million Americans are affected by obesity, constituting almost one-third of the overall population. According to the WHO, childhood obesity is rising at an alarming rate and figures of the US Surgeon General reveal that the number of overweight adolescents in the US has trebled since 1980.[8]

Countering the growing criticism, PETA released an official statement in which they justified their campaign by reminding people that "studies show that vegetarians are, on average, about 10 to 20 pounds lighter than meat-eaters" and are at lower risk for heart diseases, diabetes, cancer, and infertility.[9] In August 2009, the OAC and Ingrid Newkirk discussed the billboard on an American radio show. After hearing about the emotional turmoil the campaign had caused, Newkirk announced that PETA would take down the advertisement. The OAC's enthusiasm, however, was only short-lived as PETA immediately replaced the billboard with a new one stating, "Gone – Just like all the pounds lost by people who go vegetarian." (For images of both billboards, enter Save the Whales and PETA into Google.)

PETA's anti-fur campaign

One of PETA's most widely recognized advertisements is its "I'd Rather Go Naked Than Wear Fur" campaign which was first launched in 1991 to raise awareness about fur farming and animal killings for the fashion industry. In order to appeal to a broad audience, PETA relies on celebrity endorsement and features (inter)national stars in its campaign who are willing to bare their bodies.

The campaign, however, aroused criticism as some feel that these portrayals of nudity are sexist and degrade women. The National Organization for Women and Lilith eZine, a collective group of editors and writers who promote social causes, have publicly spoken out against PETA's campaign and labeled the photographs "disturbing and problematic."[10] They point out that PETA stereotypes women by only depicting young, beautiful, thin, and cosmeticized female bodies as a means to convey its message. Furthermore, they seem concerned with how disadvantaged consumers such as illiterate people, non-English speakers or young children react to this campaign as they only see soft pornographic images and fail to understand PETA's deeper message.

Newkirk argues against these allegations and remarks that she herself as well as men engaged in similar campaigns in the past. Furthermore, she points out that the models participate voluntarily and are not coerced or exploited to do the ads. In a 2008 interview with Mother Jones, a non-profit news organization, Newkirk declared that PETA's ads are not sexist as "no woman has ever been paid to strip. She has decided to use her body as a political instrument. That's her prerogative and I think it is anti-feminist to dare to tell her that she needs to put her clothes back on."[11]

PETA's recent campaign

For the 2011 Super Bowl game, PETA developed a TV ad "Veggie Love" that was not accepted by the networks as the commercial was deemed too risqué because it featured models with vegetables in compromising situations. Despite the TV ban, the PETA website features a "casting session" which shows the models in both video and still situations with various vegetables including broccoli, cucumbers, and squash (http://features.peta.org/casting-session/). This and other recent sex-oriented campaigns by PETA that use celebrities and models to promote the rights of animals have generated significant controversy and negative attention. PETA has acknowledged that this tactic has drawn detractors by including "Why does PETA sometimes use nudity in its advertising campaigns?" as one of the frequently asked questions on its website.

Questions

1. Is it ethical for a nonprofit organization like PETA to use strong sex appeal advertising campaigns?
2. Should PETA move away from use of "shock" advertising and marketing? Why or why not?

11 Drug testing in India[1]

Nicholas J.C. Santos and Jacob Bagha

The country that has emerged as the fastest growing destination for clinical drug testing during the first decade of the new millennium is India. Partly responsible for this development is the enactment of a new ruling in 2005 that permitted foreign pharmaceutical companies to conduct phase II and III trials of new drugs in India concurrently with trials of the same phase conducted in other countries.[2] Previously, phase II and III trials were only permitted in India after they had been already completed in another country. Phase II and III clinical trials both involve testing on human volunteers to ensure suitability to sale. Phase II trials focus on dosage levels and overall efficacy, while phase III trials deal with regulatory approval. Phase III trials in particular, are considered expensive, time-consuming, and very difficult to run.

LMN Pharmaceuticals,[3] a multinational pharmaceutical company headquartered in Europe, decided to conduct phase II and III trials in about a dozen locations in India of a drug that was in the clinical pipeline, being tested to treat a medical condition that was increasingly common in populations residing in Europe and North America. The attractiveness of India as a site for clinical trials owes to a number of factors: (a) a population of over a billion people; (b) the availability of a skilled workforce to conduct trials at a fraction of the cost compared to Europe or the US; (c) treatment-naïve patients who ask fewer questions; and (d) lower ethical requirements than in Europe or North America.

The last official census survey in India conducted in 2001 reports India's general population to be about 1.02 billion. The population projection for 2010 was estimated at 1.18 billion.[4] According to a report released in July 2010 by the Oxford Poverty and Human Development Initiative, about 55 percent of the Indian population lives in poverty.[5] This statistic is computed based on the multidimensional poverty index (MPI) that uses 10 indicators to measure poverty in three dimensions: education, health, and living standard. Even though India has become a hotbed for Foreign Direct Investment (FDI) from the West, many in India still cannot find work. Eleven percent of a nearly 500 million-person labor force were unemployed as of 2009[6]; meaning nearly 50 million Indian laborers had no regular source of income. The 2008 financial crisis had also curtailed India's ability to export, pushing the nation's budget deficit to 6.8% of GDP in FY2010.[7] India features a national healthcare program run and administered by individual states and territories. Still, 75% of healthcare expenditures in India are done so out of pocket and administered by private agents.[8] Most of the population categorized as "poor" in the Oxford study cannot afford medicines or healthcare and relies on the government to provide these. In many cases, the delivery of medical services by the government is very dismal. This situation is especially true of rural or semi-urban areas, in which about 70 percent of India's population resides.

The plight of the lower classes in India was exacerbated in the states in which LMN was to focus its first wave of clinical trials. For example, in the state of Bihar, which was to be one of the first testing locations, 85% of the population lives in villages, with what are considered to be basic utilities, such as electricity, reaching less than 50% of the state beyond the relatively prosperous capital of Patna. Disparate situations like this were the norm in India, where an emerging free market economy is juxtaposed over a long-embedded caste system. Even with 55% of the population living in poverty, India still boasted 58 billionaires as of 2010.[9]

Almost all the hospitals chosen for clinical trials by LMN were in these semi-urban or rural areas, such as those in Bihar. While costs were lower across the board in India, costs and political access were even more favorable in these areas. For each person enrolled in the trial, the hospital would receive about USD 1,000 (equivalent of roughly 45,000 Indian rupees). The doctor conducting the trials was to receive compensation of about $5,000 a year (about 250,000 Indian rupees) and a one week all expenses paid vacation at a holiday resort in Hawaii if he/she was able to recruit at least 100 subjects for the trial. Patients enrolling in the trials received the drug free of cost. Also, the hospital would provide two free physicals to each patient every year for the duration of the trial. To abide by new rules enacted by the Government of India, LMN required all doctors conducting trials to inform patients of all possible side-effects of the drug. LMN also publicized on its webpage that it spared no efforts to be totally transparent about side-effects of the drugs being tested. Patients were asked to sign a 10-page document that outlined all the risks of taking part in the trial. Of course, as almost all the patients were illiterate they could not read what the document contained and relied on the doctor to explain it to them. In most cases, the patients were so eager to get enrolled in the trial, especially because of the free physicals, that they did not care about any negative side-effects of the drug.

As monitoring and evaluating clinical drug testing was becoming a thorny issue, LMN paid a local agency to audit the trials so as to ensure conformity with existing regulations. LMN required the audit reports to demonstrate to the government agencies in Europe and North America that the company had complied with all the requirements set out by them for clinical trials. With all costs taken into account, including amounts paid to the audit agency and gifts to government officials, the total cost of the clinical trial worked out to about $2000 per subject. This was much lower than the $20,000 per subject cost that LMN incurred in clinical trials in Europe or North America. LMN decided to outsource more of its clinical trials to India and to push for legislation that would allow even phase I trials—which determine the initial safety of a drug or treatment—to be permitted there. From its experience in India, LMN was confident that it could entice a growing number of people to participate in its clinical trials even though almost all these people would not be able to afford the drugs that the company would roll out on successful completion of the trial.

Questions

1. What are some of the advantages of outsourcing clinical drug tests to India for different stakeholders: subjects in India, Indian hospitals, the Indian government, the pharmaceutical company, and potential users of the drugs?
2. What are some of the problems that you see in LMN's approach? Briefly mention these and state what could have been done differently.
3. How might Kantian ethics be applied to this situation?
4. How does a company refrain from taking undue advantage of the constraints facing subjects such as lack of income, poor access to medical services, or illiteracy?

12 Tough decisions

Something to snack on[1]

Brendan D. Murphy
and Patrick E. Murphy

Major players

Breston's = Salty Snacks producer
Charles = Breston's Category Advisor for salty snacks
Deke = salty snacks' Account Manager for Breston's
B&M = Breston's main competitor
SuperSaver = major retail chain
Alice = Buyer for SuperSaver

Introduction

Deke couldn't believe his eyes as he reads the sheet of paper handed to him by Charles during their weekly meeting. He studies the POG[2] and realizes he is losing four SKUs[3] of his company's branded product, while the competitor, B&M, was gaining five. "How could you do this to Breston's?" Deke shouts. "There is no way I'll be able to hit my Fiscal 2012 sales goals with all of this distribution loss!"

"B&M's product introductions are simply stronger and they had a better year," Charles replies. "I have to give the extra shelf space to the stronger brand. If Breston's has a good year this year, we'll take another look at the shelf and reallocate where necessary."

Background of characters

To understand the implications of Charles' decisions, it's first important to recognize the background of his situation. He had been working at Breston's for three years, primarily in a Category Adviser capacity. As a Category Adviser for the national grocery chain, SuperSaver, Charles is in charge of properly allocating shelf space to each product and brand in the POG. He analyzed unit sales, dollar sales, price points, and sales velocity for each of the SKUs in his category, and makes decisions based on his analysis about how products are performing ranging from adding and deleting to increasing and decreasing shelf space. Charles is incented on the growth of the overall category, not just Breston's products.

Although he had only worked at Breston's for a few years, Charles was considered a rising star at the firms. This was his first role out of graduate school, earning his MBA at Wharton, and graduating second in his class. Prior to business school, Charles traveled the world as a consultant for McKinsey, but grew tired of the hours and living out of a suitcase. He was inundated with offers from banks as he wrapped up his MBA, but was intrigued by the possibility of working with products used in virtually every household across the country, so he decided on the food industry.

Charles had a strong relationship with the Salty Snacks buyer at SuperSaver, Alice, who often gave Charles autonomy over making decisions that were best for the category. Because of the overwhelming responsibilities of being a Buyer at a major retailer, it is common for the buyer to lean on their larger vendors for category advice. Charles had a strong track record of making excellent decisions for the category, which had grown 4% versus prior year, as compared to –1% at SuperSaver's major competitor, BullsEye Markets.

Charles and Alice get along so well because they actually had a history together—they had worked on several projects at McKinsey prior to their current jobs. She has only been with SuperSaver a little over a year, coming out of a top business school herself. While they were pleasantly surprised to find out they were working together, they had a strictly professional relationship and never blurred the lines between friendship and the office.

Deke is one year out of a Midwestern state university where he majored in marketing. He is the first of his family to attend and comes from a rural background. He is known around Breston's as a hard worker and someone willing to put in extra hours on nights and weekends to get the job done. Deke impressed his supervisors during the summer internship he received at the company during his college days. Thus, he was offered a full-time position and accepted it. His compensation is based on his hitting the target goals for Breston's snacks.

Salty Snacks category

Breston's is a $16B company, with particular strength in the Salty Snacks category. The firm has a wide array of products in potato chip (crisps), pretzel, and tortilla chip segments, historically achieving targeted annual sales growth of 4–5%. In 2010, Breston's fell slightly short of their annual target, growing 3% overall. For the most part, the company relied heavily on their established items in the potato chip segment, and had become relatively stagnant on new product introduction. While Breston's saw overall growth in their most recent fiscal year, they lost over one full point of share in the Salty Snacks category. Even with this share loss, however, the firm holds a strong 42% share of the category nationally.

Breston's major competitor is B&M, which began operations in the late 1990s, but had quickly made a name for itself in the highly competitive Salty Snacks category. B&M initially relied on its formidable potato chip SKUs, but in recent years had developed a strong presence in the reduced fat Salty Snacks segment, as well as serious R&D investment in other healthy segments. The firm was quick to react to the changing environment of the category, and while they currently held a 22% category share, they had steadily gained share in five consecutive years.

The rest of the Salty Snacks category was divided up among a number of smaller, regional players. None of these players held over a 5% share because of limited supply chain abilities.

National retail landscape

SuperSaver was the nation's third largest retailer with just over $60B in sales annually, growing at an average rate of 2% per year. 2010 was a particularly strong year for SuperSaver, experiencing 4% growth, and outpacing its major competitor, BullsEye Markets. SuperSaver's store format was simple, and succeeded on its core principle of offering consumers low prices every day.

BullsEye had a tough year in 2010, with declining sales by 1%, but was still almost twice the size of SuperSaver at $115B in sales annually. It was considered more chic than SuperSaver, offering consumers trendy new products, and staying on the cutting edge of not only food, but also fashion. When the economy was performing well, BullsEye also thrived, as consumers "traded up" to the trendy retailer. When the economy was down, however, consumers perceived SuperSaver's simple format as translating to lower prices, and shifted their loyalty to it.

Breston's sales department structure

Charles worked in the sales division at Breston's, where employees were divided up by retailer and allocated personnel by size of that retailer's business. Employees of Breston's were hired to work in one of two capacities: direct sales or category management.

> The sales teams, or Account Managers, are responsible for compiling an annual plan of promotions and selling to the buyers by trying to outbid competitors for optimal ad space and timing of promotions. Deke was the Account Manager for Breston's Salty Snacks products with responsibility for selling to SuperSaver.

> The category management team, called Category Advisers, work hand-in-hand with buyers at retailers to make decisions that were best for the category as a whole. This team regularly interacts with Account Managers, but ultimately is expected to make unbiased decisions that will grow the total category at that retailer. Charles was the Category Adviser from Breston's with responsibility for the Salty Snacks category at SuperSaver.

Fiscal 2012 Salty Snacks category review

At one of their bi-weekly meetings, Alice told Charles that she would like to take a close look at the sales numbers from Fiscal 2011, and to see which competitors had performed best and how he thinks they are likely to perform in 2012. Charles prepared a thorough analysis which showed that B&M had achieved 8% growth in the Salty Snacks category in F11, whereas Breston's was only growing at 4%. In addition, as Category Adviser, Charles had gained knowledge of new product lineups for both Breston's and B&M. Breston's new product introductions were weak, only offering line extensions of their current brands, such as Salt & Vinegar Chips, and Mustard Pretzels. B&M, on the other hand, is offering groundbreaking products that are designed to introduce new consumers to the Salty Snacks category. One of the main introductions B&M was most excited about was a 100 Calorie Potato Chip that had all the flavor of regular potato chips, with a fraction of the fat. This is an item that Alice was particularly excited about and is considering allocating a significant amount of space to all three flavors (i.e., plain, sour cream and onion and cheesy tomato) of B&M's new 100 Calorie Packs.

Charles' draft recommendations

When it came time to allocate the space on the new POG, Charles proposed reducing Breston's to 12 SKUs, down from 16 in 2010, a 25% reduction in total SKUs. He contemplated B&M taking all of that space in addition to taking one facing[4] from a local regional competitor, going from 10 SKUs to 15. With this change in shelf space allocation, B&M stood to gain significant ground in the share of the category in 2012.

At the same time, in one of his regular meetings with Alice, Deke discovered that Alice was undergoing a Fiscal 2012 Review and Reset,[5] and that Charles' recommendations would play a major role in the decisions. Upon returning to his office, Deke gave Charles a call. "Breston's could really use some help with this reset. You know we've had a tough year, and it's only going to get worse if we keep bleeding distribution like this. I also know you were in the big product development session, so you know our R&D team is working hard on coming up with our very own 100 Calorie Packs ... You just have to give our folks a little more time. You do work for Breston's, after all, you know?"

Charles hung up the phone and got to work on the POGs. He knows that he already has to answer to two companies and this situation is making it more difficult for him. He wonders whether he should revise his proposed recommendations to Alice.

Questions

1. What should Charles do? Should he allocate the facings on the POG to maximize SuperSaver's sales, as Alice expects? Or should he rework the POGs so that his own company, Breston's, can turn things around?
2. What are the short- and long-term risks and benefits of the decisions that Charles makes?
3. What are the potential personal risks and benefits for Charles?
4. Is Charles's personal relationship with Alice potentially affecting his judgment in this situation?
5. If Charles makes the decision to reduce the SKUs for his products, should Deke take any action?

13 Honest Tea and Coke

An unlikely couple[1]

Mark Vander Heiden

Honest Tea background

Honest Tea is a bottled organic tea company based in Bethesda, Maryland. Founded in 1998 by Seth Goldman and Barry Nalebuff, Honest Tea, with over $47 million in revenue in 2009 and products in tens of thousands of stores across the US, has blossomed into one of the best-selling organic teas in the country.[2]

Honest Tea was born as a result of a lack of alternatives to sugary drinks that failed to quench one's thirst. Goldman, an active person who drank a lot of liquids, would experiment by combining several different beverages to cut the sweet and intensify the flavor. After several failed attempts to create a mix that would quench his thirst, Goldman concluded that he would have to create an original drink. He contacted Nalebuff, one of his business school professors at Yale, who also shared a passion for the idea of a less sweet, yet tasty beverage. Coincidentally, Nalebuff had just returned from India where he was examining the tea industry for a case study. What he found was that most of the tea purchased for bottling in the US was made from lower quality dust left after quality tea had been produced. This presented a prime opportunity to create an all-natural brand with real tea leaves.

After quitting his job to brew batches of tea in his kitchen, Goldman received an opportunity from Fresh Fields (part of Whole Food Markets) to test his product. During their initial meeting, Fresh Fields ordered 15,000 bottles and after only five weeks from their discussion on the tea industry, Goldman and Nalebuff were in the tea business.[3]

Since the Company's inception, Honest Tea (as the name implies), has been committed to creating healthy and honest relationships with its customers, suppliers, and the environment. Its mission is as follows:

> Honest Tea creates and promotes delicious, truly healthy, organic beverages. We strive to grow with the same honesty we use to craft our products, with sustainability and great taste for all.

> We will never claim to be a perfect company, but we will address difficult issues and strive to be honest about our ability or inability to resolve them. We will strive to work with our suppliers to promote higher standards. We value diversity in the workplace and intend to become a visible presence in the communities where our products are sold. When presented with a purchasing decision between two financially comparable alternatives, we will attempt to choose the option that better addresses the needs of economically disadvantaged communities.

> A commitment to social responsibility is central to Honest Tea's identity and purpose. The company strives for authenticity, integrity, and purity, in our products and in the

way we do business. In addition to creating a healthy alternative beverage with a lot less sugar than most bottled drinks, Honest Tea seeks to create honest relationships with our employees, suppliers, customers, and with the communities in which we do business.[4]

The mission statement sets high expectations for the company; however, Honest Tea has honored its commitment. In its quest to be an ethically ideal organization, Honest Tea has expanded its certified organic, lower sugar offerings. This has helped to eliminate the need for thousands of pounds of pesticides and other chemicals that can disrupt the ecosystem. The firm has also significantly increased the number of Fair Trade Certified offerings and strives to partner with growers who practice sustainable agriculture. Honest Tea is very active in promoting recycling in local communities and has reduced the weight of its plastic bottle by 22%.[5]

As Honest Tea expanded, one of the most difficult issues the company faced was building distribution and gaining shelf space. Many retailers and distributors charge slotting allowances, which are additional compensation (in the form of money or free goods) to take on a new item in their warehouse or store.[6] These fees can cost thousands of dollars to producers, prohibiting many of them from introducing new brands to the market. According to Goldman, "There's no question that we've had opportunities that we've just had to forgo around the country because either we have not been able to, or not willing to, pay what it takes to get there."[7]

Fortunately for Honest Tea, it has still been able to grow and gain negotiating leverage due to consumer demand for organic products. However, coming up with cash is still difficult, so the company might throw in a free case of tea for every flavor that each store picks up. According to Goldman, "It can add up to tens of thousands of dollars."[8]

Goldman and his employees fought for nearly a decade to establish shelf space at distributors and retailers. Over this time frame Honest Tea achieved a compound annual growth rate of 60 percent and expanded its distribution to approximately 15,000 outlets.[9] Despite this growth, Goldman was still not reaching all the people he wanted to; but this was about to change when Honest Tea met the largest soft drink distributor in the world.

The Coca-Cola Company (Coke)

Coca-Cola is a carbonated soft drink sold in stores, restaurants, and vending machines across the world. Developed in 1886 by John Pemberton, an Atlanta pharmacist, Coca-Cola was originally intended for medicinal purposes. From 1888 through 1891, Asa Griggs Candler secured the rights to produce Coca-Cola for $2,300. Under Candler's leadership, Coca-Cola was transformed from an experiment to a business. Since the company's inception, it has produced over 10 billion gallons of syrup and has dominated the world soft drink market throughout the 20th century.[10] Beverages bearing Coke's trademark are sold in more than 200 countries and account for 1.7 billion of the 55 billion beverage servings of all types consumed worldwide every day.[11]

Coca-Cola and many other beverages under the Coke trademark are produced and distributed primarily under the franchise model. Coke produces syrup concentrate, which it sells to its more than 300 bottling partners across the world. The bottlers hold the rights to distribute Coca-Cola in one or more geographical areas. The final drink is produced by mixing the syrup concentrate with filtered water and sweeteners. The drink is then carbonated and bottled or canned for sale and distribution to retail stores, restaurants, and vending machines.

Over the last 100 years, Coke has evolved into a model company for distribution and branding. Coke has ballooned from a single product line in its early years to a company with a portfolio of more than 3,500 beverages.[12] Although the company has developed some of the most popular brands in the world, Coke has received its share of criticism for the ingredients it uses in its products and its environmental footprint.

Since 1985, Coca-Cola produced for US consumption has been made with high fructose corn syrup (as opposed to sucrose) to reduce cost. This is of concern to some people as the corn used to produce syrup often comes from genetically altered plants. More importantly, nutritionists believe high fructose corn syrup may lead to adverse health consequence such as obesity and diabetes. Due to increasingly health-conscious consumers, Coke has faced challenges with a shrinking soda market. Alternatively, the market for bottled water and less-sweet, low-caloric drinks is on the rise.[13] This factor, coupled with increasing consumer demand for products sold by socially and environmentally responsible businesses, forced Coke to take measures to further diversify its beverage portfolio.

Coke swallows Honest Tea[14]

On February 5, 2008, Coke announced its purchase of a 40% stake in Honest Tea for $43 million. Just over three years later Coke would exercise its option to purchase the remaining portion of the Company. When the initial deal was first announced, many people were stunned that these seemingly different companies were joining forces. However, transactions like this have been quite common in the world of organics and socially responsible business. Whether its Unilever acquiring Ben & Jerry's, Stonyfield Yogurt selling to Group Danone, or General Mills purchasing Cascadian Farm, successful small companies cannot resist being swallowed by giant ones offering wider distribution and mass marketing.[15]

While people criticized Honest Tea for selling out to Coke, Goldman believed it would not only boost business, but also help the Company's social mission. With its drinks reaching more consumers, Goldman believes Honest Tea can influence a shift to healthier diets. He also believed he could use Coke's marketing influence to encourage more sustainable agriculture.[16] According to a blog posted by Goldman and Nalebuff's, "While Coke is now our largest shareholder, the agreement was negotiated to ensure that Honest Tea will not be managed and controlled by Coke. We will continue to operate as an independent business with the same leadership and mission."[17]

A few months after the initial deal, Coke expressed concern to Goldman over Honest Kids' packaging, which had prominent lettering on its label that stated: "no high-fructose corn syrup." Executives at Coke took the phrase as an implicit admonishment of its products, many of which contain the controversial synthetic syrup. "We got a strong request to change the wording," said Goldman.[18]

Questions

1. How should Seth Goldman respond to Coke's request?
2. How have the large multinationals mentioned above handled their smaller subsidiaries that have a strong ethical posture?
3. Go online and examine Coke's sustainability and corporate responsibility report. Are you impressed with the company's commitment to these areas?

Part 3
Longer cases

14 Another day in paradise?[1]

Jared Benson and Rachel Fisher

Introduction

It was 5:30 PM, on a perfect Hawaiian evening. The ship's whistle had sounded as the Pride of Honolulu, Hawaii's largest and most successful dinner cruise, pulled away from the docks near downtown Honolulu. The weather and the waves appeared to be calm, providing the perfect environment for tourists to have a memorable dinner cruise. Jerry Smith, the founder, president and owner of the Pride of Honolulu's parent company, Paradise Cruiselines, Ltd., was happy to see yet another sold out cruise. It had been a long difficult struggle to bring the company back from the tragic slump in business that followed the attacks on 9/11. An uneasy feeling was in the air, however, as Jerry began thinking about the internal management problem that had surfaced earlier in the day.

Information from one of the company's middle managers in the food and beverage department was particularly troubling. According to the information, Joe McArthur, director of the food and beverage department, had been frequently accepting gifts from suppliers and distributors in return for continuing business relations. Joe, a forty-year-old hard-working man, had been an integral part of the company for the past six years. The news about him accepting inappropriate gifts was a disappointment to Jerry.

Jerry was faced with a decision he did not want to have to make. The company's long-standing, but unwritten, policy on receiving gifts was that every gift must be declared to upper management (most gifts were to be rejected altogether). In fact, most gifts that could not be shared among employees were re-gifted during the company's annual holiday party. The policy was in place to prevent employees from accepting anything that would cloud their decision making.

Complicating the matter was the fact that Hawaii's unemployment rate was the lowest it had ever been. Joe was a very competent director, who had brought many good changes to his department and added value to the company overall. It would be almost impossible to replace an employee like him. It was extremely difficult to even hire and retain entry-level employees.

As Jerry left the docks, he was running through the options. He questioned the company's longstanding policy (established in 1982), taking into consideration competitors' overall handling of gifts. Many other companies in the industry had embraced gift-giving for years. Paradise Cruiselines' sales force had complained that not being able to exchange higher value gifts hurt client relations and lost business. Although there may have been some truth to their claim, Jerry was still hesitant to consider a change, as he saw many managers from other companies fall prey to excessive gift-giving.

As Jerry pulled into his driveway, he also considered the changing nature of the tourism marketplace. In the past, Paradise Cruiselines could rely on Japanese tourists (about 50% of the total tourists in Hawaii) to fuel the company's growth. Recently, however, fewer Japanese were coming to the islands, as less expensive travel destinations like Bali and Mainland China became popular. Also, the Japanese that did visit Hawaii traveled with less money, and often demanded outdoor activities like hiking, mountain biking, and surfing, instead of a romantic dinner cruise. With the company's bread and butter—Japanese tourism—contributing less and less to the bottom line, perhaps it was time to consider other strategies to securing future business.

Company history

Paradise Cruiselines, Ltd. was founded by Jerry Smith, and his wife Chikako, in 1982. The company began with a handful of employees operating a Second World War era twin hulled catamaran with a capacity of 250 passengers. The company's sole business was providing sightseeing tours by water into Pearl Harbor to visit the Arizona Memorial. The Pearl Harbor tours could only take the company so far, so in the late 1980s, Jerry and Chikako designed and launched a product the islands had not seen yet—a sunset dinner cruise. At times, the first year of the dinner cruise business was discouraging, as the 250-passenger vessel often left the dock with as little as two passengers. The successful Pearl Harbor afternoon cruises enabled the company to continue operating its dinner cruises despite little demand.

Currently, Paradise Cruiselines is the largest and most successful player in Hawaii's cruise industry. It operates four different vessels on two islands, offering everything from whale and dolphin watch cruises, to snorkel adventures and sunset dinner cruises. The company's flagship, the Pride of Honolulu, is a 1500-passenger luxury yacht that sets sail nightly with dinner cruise passenger counts of 900+ people. Companywide daily passenger counts are well over 1200 people. The company's success was built on the backs of Jerry and Chikako Smith, along with a core of dedicated employees. Providing a constant product of high quality, playing fairly in the marketplace, and treating all stakeholders honestly were the keys to success.

The eventual success of the dinner cruise product also relied heavily on the relationships Chikako, Vice President of Sales and Marketing, had formed with the Japanese travel agents in Hawaii. She constantly struggled to persuade agents that a dinner cruise was exactly what the market needed, and that it would be the highlight experience in tourists' visit to the islands. Her efforts paid off handsomely, as more than 50% of the company's revenues originated from Chikako's relationships with travel agents.

Jerry was born and raised in Alaska, worlds apart from Hawaii's pristine beaches, transparent aqua-colored water, and tropical sunny days. At a young age, he moved to California to start his own ocean freight shipping company. He established ties to Hawaii's cruise industry through contacts he had in the shipping business. Equipped with his tireless work ethic and entrepreneurial success in the shipping industry, he moved to Hawaii in 1980, looking for another start-up opportunity.

Chikako was born and raised in the countryside of Japan, where she grew up rich in tradition and the old ways. She was often criticized by travel agents and suppliers for not embracing more fully the Japanese custom of gift-giving. She did, however, habitually send out a simple gift to all of the travel agents every year in June and December, as is customary in Japan, but would not consider relaxing the company's stringent gift exchanging policy.

Her perceived abandonment of Japanese culture was mysterious to some, misunderstood by others.

Gift-giving in Japan

The centuries-old tradition of gift-giving in Japan remains alive and strong in contemporary corporate society. The nature of this practice is highly ritualistic and regimented. Japanese people love giving gifts because it "communicates respect, appreciation and friendship."[2]

There are different times when giving and exchanging gifts is expected.

- A Japanese businessperson is expected to bring a gift when meeting a new colleague or business associate.
- A gift should not be presented too early in a trip or appointment. Instead, the best time to present a gift is at the end of a visit in an inconspicuous manner.[3]
- In June and December, Japanese give gifts to one another to commemorate the mid-year and end of the year. These times are known as "chugen and oseibo."[4]

When giving a gift in Japan, the recipient is expected to politely refuse it once or twice before graciously accepting the gift. The gift given can be of high value and will not be considered bribery, as it is the act of giving a gift that is important and not the gift itself. However, a gift-giver is not expected to give a gift of high value as this could create an uncomfortable situation for the recipient who is expected to reciprocate. A gift recipient is expected to reciprocate by giving a gift that is half the value of the gift received.[5]

If someone gives a gift to an individual, the presentation should take place in a private setting. Conversely, if a gift to a group is being presented, the group should be assembled and given the gift at the same time. Different gifts should be given to businesspeople that hold different ranks within the organization. If a gift is given to one person in a group setting, it then is customary to give gifts to everyone present.[6]

Although deep tradition exists with Japanese gift-wrapping (called "tsutsumi"[7]), it is not necessary to use these elaborate wrapping techniques when presenting corporate gifts. Instead, a gift can and should be wrapped in quality pastel colored paper without bows or other embellishments.

Certain gifts should be avoided that have bad associations in Japanese culture. Do not give lilies, camellias, lotus blossoms or any kind of white flower as they are all associated with funerals.

The color red should be avoided as Japanese funeral notices are printed on this color paper. Avoid giving potted plants, which are considered to cause sickness. Finally, do not give gift items in denominations of four or nine as this is deemed unlucky. Conversely, there are many types of gifts that are highly appreciated in Japanese corporate culture. These include, but are not limited to, prestigious brand name items, top quality wines and spirits, gourmet food, a memorable photograph, or something that is tailored to the personality and interests of the recipient.[8]

Gift-giving in the US

Corporate gift-giving and entertainment in the United States is typically used as a way to build and enhance relationships between clients, suppliers and vendors. Giving gifts can show gratitude and appreciation, but also spur future business. Rules for gift-giving in the United States revolve more around corporate policies and etiquette than tradition or rituals.

- *Corporate Policies:* Corporations see gift-giving as a cost-effective way to build their business.[9] In recent years, companies have tightened up their gift-giving policies to ensure that they are competing with rival businesses fairly and ethically.[10] The majority of large, publicly traded companies embed their gift-giving and entertainment policy into their Ethical Guidelines or Code of Conduct as part of "conflicts of interest". See the *Appendix* for a summary of gift-giving and entertainment policies for some select companies. Smaller companies may not have an official, written policy but are required to follow the IRS' stringent guidelines if they wish to write-off the expense as tax deductible.[11]
- *Etiquette for the Gift-Giver:* There are three main points for a gift-giver to follow as part of corporate gift-giving.[12]

  1. To avoid an awkward situation, a gift-giver should always research the company's rules of the intended recipient to determine whether or not they can accept the gift.
  2. Gifts should be appropriate in nature and can contain company logos or be customized to the recipient's personality and interests.
  3. When bidding for business, an outside businessperson should refrain from giving any type of gift to a decision-maker or anyone else at the decision-maker's firm.

- *Etiquette for the Gift Recipient:* Depending on the corporate policy, employees should disclose gifts that exceed $25 in value to upper management so that they can monitor this activity. Gifts that involve food should be shared with co-workers so that "back-office" employees are rewarded for their hard work.[13]

  Above all, gift-givers and recipients alike are expected to remain ethical in their decision on when and how to accept gifts.

Conclusion

After a long night of restless sleep wondering about what to do with Joe, Jerry got ready for work and headed to the office to meet with the Director of Human Resources (Chikako would also be present). Immediately following the meeting, Joe would be arriving at the office for his monthly budget review. Jerry knew that then was the time to confront and solve the problem. In his mind, there were a few options:

(a) Keep Joe as the Director of Food & Beverage, give him a slap on the wrist, but turn your eyes to his gift exchange habit.
(b) Keep Joe as the Director of Food & Beverage, but use this experience to change company policy to allow for more open gift exchanging.
(c) Place Joe on probation, monitor his accounts, and issue a written notice of the company's gift exchange policy to all vendors/suppliers.
(d) Terminate Joe, threaten vendor/supplier contracts, and establish a written gift exchange policy.

Questions

1. What should Jerry do about Joe? About the company's gift exchange policy?
2. What should Chikako do about her Japanese traditions?

3. Discuss the stakeholders in the case and what they will gain or lose with a change in company policy.
4. What are the ethical issues involved in the case? How might this case relate to your future work experiences?

Appendix

Appendix:Table 14.1

Table 14.1 Samples of *Fortune* 500 companies' gifts and entertainment policies

Company	Policy summary
Wal-Mart[14]	No gifts or gratuities, which have monetary value, are to be given, offered or encouraged in any way to any Wal-Mart/SAM'S Club Associate or potential Wal-Mart/SAM'S Club Associate. Suppliers may donate gifts for the purpose of raising funds for charities or non-profit organizations or for resale at Wal-Mart's Associate Store. Gifts or gratuities include, but are not limited to: free goods, tickets to sporting or entertainment events, kickbacks in the form of money or merchandise, special discounts to any Wal-Mart/SAM'S Club Associate, discontinued or no-longer-used samples, supplier-paid trips, liquor, food products, meals or personal services. When practical, any such item received must be returned to the sender with an explanation of this policy. Any item not returned shall be considered the property of Wal-Mart Stores, Inc.
3M[15]	*Policy statement* The term "business gifts" in this policy includes business entertainment, as well as gift items. The giving of business gifts is a customary way to strengthen business relationships and, with some restrictions, is a lawful business practice. It is 3M policy that company employees may give and receive appropriate, lawful business gifts in connection with their 3M work with commercial customers and other non-governmental parties, provided that all such gifts are nominal in value and not given or received with the intent or prospect of influencing the recipient's business decision-making. Special laws and rules apply to gifts to government employees and it is 3M policy to strictly comply with all such restrictions. Local laws in the US and around the world strictly limit gifts to government employees. These may be criminal acts, regardless of whether they are paid for with 3M or personal funds. Bribery is illegal and violates this policy. 3M policy does not allow for corrupt practices in any form, including bribery. Even when legal, employees cannot give or receive business gifts if doing so would violate this policy. Any business gifts given or received by a 3M employee must be nominal in cost, quantity, and frequency. Never accept or offer gifts of cash or cash equivalents, such as gift certificates. Never accept a gift that could be viewed as lavish. *What it means* • No 3M employee may give or receive a gift that violates the law, regulations, agreements, or reasonable customs of the marketplace. • Make sure any business gift is nominal in cost, quantity, and frequency and that the gift can withstand public scrutiny without damaging 3M's reputation. • Gifts of 3M consumer products are generally likely to be appropriate, as are gifts of items that are marked with 3M promotional labeling. • Properly record any business gift on your business unit's books and make sure that it complies with any policies of your specific 3M business unit.

(Continued)

Table 14.1 Cont'd

Company	Policy summary
	• When deciding on the appropriateness of giving or receiving a business gift, consider how the gift compares in value to the usual gift-giving practices in your industry and country, the sum of gifts to or from that entity over time, the suitability of the gift given your position at 3M, the impact of the gift on building positive business relations with the recipient, and how the gift might look to an outsider. • These guidelines apply even when no reimbursement from the company is sought. If you plan to give or accept a business gift of more than a nominal value, you must inform your supervisor. • Coffee, doughnuts, soft drinks, and similar refreshments of nominal value provided other than as part of a meal are not considered to be gifts under the gift rules for executive branch employees. Therefore, these types of nominal refreshments may be provided to executive branch employees. Do not be offended if they seek to make reimbursement, however, and accept any such payment. • Consult with your assigned 3M legal counsel before giving business gifts to consultants and employees of state and local government agencies. *What to avoid* • Giving or receiving money or other cash equivalent as a business gift. • Unless it is clear that applicable laws and regulations permit it or prior approval has been obtained from assigned 3M legal counsel, offering business gifts to US government employees. Although US executive branch employees may lawfully accept some nominal gifts, the gift rules for US judicial and legislative branches differ from the executive branch and are sometimes even stricter. Because of these strict limitations, 3M employees should avoid giving gifts to any US government employees, including military personnel, regulatory agency employees, and US government employees located outside the US. • Giving or receiving gifts that are too costly or frequent to be within the customs of the marketplace. • Giving any gift to reward a government employee. • Giving or receiving gifts that influence or give the appearance of influencing business judgment. • Offering a gift if you know it would violate the recipient's policy to accept it. • Giving or receiving entertainment, such as tickets to a sporting event, where a representative of the company offering the gift will not be accompanying the recipient to the event.
Chevron[16]	Any activity that has the appearance of a conflict of interest—regardless of whether an actual conflict exists—must be avoided. Any potential conflict of interest should be reported (refer to the sidebar). Avoid accepting gifts, fees, favors, or other advantages: We are not allowed to receive compensation beyond that provided by Chevron for any services rendered to any person or organization on behalf of Chevron. Therefore, the following are prohibited: • Accepting fees or honoraria in exchange for services provided on behalf of the company; • Accepting gifts or entertainment or any other services of more than nominal value from anyone doing or seeking business with Chevron or any of its affiliate companies; • Benefiting by personal gain, opportunities, or advantages through our position within the company or through use of the company's property (including intellectual property), information or influence. When we believe it may be inappropriate under certain circumstances to reject a gift, we should seek guidance to determine an acceptable course of action. Accepting or offering bribes and payoffs to induce a business deal violates company policy and may be illegal.

Table 14.1 Cont'd

Company	Policy summary
Ford Motor Company[17]	Receiving gifts or favors

Accepting gifts or favors from a business contact, such as a supplier or dealer, can cloud your judgment when making decisions for the Company, or give the appearance that the supplier or dealer is "buying" favorable treatment. Always follow the Company's limitations and conditions on accepting gifts or favors from individuals or organizations that do business with the Company, or that are actively seeking to do business with the Company.

Core requirements
- Do not use your position at the Company to privately enrich yourself or others (such as family or friends). in fact, you should avoid situations that could even look to outsiders as if you are doing something improper.
- Never ask for a gift or favor from an individual or organization that does business with the Company, or is actively seeking to do business with the Company.
- Accept a gift or favor that is freely offered by suppliers, dealers, and others only if it is of nominal value, involves a normal sales promotion, advertising, or publicity, and there is a legitimate business purpose. in the US, $50 is considered to be nominal value. See your local appendix, or ask your human resources representative to find out what is considered "nominal value" in your country.
- Never accept any of the following types of gifts or favors from an individual or organization that does business with the Company, or is actively seeking to do business with the Company:
  - Cash, gift certificates, or a gift of packaged alcohol (including beer or wine)
  - Tickets to any event, unless the supplier is in attendance and the situation meets all other entertainment limitations
  - A loan, unless it is from a regular financial institution on normal terms
  - Discounts on goods or services, unless the supplier makes them generally available to all employees in the Company
  - Gifts or other donations for parties or social events attended principally by Company personnel (for example, retirement or holiday parties)
- Return inappropriate gifts with a polite note explaining the Company's policy. If it is not possible or practical for you to return the gift, consult your local Human resources representative to determine what to do with the gift
- Ask if you are not sure if something is appropriate. You may ask your manager, your local Human resources representative, the office of the General Counsel, or your local legal office

Entertainment and social events
Socializing with suppliers, dealers, and other business contacts (referred to below simply as "suppliers") can be helpful in cultivating a good working relationship, but there are limitations on what types of entertainment and social events are acceptable. You must always remember to act in a way that promotes the Company's best interests, and that protects the Company's reputation. Social activities with business associates must be appropriate and limited. You should only accept invitations that are business-related and freely offered. You should never accept an invitation that would create an appearance of impropriety. Always follow the Company's limitations on attending supplier-paid activities.

Core requirements
- Know and follow Company policies regarding accepting refreshments, entertainment, and other social events associated with your work at the Company:
  - You may accept refreshments provided by a supplier while attending a business meeting.

(Continued)

Table 14.1 Cont'd

Company	Policy summary
	− You may accept only one meal per quarter per supplier.

− You may accept only one meal per week, in total, from all suppliers.

− You may accept up to two entertainment events (such as a golf outing, or a sporting, theatrical, or cultural event) per calendar year, per supplier, provided that the supplier is in attendance and the event does not require extensive travel or an overnight stay.

- Do not attend an event that involves adult entertainment when you are on Company business.
- Do not travel on a supplier's aircraft or vehicle for transportation unless it is an authorized Company business trip (such as a trip to a supplier's plant for a quality review, or a local social event that complies with the Company's entertainment policies). Additionally, any travel on a supplier's aircraft must meet the requirements of directive a-110.
- Although you may accept invitations from multiple suppliers, remember that frequent acceptance of gifts or invitations (even if within policy limitations) may create an appearance of impropriety.
- You may accept a gift while at a supplier-paid event, as long as the gift is of nominal value. Remember, prizes given out at such events are considered gifts. Therefore, you may not accept a prize of greater than nominal value, even if you win a contest to qualify for the prize. See your local appendix, or ask your Human resources representative to find out what is considered "nominal value" in your country.
- Use good judgment when you are offered gifts or invitations. If there is any doubt whether the conduct is appropriate, you should consult your Human resources representative or pay your own way.

15 Montenegro Electronics, Ltd.[1]

Jacob Bagha and Gene R. Laczniak

At 28 years old, Mirko Markotitch had reached the first plateau in his strategy for launching a career in international business. Two months ago, he had been transferred to the Serbian International Headquarters of U.S. Electronics Enterprises, Inc. (USEE) to assume responsibilities as a sales representative working out of the company's international sales offices in Belgrade. Having been raised in Bor and educated in Belgrade, this assignment was a welcome return "home" after five years in the US, first as an MBA student in a leading American business school and then as a trainee and sales representative in the New York sales division of USEE. Mirko's decision to work for USEE was based on his perception that this billion-dollar, multinational company would offer challenging opportunities for him to gain experience and earn advancement in the field of international business.

USEE is a major worldwide supplier of electronics components for industrial applications. USEE conducts its business through its own subsidiaries and through its highly developed network of exclusive distributorships in non-subsidiary regional markets. Although this system of regional distributors did not provide as much control over business operations as did the company-owned subsidiaries, the distributors provided a practical alternative in areas where the business short- and mid-term potential did not warrant costly subsidiary coverage. In each of the assigned regions, the independent distributor acted as the exclusive representative of USEE for all its electronics products. Distributors were not required to make heavy investments in electronics inventories and business facilities, but they were expected to maintain close working relationships with industrial users of electronic components. As the regional representative, the distributor also should be well versed regarding local business regulations, practices, and political realities. It was not unusual to have a distributor who was "well established" in relation to both business and government contacts.

In his new position as the regional sales representative for all sales in the regions directly south of Vojvodina (which was considered an autonomous region), Mirko was responsible to the distributors for developing and maintaining the electronics components business with approximately 70 industrial accounts ranging from the Serbian capital of Belgrade to the country of Montenegro which had once been politically joined with Serbia. Mirko worked through the local distributors in the area to promote USEE business with the local manufacturers of electronics products. In spite of its small size, Montenegro was developing a thriving manufacturing business in electronic products (MP3 players, televisions, Blu-Ray players, music systems, and so on) for Eastern European and Middle Eastern consumer markets. Shortly after assuming his new responsibilities, Mirko decided to make an initial tour of his new sales territory to introduce himself to his industrial customers and to his distributor partners. It was in Montenegro that Mirko was confronted with a situation that caused him to reexamine his company's policies and his own.

On arrival in Montenegro, Mirko was met by the local distributor, Dragan Petrović. Dragan had represented USEE in Montenegro for over 20 years, and Mirko was pleased to note that during that period, USEE's business had grown steadily from virtually nothing to its current level of significant sales revenue. Dragan was quick to point out that this success was due in part to his own excellent working relationship with Mirko's predecessor in the job, Kristina Cetnik. According to Dragan, Kristina was an experienced, charismatic woman who understood the realities and nuances of doing business in a close-knit society where "business is not always conducted in the most sophisticated manner." Dragan went on to observe how unfortunate it was for everyone that Kristina was stricken with a serious heart problem at such an early age. "One day she was here, healthy and vibrant. Two weeks later, we heard that she had been hospitalized with little chance that she will be back with us again. Ah, what a tragedy! What a nice woman!"

From the outset, Mirko was impressed with Dragan in terms of his sincerity and his con-geniality. Not only was he a conscientious host, but he gave evidence of being an astute businessman. Early in their discussions, Dragan pointed out that his success was also the result of the Montenegro government's commitment to develop an industrial base for the country, which historically had been a farming and sheepherding economy. One of the major industries receiving government support was electronics products manufacturing, and fore-most among the several companies in this business was Montenegro Electronics, Ltd, one of USEE's major customers in the area. Dragan pointed out that Montenegro Electronics had purchased more than $2,000,000 worth of electronics components from USEE during the previous business year. In view of the importance of this account to USEE and to his own distributorship, Dragan suggested a dinner meeting with Anton Jovanović, the director of purchasing at Montenegro Electronics. Dragan pointed out that, as far as USEE was con-cerned, Anton was the key man at Montenegro Electronics. Kristina had developed a close personal relationship with Anton over the years. Dragan pointed out that, as a member of one of the leading families in Montenegro, Anton participated actively in the social and political activities of his small country. His brother, Ivan, was an elected member of the Montenegro Council, the 24-member council that governed this small nation. Dragan had planned the Wednesday dinner meeting so that Mirko and Anton could get to know one another in a relaxed social setting prior to their business meeting on the following day. Mirko was quite conscious of the Thursday meeting at which they would be discussing Montenegro Electronics' requirements for next year and the renewal of their contract. This would be Mirko's first major negotiation in his new position, and he was keenly aware of the importance of the Montenegro Electronics business.

At the dinner meeting on Wednesday, Mirko was impressed with the cordial reception he received from Anton. On being introduced to Mirko, Anton was quick to express his appre-ciation of USEE and Kristina for the excellent support that they had provided over the years and also for the enjoyable "USEE Customer Appreciation Weekends" in Belgrade, Budapest, and Larissa that had provided much needed relaxation for Anton and his small family. In his subsequent conversation, it was clear that Anton was a person of warmth and culture.

During dinner, both Anton and Dragan discussed with pride the strides that their country was making in emerging from a simple farming society to a more industrialized economy. Anton observed, however, that progress has its price: "Although we from Montenegro are happy with our economic progress, we are also concerned with maintaining our ancient customs."

As they were enjoying their after-dinner brandies, Mirko commented on the fine meal and the excellent wine. Anton's response caused Mirko to deliberate: "Ah, Mirko, it must be good for you to be back home after your five years in America—back to where people truly know how to prepare and enjoy delicious cuisine. Now, I have nothing against Americans—except that they know nothing about good food and fine wine. They are more interested in the quantity of food that they are served at a meal rather than the flavor. They know little about the careful preparation of food and the skillful blending of the ingredients. It is the seasoning that is important. Good food as well as good business requires discreet seasoning, appropriately applied."

While Mirko was pondering the reference to "discreet seasoning" as it related to "good business," Anton continued in a more explicit way: "Has Dragan discussed with you the arrangement that we have had over the years, Kristina and myself? Yes, yes, Kristina appreciated the significant business that we were able to give to her—and to USEE. She was generous in her 'seasoning'—ah, I believe she called it 'our komisija.'[2] He said, 'One half per cent is a small amount to pay to such a loyal friend.' I am assuming that you will wish to continue this arrangement, Mirko." As Mirko hesitated in responding, Anton turned to Dragan and said, "That was the way we worked wasn't it, Dragan? Kristina would give me my envelope with the one-half percent cash payment for each previous order. Unfortunately, she was not able to give me the payment for our last order, but we will forget that. I am an understanding man, if not the most patient one. If you wish to continue this arrangement, we will work out the details of the order at our meeting tomorrow, and you may pay me my komisija on your next visit. That is the way the arrangement works, isn't it, Dragan?"

"That was really between you and Kristina," Dragan responded. "Of course, you know that we value you as a key customer, and we want to keep you as a customer."

Noticing Mirko's surprise and uncertainty, Anton stood up and extended his hand: "Perhaps you would like to think about this overnight, Mirko. We can confirm it at our meeting tomorrow. Thank you, Mirko and Dragan for a most pleasant evening."

When Anton had left, Mirko turned to Dragan: "What the hell is going on here, Dragan? What that man is asking for is outright bribery. You know that it is strict company policy not to pay any form of bribery. It's hard for me to believe that Kristina would go along with such an arrangement."

"Relax, Mirko. You are not in America now. You are in Montenegro—and this is the way business is done in Montenegro. This is nothing more than an extension of your company's 'Customer Appreciation' program."

"I am sorry to disagree with you, Dragan, but this is bribery—and bribery is illegal everywhere that I know of."

"Yes, Mirko, this type of 'komisija' bribery is regarded with some concern in the United States, but in other parts of the world it is a long-standing way of doing business. If you do not wish to continue the arrangement, someone else most certainly will be more flexible in order to get the Montenegro Electronics' business. Please, Mirko, we have a lot at stake here. USEE wants this business. They will not be happy to lose a customer who gives them over two million dollars worth of business a year. I also need this business. Montenegro Electronics is my largest customer. I do not think I will be able to survive without them. And you, my young friend—you are just starting in your career. How will it look if you lose this most valued account? And how will it affect your sales komisijas? In situations like this, the best rule to follow is 'When in Rome, do as the Romans do.'"

"Dragan, you know and I know that it is against company policy to pay bribes in order to get business. This was really stressed in our company-training program; in fact, we had a separate session on this subject, and the vice president of sales came to our session to state the company's position in person. He emphasized that bribery was not only bad business but also illegal under the Foreign Corrupt Practices Act."[3]

"Mirko, even the Corrupt Practices Laws allow for some exemptions in situations where companies would be put at a severe competitive disadvantage. The reasoning is, I believe, that if commissions to company or government officials, though illegal in some countries, are customary practice, then sellers should be allowed to compete on an even basis."

"That may be so, Dragan, but our company does not allow this sort of practice, and they are clear about warning us that it could cost us our jobs. The company believes that we should make excellent products and sell them at competitive prices. There is no room for payoffs."

"Mirko, I am distressed that you see it this way. Kristina understood that this was the way to do business here. She worked out a fair arrangement with Anton. It was no big deal. I suggest that you consider the consequences of changing this arrangement. Perhaps a good night's sleep will help you to put things into perspective. We can meet tomorrow morning to discuss this before our meeting with Anton."

On returning to his hotel room, Mirko was unable to go to sleep. He had a serious problem and an important decision to make before the meeting. Bribery, even under the disguise of a "komisija," was repugnant to him both personally and professionally. And the company position on this was quite clear. Yet Kristina had been an honorable and respected USEE employee, and Kristina felt that it was a necessary accommodation. Mirko was genuinely impressed with Dragan Petrović as a person and as a businessman, and Dragan sincerely believed that the payment was appropriate in this situation.

Mirko also realized that he could not ignore the impact of the lost business on his commission earnings. When he took over the territory, he was told that Kristina had averaged between $140,000 and $175,000 (US$) in commissions annually. Although the sales commission varied on different products, the average commission to the sales rep was 2 percent. The sales quota for the territory was $7,000,000. If Mirko could sustain the 2 percent commission rate and also retain the business with his 70 assigned accounts, he could look forward to an income of $150,000 in his first year, which was a healthy increase over his income for the previous year in the New York territory. Not all his accounts were the size of Montenegro Electronics, however. Although there were three other sizable accounts in the territory, most of the customers were much smaller. The accounts ranged in size from $50,000 per year to $1,500,000, with the majority being under $150,000. As he considered the makeup of his territory, Mirko was again reminded of the importance of the Montenegro Electronics account. He wondered if he could realistically turn his back on one of his top accounts and the $40,000 komisija income generated from that account.

Mirko realized that he must reach a decision before his meeting with Dragan in the morning. He also realized that he had neither the time nor the opportunity to consult with his sales manager in the Belgrade office who was in transit to Asia. As he sat thinking about his problem, he remembered his naive reaction to the discussion of bribery in the ethics session in the training program and in his previous MBA classes. It all seemed so clear and simple then. However, no one told him that he would be called on to make these decisions under such great pressure and in situations where it was not at all clear what the appropriate business decision should be. He realized that the textbooks couldn't really prepare a person for the kind of situation that he now found himself in—one that involved a costly decision, no time to get advice, and significant financial consequences to his company, to his distributor partner, and to himself. And he was reminded that he was not dealing with sleazy people but with smart, cultured businesspeople for whom this was a way of life. The meetings with Dragan and Anton tomorrow should be quite challenging.

Questions

1. Should Mirko refuse to follow his predecessor's "customs" and run the risk of losing a large client?
2. Should Mirko inform USEE of his decision if he chooses to follow past agreements?

16 Arctic Desert[1]

Katie Hesemann and Rachel Mellard

The assignment

Jennifer has recently received a job offer to work within the service division of a large heating and cooling company, Arctic Desert. Her responsibilities include understanding the service network to which the company outsources their in-home service needs and fostering a relationship with the individual companies. The top executives at Arctic Desert believe they are underperforming in comparison to their competitors in the heating and cooling industry. They feel it would be an important strategic position if they could be known in the industry as the company that stands behind their brand and cares about the customer through the entire product lifecycle.

The biggest challenge of her position is that the service network consists of approximately 6,000 in-home service companies. The industry is extremely fragmented which means that it is hard to keep control of the many companies and how they are treating Arctic Desert's customers compared to their competitors. In order to understand how Arctic Desert stands in comparison to the other heating and cooling companies, Jennifer decides to conduct a couple of market research studies. She wants to do two studies: one will survey the customers who have recently had service on their products and the other will be to a sample of the service repair companies. The survey for the service repair companies will target three job areas in the company: the owner, the servicer and the back office support in an effort to fully understand the similarities and differences of Arctic Desert's policies versus other companies.

Hurst Evans Associates

Jennifer learns that Arctic Desert has an exclusive contract to work with a local market research company, Hurst Evans Associates. Arctic Desert is a *Fortune* 500 company and the executives previously realized that they were wasting both monetary resources and valuable time on duplicate market research reports because of the corporate silos. To cut down on duplication, Arctic Desert decided to work with a single company who would be responsible for managing all of the research and leverage findings across all business units. Both Hurst and Evans, the owners, are former employees of Arctic Desert so they have a solid understanding of the industry and needs of the company. This provides a good fit for the companies to work together and develop positive relationships.

The project

Jennifer first works with Hurst Evans to develop an RFP (request for proposal) and begins the assignment. The cost comes back as $75,000 for the customer survey because they will have to buy the customer list and send it to a large number of people in order to get statistically significant data. She knows these findings will be purely directional anyways because customer surveys lend themselves to frequent errors. Costing $15,000, the second proposal is for the in-home servicer survey and the list of contacts who will likely take the survey will be provided by Arctic Desert. Jennifer's boss signs off on both expenses and she is on her way to meet with Hurst Evans to begin collecting the data.

Brad works at Hurst Evans and is assigned as the account manager for the research. Jennifer first set up a meeting with Brad, herself, and her management team to outline the priorities and goals for the research. She makes it very clear that her objective is to understand Arctic Desert's position within the in-home service market and to be able to benchmark the company against competitors. In addition, Jennifer's boss explicitly states that this research needs to be a priority and requests that it be completed in three months, an unusually quick turnaround for Hurst Evans to do such a study. Regardless, Brad seems happy with the discussion and sets off to write the surveys. Meanwhile, Jennifer is nervous because she can tell that this is Brad's first assignment as account manager and lead of a project. She also knows that this is the first study Hurst Evans has ever done on the in-home service side of the business.

Brad sends Jennifer a copy of the proposed surveys three days later. She sees the email and is pleased that he has done a substantial amount of work so quickly. As she begins reading through the surveys, she makes it past the poor grammar and incorrect word choice and notices that Brad has missed the project's objective of comparing Arctic Desert to the competition. She sets up a two-hour meeting immediately to review the surveys with him and, at this point, she realizes this project is going to require substantially more project management and hand holding on her side than anticipated.

Three weeks later, Jennifer receives an email from Brad asking for approval to field test the customer survey. She reflects on the 14 versions they have been through and the countless hours she has spent reworking every question for grammar, clarity and purpose—this project now consumes 55% of her time. Recognizing that the deadline is quickly approaching and work on the in-home servicer survey has not begun, she immediately stops what she is working on to review the customer survey then sends it off to the business unit heads for approval. Two days later, the survey is sent out to the customers and she moves her focus over to the second part of the project.

Similar to the first set of surveys, upon receipt of the in-home servicer ones, Jennifer recognizes that a substantial amount of time will be required to perfect these so she immediately pulls out a red pen and begins the corrections. After four meetings with Brad and countless emails she feels it may be ready to field test. Because of the importance of this survey, she calls on a co-worker to serve as an additional reviewer. With an understanding of the project's goals, this co-worker can provide a reasonably fresh perspective on it and ensure that she has not missed anything important. After several small revisions, it's finally ready to go.

Seven days later, Jennifer receives an email from Brad to inform her that Hurst Evans was not able to get enough customer respondents so they need to send another batch of surveys out. This will cost an additional $10,000. At this point, Jennifer grows frustrated because she is paying so much money for Brad to facilitate and conduct this research but feels like she has done all of the work. Regardless, she cannot back out now because they have already spent $75,000 on the survey and need the data. She approves the additional cost and moves on.

Upon feeling pressure from her boss to present the research findings several weeks later, Jennifer emails Brad to find out where they are in the process and how quickly they can wrap it up and complete the analysis. He promises the customer survey data in two weeks and the servicer survey the following week. Jennifer feels a sense of relief to know that the end is in sight.

Getting the results

On Friday, Jennifer receives Hurst Evans's presentation of the findings for the customer survey. She sits down that night with a glass of wine and a sigh of relief to go through the PowerPoint deck. Page by page, a sense of frustration and concern begins to grow inside as the presentation is all wrong! The data are cut to provide customer preferences and customer satisfaction rather than indicating customer's perceptions and feelings about Arctic Desert as compared to the competitors. In hopes that only the recommendation pages are incorrect, she continues to turn the page, but quickly realizes the entire report needs to be redone.

Simply stated, the most important desired findings from the research, of which were explicitly told to Brad, were not even shown in the data. All of her hard work and long hours spent coaching Brad and helping him understand the project's goals were wasted. This is the result? Jennifer is in total disbelief.

First thing Monday morning, she informs Brad over the phone that she is unhappy and the presentation is nowhere near ready to be presented to her boss. On Wednesday, the day of their scheduled meeting, she incidentally receives the presentation for the second part of the project, the servicer survey. At the meeting with Brad, she spells out the changes that need to be made and the way the data need to be re-cut. In addition, she indicates her decision not to look at the second presentation received that morning until it has been cut and presented the correct way. Jennifer is visibly angry but understands that her anger is not directed at Brad and his inexperience; but rather, she is frustrated with Hurst Evans for giving her an account manager that has neither experience nor training on such an important project. The implication of this has required her to complete 80% of the upfront work. Jennifer should have paid herself or saved the money for Arctic Desert and conducted the research on her own!

Presentation to the boss

With her boss breathing down her throat looking for the report, Jennifer chases Brad down for the final report and sets up an official meeting to review the findings. With nervous chills circulating her body, Jennifer enters the meeting ready to take over at any point. She recalls the history of the project, but knows how picky and experienced her boss is with research. Without her knowledge, Brad has put together a short deck that combines the results of both studies, causing the meeting to start off shakily. As he continues, she realizes the new deck does not make any sense so she quickly jumps in and asks to review the two research presentations instead. Once she begins to take control, the meeting changes direction and is smooth sailing from there. Jennifer's boss provides several recommendations on preparing the data to show the CEO; but, regardless she seems pleased. Several key learnings have surfaced from the studies and she feels that the data can be used to make changes.

All in all, Jennifer, in turn, is pleased with the outcome of the research. The memories of the struggles she went through with Brad fade away as she sees the good information they are getting from this. Arctic Desert begins implementing a few policy changes and life continues on.

The bill

Three weeks later, Brad sends an invoice to Jennifer. She mindlessly opens the envelope expecting the total to equal $105,000: the $75,000 original fee, the additional $15,000 for the second set of recruited respondents and the $15,000 for the servicer research. Slightly over the standard amount, the cost is worthwhile because the findings are helpful. The amount payable catches her eye—it reads $120,000. In a state of confusion, she calls Brad immediately.

Brad explains that the additional cost is from the additional hours recorded to rework the surveys, re-cut the data and reconstruct the final presentation after Jennifer had rejected the first version. He indicates that the original proposal only allowed for 20 hours of front end work and 20 hours of analysis on the back end. The actual logged hours came out at 48 for the survey creation and 34 for analysis. From Hurst Evans's perspective, Jennifer was the party not happy with either the surveys or the findings. The reconstruction and additional analyses of both took time and energy but they were willing to do whatever it took to make her, the client, happy. She should have known that this would cost more and factored that into her expectations of the final cost. Brad and fellow associates completed the work and for that they should be compensated at the prearranged rate.

Jennifer, once again, is in a state of disbelief. She feels angry that they never mentioned the potential for additional cost in the contract or what the maximum hours that could be spent on it would be. She also knows that if Hurst Evans assigned a seasoned account manager to her, it would never have taken that long. Plus, she would also not have had to do so much work herself!

The alternatives

(a) Pay the bill and accept her frustration with the whole process. The top executives were responsible for the decision to work only with Hurst Evans so this is out of her hands.
(b) Refute the hours spent on the survey to see if they can come up with a prorated cost and log some of the hours as training for Brad.
(c) Call a meeting with management at Hurst Evans and your own management team to express disappointment in both the work and the hidden costs. Tell Hurst Evans you will pay this time but expect more clarity next time.
(d) Go to Arctic Desert's executives and plead a case for firing Hurst Evans and refuse to pay a penny more than $105,000.

Questions

1. What should Jennifer do?
2. Which ethical theory best supports her discussion?

17 Superior Services

Should short skirts sell software?[1]

Lori Lepp Corbett

Elizabeth once again smoothed her skirt as she crossed her legs and tried to redirect the gaze of her potential client. She was unsuccessful in making eye contact with her customer, so she then stared at the clock over his shoulder, squirming as the seconds slowly passed. Skip, one of her first sales calls ever and an important customer, was the CEO of the Community Bank Savings Bank (Indiana, US). He was in the process of telling yet another story about "the good old days" when he was president of "Lamda" fraternity at Rutgers University. He kept standing up, supposedly to point out souvenirs on his wall, although more likely to try and look down the front of her dress. He seemed to focus 100 percent of his attention on Elizabeth's chest or legs instead of on her face or, more important, on the software bid she had put in front of him over an hour ago. After what seemed like an eternity and easily four years' worth of "frat boy" antics, Skip decided he and Elizabeth should step across the street for a bite of lunch. Elizabeth stood up with relief, thinking that maybe a change of venue would help Skip regain some focus regarding the topic at hand—adding a debit card product and its management software to the First Community Bank line of retail banking products.

Unfortunately, over lunch Elizabeth had another rude awakening. Instead of discussing business, Skip wanted to have drinks at lunch and continue regaling her. For another two hours, the CEO talked about the frolics of his college days while he slowly got drunk on vodka martinis. He continued to leer at Elizabeth, while he made innuendoes about his preference for younger women and his particular interest in 24-year-old blondes like her. Finally, as time approached 4:00 P.M., and after repeated attempts to steer the conversation back to her product offering, Elizabeth decided she didn't care anymore about the outcome of this sale. She stood up, thinking she would just walk out of the restaurant if he insisted again that she didn't really have to go back to her office. His last remark to her as she walked out the door was, "Liz, don't worry, and for God's sake, please lighten up; I will sign that contract you left me, just as long as you are cuter than that little rep from ATN Corp. You know I make all my decisions based upon the physical attributes of my vendors." Elizabeth was fuming as she pulled out of the parking lot. In fact, she was so distracted that she bumped into the back of another car as the crudeness of Skip's final comment rang inside her head. Elizabeth sat on the side of the road, crying as she exchanged phone numbers with the other driver. She couldn't wait to get back to the office to tell one of her co-workers that this man was a jerk. (Her local office was mostly women, which was typical for her firm.)

Elizabeth's sales manager, Maria, was also her mentor. Maria, had started as a sales rep with a terrific reputation for closing deals. And, she had been Skip's key contact until Elizabeth had been assigned the account. Elizabeth liked and respected Maria, who seemed both capable and sophisticated. So once Elizabeth returned to the office, she practically ran into Maria's office to tell her about this creepy buyer and to propose letting him go as a customer. She was shocked as Maria started to nod her head knowingly, saying, "Oh sure, I know Skip loves to drink at lunch, and he loves our Superior Software girls. That's why we sent you out there, Elizabeth. As long as you go to see him once a month, wear a short skirt, let him gape at you for an hour or two, and buy him a few drinks, he will always extend his contracts with us and consider purchasing more upgrades. He makes his decisions based upon the appearance of his reps and the attention they give him. So I want you to use your resources, go visit him occasionally, wear a short skirt, maybe loosen your blouse a bit, and don't get too hung up on his inane comments. Skip is clumsy and harmless; if he was a problem, I never would have put you in that situation."

Elizabeth looked at Maria quizzically and was speechless; Maria reacted after a brief pause. "Liz, you don't quite get it, do you? Our top management may be too conservative to use sex appeal to promote our software, but we sure can use our assets when calling on customers. Have you noticed that eight of our ten reps are female and good looking? Small savings bank and credit union managers are mostly middle age men who are always very busy; your 'looks' can get you the necessary face time required to pitch our excellent product line-up. Drug companies have used this strategy for years with physicians when detailing new drug products. You should never do anything improper or something that makes you feel uncomfortable. But realize that a little friendly banter with old guys like Skip makes them feel a little younger. Eighty percent of these small financial institutions are managed by older men like Skip and a little banter with an attractive rep always will make a sales difference at the margin. So, grow up Liz!"

Elizabeth went into her office thoroughly confused and trembling. She didn't want to ever see Skip again. But maybe Maria had a point: wearing a short skirt might be an easy way to extend some service contracts. And surely if other companies like ATN were using the exact same tactics, Superior needed to compete. Elizabeth knew she would have to make a very difficult decision—could she use her short skirt to sell software? Was this an ethical way to close a deal?

Facts about Superior Services

Superior Services is a subsidiary of Consolidated Financial, a large commercial banking corporation based in the Midwest. Consolidated first opened their doors in 1863 when a group of businessmen started the bank inside a Masonic Temple. The goal of the original firm was to serve the Ohio River trade. The company grew rapidly through the next century, primarily through acquisitions, although the addition of innovative new products and services also helped add revenue as customers switched to the Consolidated. In the early 1970s, the firm reorganized in order to keep current with industry trends. As part of the restructuring, the bank switched their emphasis from commercial loans to consumer credit. As part of this new focus on the individual consumer, one of the senior officers of the bank realized that the future in retail banking was to move away from branches and introduce technology-oriented banking alternatives. This executive proceeded to develop his idea while having drinks with the CEO after a golf game—that was how things got done in those days. Their cocktail napkin sketch outlined a technology subsidiary that would support credit and debit card processing services. Out of their discussion came Superior Services, a data processing and information services provider. The division had expanded nationally to include a suite of software products used to manage deposit, loan and trust systems for other financial organizations. For instance, Superior offered software to manage image-based processing, electronic funds transfer and a variety of other products to oversee and analyze credit and debit management initiatives.

By 2000, Superior Services had expanded into a dominant credit and debit card processor in the United States. Superior drove ATMs for more than 1,000 banks and credit unions and processed credit cards for over 20,000 merchants around the world. Their sales revenue had grown at a rate of 30 percent annually, an aggressive growth rate that the Superior team managed to maintain year after year. On the balance, the Superior profit margin was one of the highest in the industry. Superior provided 25 percent of total revenue for the bank, and Consolidated profited $0.25 for every dollar invested in Superior Services.

Consolidated had an extremely aggressive executive vice president, Tom Griffith, overseeing the technology subsidiary. He had specifically singled out Maria for her consistently above quota sales results in the company newsletter. And, he compensated his staff extremely well for their work; however, he demanded absolute dedication, 80-hour workweeks, weekend assignments, 24-hour on-call, and limited vacations. Elizabeth herself had already had a vacation cancelled because one of the executive's favorite customers asked to see her on a particular date, and the executive vice president "just couldn't say no." His staff was not happy with the work environment, but everyone was pleased with their paychecks, which were significantly above industry average.

Employee training and compensation

Elizabeth had started work at Superior Services directly out of undergraduate school. She began a management training program that lasted for one year. During her training as a Superior associate, Elizabeth had the opportunity to learn about various aspects of the business, including legal, billing, sales protocol, software development, and customer service. In each of these rotations, Elizabeth was able to refine her project management, problem-solving, and customer attention skills. She learned how to calm down an irate customer as well as how to close the deal with a customer who was hesitant.

After her full year of training, Elizabeth was promoted to consultant, and her responsibilities changed. She began to run system implementations, managing the entire software integration process. She coordinated tasks for the programming staff, she trained new customers on the applications, and she went on-site to trouble shoot the implementation. It soon became clear to management that Elizabeth had a terrific ability to develop customer relationships. When she was done with an implementation, every customer wanted her to come back as the relationship manager. So, after nine months, Elizabeth was promoted again to senior account manager. She handled key regional accounts, managing technical issues, billing complaints, and new product development. She also began to cross-sell and negotiate contracts. Skip, the CEO at the First Community Bank, was one of her first major sales calls.

Elizabeth's compensation was based upon the following measures:

- Her base salary was $45,000, which was compensation for her day-to-day systems consulting and account oversight tasks.
- A profit-sharing bonus, a percentage that was determined annually by the CEO of Superior Services. The percentage was then applied to each employee's base salary to determine the dollar value of the bonus. The bank had been so successful in the past several years, that the 15 percent profit sharing had become an expectation, not a bonus.

- A bonus of $1000 per deal closed, plus a percentage of future earnings from the new sale (expectation of 0 to 10 deals per year—10 deals closed would be an outstanding year). By Elizabeth's calculation, the sale of debt card software to Skip would be worth $1000 to her immediately and as much as another $2000 down the line.
- Elizabeth did not receive stock options since she was not an officer in the bank, although this was a very valuable aspect of the compensation for officers. Elizabeth could expect to make officer (according to her manager) after being with the bank for four more years.

So, Elizabeth's compensation as an employee with only two years of work experience was projected this year as a respectable $65,000 assuming $8000 in profit sharing and $12,000 in closed deals. This was well above average for a 24-year-old employee with a liberal arts undergraduate degree in Economics.

The ethical dilemma

At this time, Elizabeth had a very difficult decision to make. She was uncomfortable using the sales tactics being recommended by her sales manager/mentor. While Maria seemed to think that sex appeal could sell software, Elizabeth believed in the quality of her actual product. She didn't think she needed to use gimmicks such as short skirts or low-cut blouses to close a deal. Elizabeth thought this might be compromising her principles just for the sake of a thousand bucks. On the other hand, Elizabeth did like her job. She was very busy, always learning new technology, traveling all over Central US, and meeting new people. And, of course, she was very well compensated for her work and on the fast track to upper management. When she sat down to review her alternatives, she decided she had three options:

(a) Confront her manager Maria and refuse to call on this customer again.
(b) Pull out that short skirt, run over to First Community Bank, and "close the deal" by flirting a little with Skip and asking him to sign the contract.
(c) Quit Superior Services and find a job somewhere where she would not have to compromise her ethical principles just to close a sales deal.

Elizabeth thought she would go home for the evening and think about all of this. But tomorrow she was going to have to make a decision.

Questions

1. Which option should she choose, and why?
2. Can you think of another way that Elizabeth might resolve this matter?
3. What ethical principles exactly, if any, are at stake in this situation?

18 Facebook[1]

Urvashi Mathur and Ryan Mack

"Facebook's mission is to give people the power to share and make the world more open and connected"

—Facebook's Mission Statement

A Facebook story

Daniel and Jane had been dating for three years when Daniel decided to purchase an engagement ring for Jane. With the big surprise proposal only a few weeks away and after searching through hundreds of engagement ring websites, Daniel finally purchased the engagement ring through a trusted website. Both Daniel and Jane were avid users of Facebook, and of course, were listed as "In a relationship" with each other on their profiles.

Daniel returned home from work one evening and sat down in front of his computer to check his Facebook page. Upon viewing the latest update on his profile, Daniel was shocked at what he found. The following was posted on his profile in capital letters: "Daniel purchased an engagement ring from our store! Click below to see his purchase." Attached was a link to a picture and details of the engagement ring with the price listed directly below. Since Daniel forgot to log out of Facebook before purchasing the ring online, Facebook picked up on his purchase and logged the information on his profile.

He quickly removed the wall post from his profile after the initial shock of what had happened. Horrified that Jane had recently viewed his profile and that his surprise was ruined, Daniel immediately called Jane to check when she last logged on to Facebook. This was his lucky day. Jane had been too busy with work to check her Facebook for the past few days. This time he decided to log out of Facebook, only to realize that he didn't even know where the log out button was placed on the page. After searching for over 15 minutes, he figured out that in order to log out successfully, he had to click on the Account button in the top right corner, and then scroll down to the log out button, which was the last option in the menu.

Later that night, Jane decided to finally log into Facebook to catch up with friends and post some new pictures from her weekend trip. When she logged on, the first thing that popped up was a personalized recommendation from Facebook that read, "Hi Jane! Daniel recently purchased an engagement ring from this website! We thought you might like it too." Attached was a link to the engagement ring.

Although Jane was ecstatic to learn that she would soon be engaged, she was enraged that Facebook informed her of what was supposed to be the biggest surprise of her life. The couple eventually got engaged, and in order to announce it to their friends, they changed their relationship status on Facebook from "In a relationship" to "Engaged." After this change, Jane noticed ads on her profile such as "80% off wedding dresses" and "Lose weight before your big day!" She wondered how Facebook knew she was worried about the cost of her wedding dress as well as losing weight in time for her wedding. Upon scanning her wall posts to friends, she realized she had recently written on her friend's wall about trying to save up money to buy her dress and that she hoped she would fit in to the dresses.

This case is based on two true stories that were posted on blogs during the time of Facebook Beacon (explained below). One of the experiences was documented by a *Washington Post* article found here: www.washingtonpost.com/wp-dyn/content/article/2007/11/29/AR2007112902503.html

A brief history of Facebook

It all began in 2003, when Mark Zuckerberg began attending Harvard University as an undergraduate. After developing a program that allowed students to see which other students had signed up for a class, Zuckerberg created a program to rate girls at Harvard to share with all of his male peers. He named this program "Facemash." This expanded from within Harvard to all Ivy League universities, and from rating girls to a full social networking platform called "thefacebook.com."[2] In 2004, Zuckerberg bought the domain name "Facebook.com" for $200,000 and opened the network up to anyone with a valid university email address. By 2006, Facebook was open to anyone above the age of thirteen with a valid email address. What started as a company of three people and orders from Harvard to shut down the original site, Facebook now has over 800 million members worldwide, has 3,000 employees and was valued at $50 billion in 2011.[3] The company is headquartered in Palo Alto, California, Dublin, Ireland and Seoul, South Korea, and is led by Founder and CEO Mark Zuckerberg, Vice President of Product Chris Cox, and Chief Operating Officer Sheryl Sandberg. Zuckerberg is one of the world's youngest billionaires, with a net worth of over $13.5 billion, making him the 52nd richest person in the world as of March 2011.[4]

Ever since the launch of Facebook, the company has constantly faced challenges regarding the privacy of users. While privacy is a concern, the company has consistently grown revenue through targeted ad placements on its site. Today, the Facebook privacy policy is longer than the United States Constitution. Below are the different attempts made by the company since 2007 to take advantage of the massive amount of user data and preferences it generates. Along with each description of the platform are relevant pieces of information quoted directly from the privacy policy page (www.facebook.com/policy.php).

Facebook Beacon

From 2007 to 2009, the company had a data sharing system called Facebook Beacon, which sent data about Facebook users and their consumer behavior from other websites to Facebook. This information would then be published to a user's news feed or profile. Forty-four companies were partnered with Facebook Beacon. Although Facebook claimed that the company would not receive any information about the user's external activity without their consent, a security researcher who was testing the system found that data were being sent to Facebook regardless of consent. Although Zuckerberg responded by adding an option for users to turn Facebook Beacon off completely, it was clear that most Facebook users did not even know what Facebook Beacon was. Due to several lawsuits and litigation, Facebook Beacon was eventually shut down in September 2009.

Facebook Connect

In late 2008, Facebook launched Facebook Connect, which enables its users to log into external websites with their Facebook accounts. However, most users do not realize the extent to which their information is available for these websites to access. Also, even if they personally do not use Facebook Connect, but a friend of theirs does, the website automatically has access to their information as well. In the Facebook Privacy page, the following is written about Facebook Connect:

> When you connect with an application or website it will have access to General Information about you. The term General Information includes your and your friends' names, profile pictures, gender, user IDs, connections, and any content shared using the Everyone privacy setting. We may also make information about the location of your computer or access device and your age available to applications and websites in order to help them implement appropriate security measures and control the distribution of age-appropriate content. If the application or website wants to access any other data, it will have to ask for your permission.[5]

> If your friend connects with an application or website, it will be able to access your name, profile picture, gender, user ID, and information you have shared with "everyone." It will also be able to access your connections, except it will not be able to access your friend list. If you have already connected with (or have a separate account with) that website or application, it may also be able to connect you with your friend on that application or website. If the application or website wants to access any of your other content or information (including your friend list), it will have to obtain specific permission from your friend. If your friend grants specific permission to the application or website, it will generally only be able to access content and information about you that your friend can access. In addition, it will only be allowed to use that content and information in connection with that friend. For example, if a friend gives an application access to a photo you only shared with your friends, that application could allow your friend to view or print the photo, but it cannot show that photo to anyone else.
>
> The website's privacy policy provides solutions for users to limit information received by external websites. These solutions include the ability to limit *some* of the information communicated, or to completely remove the friend from your network.

Instant personalization

Facebook states that if a user is still logged on to Facebook and simultaneously visits a third party website that is partnered with Facebook, the company can provide certain information to the third party site. The policy is detailed below:

> In order to provide you with useful social experiences off of Facebook, we occasionally need to provide General Information about you to pre-approved third party websites and applications that use Platform at the time you visit them (if you are still logged in to Facebook). Similarly, when one of your friends visits a pre-approved website or application, it will receive General Information about you so you and your friend can be connected on that website as well (if you also have an account with that website).[6]

One must keep in mind that logging out is not the same as simply exiting out of the window. In order to successfully log out of Facebook, a user must select the option from a dropdown menu provided in the top right hand corner.

Advertisers on Facebook

Advertising is a key part of Facebook's strategy and it is the most obvious way for the social networking site to monetize the seemingly endless amount of potential consumer data that users make available on their Facebook pages. From Facebook's perspective, allowing advertisers to collect data from users based on which ads they click on has a number of benefits. According to Facebook's overview of its ad program, advertisers can "choose their audience by age, location and interests." The overview goes on to say, "people treat Facebook as an authentic part of their lives, so you can be sure you are connecting with real people with real interest in your products."[7] From the perspective of a consumer—a Facebook user—you only see ads for products or services that are likely to interest you, at least according to the advertiser paying for the placement of the ad.

Facebook has gone to great lengths to try to make its over 800 million users feel confident that information that would identify a specific user, rather than a broadly targeted age or interest group, is never transmitted to advertisers. Yet, there have been numerous reports of leaked user identification (UID) numbers. In late 2010, it was reported that certain Facebook applications were sending unique Facebook ID numbers of users to roughly 25 different advertising firms.[8] The company quickly responded by assuring Facebook's users that it will add safeguards to stop the breach and promised to terminate advertisers that were violating the company's policies in this regard.

Mark Zuckerberg tried to alleviate concerns over privacy issues by saying, "we don't give any information to advertisers. They come to us and we target the ads."[9] However, skeptics remain and the debate over privacy has split into a few different camps. Some argue that Facebook is indeed collecting massive amounts of personal information in order to better target ads and, therefore, charge advertisers more money. Others believe that Facebook may be well intentioned in its claims that it would never release or sell private information, but that the company simply cannot avoid data leaks—whether they are accidental or caused by outside hackers with motivations of identity theft or even blackmail.

Aside from the threat of cyber thieves, advertisers and data collection companies can use Facebook's by-the-book ad targeting methods to discern very private information like sexual orientation from users. A study detailed by the *New York Times* in 2010 showed that advertisers could create extremely narrow targeting criteria for an ad aimed at someone who indicated that they were "interested in" the same sex.[10] Then, if the ad was shown to a given account in the narrow target range of, say 10–20 people, the advertiser would know that person was gay, because no other users shared the specific attributes requested in the targeting process.

Facebook changed its targeting system so that advertisers could not create target criteria that narrowed the targeted users to fewer than 20 people. However, those conducting the study argue that an advertiser could create 20 fake profiles with the same desired attributes and the then target to the group of 21—one of the profiles being the real user and the other 20 being fake—in order to identify the specific user.

Issues like this continue to be brought up and Facebook clearly faces a cat-and-mouse game to try to stay ahead of these concerns, or at least respond as quickly as possible. Yet, it is hard to imagine that privacy leaks or gaps in Facebook's policies will become less of an issue as the social networking site continues to add upwards of 700,000 users every day and each of these users is constantly posting information and indicating their unique preferences—information which is stored for an indefinite period of time on Facebook's servers.

Of course, the other side of the Facebook privacy argument is that users *choose* to place information on the site. Facebook certainly does not force anyone to share your sexual orientation, religious preference or birthday. Yet, in today's society users seem compelled to do so.

Some Facebook users do not even use the available safeguards for their data. As of 2009, a study concluded that 58 percent of users restrict their social network profiles in some way.[11] However, that figure is up sharply from 2007 when only 20 percent applied similar restrictions to their information. Perhaps Facebook is doing a better job educating its users about the site's privacy settings or, more likely, users are being swayed by the frenzy of media attention over privacy issues.

In addition to media attention, Facebook has been receiving increasing attention from lawmakers and regulators over privacy concerns. The Federal Trade Commission has launched an investigation into the company's privacy policies and several lawmakers, including Senator John McCain, have moved to introduce legislation that would establish a consumer bill of rights.[12] Thus far, Facebook has had a rather weak presence in Washington. Yet, with mounting attention from lawmakers the company has recently increased the number of lobbyists it employs in its D.C. office. However, the company has a long way to go to catch up with its peers. Facebook spent less than 7 percent of the amount Google did last year on lobbying and only 5 percent of what Microsoft spent.[13] Certainly the interaction between Facebook and policy makers, not only in the US but around the world, will become increasingly important as the company seeks answers over user privacy.

What is clear is that there does not seem to be a definitive solution to the balance between user privacy, advertiser targeting and the basic premise of social networking: to share information and be connected with other people through the internet. Since these two ideas— privacy and social networking—appear to be in conflict, it will be up to users to determine how much of each they are willing to sacrifice in the end.

Questions

1. Where do you draw the line between general information (age, gender, etc.) that can be shared and personal information that should never be given to an advertiser?
2. How much responsibility falls on Facebook users? Advertisers? Facebook itself?
    Do you know of examples of how Facebook's ever-changing privacy policy has affected you or your friends, like it did for Daniel and Jane in the story at the beginning of the case?
3. In what way do you think Facebook's growth around the world both helped and hurt its ability to protect its users? What are the costs and benefits?
4. Is Facebook, a company whose mission is to make the world more open, in conflict with its own identity when it tries to restrict access to user information?
5. Despite criticism and even news of user information leaks, Facebook continues to grow exponentially. As a result, have Facebook users become too "hooked" to forgo social networking even if their privacy is sacrificed? How dependent are we on Facebook?

19 Auchan (France)[1]

Geert Demuijnck

Auchan and its roots

Auchan was created in 1961 as a single supermarket in Roubaix, France. Now, the retailer operates supermarkets and shopping malls in 12 countries with a business turnover of €39.5 billion (2008). It employs 209,000 people, 116,000 of whom are shareholders (in eight countries). Employees currently hold 13% of the shares. The other shares are still owned by the (now hundreds of) members of the founding Mulliez family.[2] Auchan is now the second largest retailer in France with €39.7 billion in revenue before tax in 2009 (source: Auchan website Auchan.com, accessed January 10, 2011). The largest, Carrefour, is twice as big, holding a 23% market share.[3]

Auchan had a strong reputation for social responsibility from the start, and, moreover, developed a management style which strongly motivates employees by offering them significant responsibilities. By also giving them the opportunity to become shareholders and to take advantage of the growth of the company, the Mulliez family showed their commitment to Catholic Social Teaching. In a nutshell, there are several key ideas of this teaching which are relevant in this context: making profit is imperative for the survival of a firm, and therefore a legitimate aim, but it has to be done properly. Private property is morally correct if this property's ultimate aim is the "common good." That is, roughly translated, if it is used in a socially responsible way. Since employees are considered to be persons, the principle of a morally defensible society based on private property also applies to these employees; therefore, they are able to become owners as well.[4] In general, business should be run honestly with a deep respect for clients and employees.

The process of ethical reflection in the company had strong underpinnings. The Catholic background of the Mulliez family, the founding shareholders of Auchan, goes back to their parents and grandparents. They are direct descendants of and related to the families who owned the once quite important textile industry in the Lille area. These families were deeply influenced by the more "progressive"—at least in social matters—Catholic movement inspired by the *Rerum Novarum* encyclical published in 1891. As a consequence, the set of Christian values and Catholic Social Teaching formed the normative background of the "culture" of the company.

Therefore, Catholic Social Teaching, and Catholic values in general, both progressive and conservative, were still a strong influence in the first decade of Auchan's development. A striking example of the more progressive sense is the employee share ownership that was developed in the early seventies in Auchan. The leaders of Auchan introduced employee shareholding at a time when it was quite revolutionary for two reasons. First, the company was starting to make substantial profits, but, at the same time, it was quite demanding with respect to its employees. The leaders, who were also the shareholders, judged it as unfair not to share these results with their collaborators. Second, rather than increasing wages, they opted, under the direct influence of *Mater et Magister* (1961), for sharing stock with the employees. For more than 30 years the system has functioned very well and was referred to as an example to be followed during the political debates that preceded the 2001 law which stimulates employee savings and investment in stock.[5]

Business ethics in Auchan

During the 1970s and 1980s, the company grew rapidly. Preserving the "values" became one of the worries of the shareholder family, albeit in a more secular and open-minded way. The need for a broader ethical framework became obvious in a growing company with more and more employees from different backgrounds of the quickly evolving French society. As a result of these changes, a project to implement business ethics in the firm was initiated in 1992. Initially, there were two steps: the first consisted in creating a code of ethics and the second step involved establishing an "ethics committee" which would supervise compliance with the code.

The 11 committee members are: the CEO of Auchan, one store manager, the head of the legal department, a person from the supply branch, the head of external communication, two shareholder family members, the executive in charge of sustainable development, the secretary general (who represents the president) and two external members. The author is one of the external members of the committee. In addition to the permanent committee members, two or three other people are usually invited, in order to consult on a particular topic that is to be discussed.

Levels of responsibility

Over the years, several recurrent scenarios have surfaced in the discussions within the Ethics Committee that can be ranked according to the different level of "space of freedom" the company has with respect to the issue at stake.

The first scenario is one in which an ethical issue can be dealt with, creatively, in a way which benefits (almost) all stakeholders, certainly in the long run, sometimes in the short run. These cases are totally unproblematic, but sometimes interesting. An example is the decision to print the content of small cardboard boxes in Braille. As a result, blind people no longer confuse salt and sugar. Auchan won several prizes for this initiative which was, after all, beneficial for the company.

In a second scenario, an ethical issue can be dealt with, but there is some cost— and it is totally unclear whether or not this cost will be compensated for, even in the very long run. Nevertheless, the firm decides to accept the ethical constraint and to face the loss it causes. There are some examples of such decisions. Some years ago, the committee debated the sale of violent video games.[6] Some extremely violent games (with racist allusions) had been submitted to the ethics committee, and it was recommended that they should not be sold. The market share of Auchan for videogames is known. However, the total number of these games on the French market (sold in 2003–4 by competitors like Leclerc and the specialized Micromania) was made public and the shortfall could be calculated. However, Auchan followed the recommendation of the ethics committee and did not reverse its decision.

Third, the company faces a huge social problem, for which it is not (causally) responsible. However, the company is aware of its potential role as a "big player" in the social field and decides to act in a responsible way, although the outcome in financial terms is unclear. An example here is the signing of a "code of diversity" by several big companies in France (Auchan among them) which committed them to be extremely cautious about forms of implicit discrimination.

In a fourth scenario, the cost is too high for the company, but there is something that needs to be done, and more can be done indirectly, by lobbying. An example concerns the unacceptable working condition in suppliers' firms in Asia. When some competitors buy from suppliers with unacceptable working conditions, there is inevitably a loss of competitiveness for the company which refrains from such practices. The answer here lies in close cooperation among competitors. Auchan collaborates with other major retailers in the field (a collective database of social audits was established in the French Federation of Trade and Distribution), as well as at the European level, since no company has enough power to impose its rules in this context. Nevertheless, Auchan developed a commercial code with ethical requirements (and sanctions) in this area. Auchan has also increased the number of supplier audits, and the firms who produce the products which are sold under Auchan's own brand name are systematically audited.

Fifth scenario: the company observes market trends that are regrettable, but that even the leaders of retailing cannot combat them without committing commercial suicide. Thus, a few years ago, Auchan refused to sell mixed drinks or energy drinks, that is, *alcoholic* drinks which are ambiguous because they are presented as soft drinks. However, the trend for cocktails consisting of fruit juice and alcohol has only grown. So, Auchan has decided to sell them, but a number of precautions have been taken, such as clearly isolated shelves so that no confusion is possible. It seems that the retailer could not escape this trend, which is much stronger than before.

The sixth scenario consists of a radical contradiction between the mission of a retailer, even as ethically conceived as possible, and the ethical challenge at stake. An example of this limit was a recent discussion focused on what to do with respect to overindebted customers (the discussion was related to the use of the shop-specific credit card). The discussion was frank but behind this issue another almost subversive question is lurking: "Why should we push economically fragile people to buy consumption goods?" This question is totally contrary to the purpose of the company. Here, there is a fundamental limit of the realm of ethical questions with which the ethics committee can deal. Such questions have to be resolved at a more general, social and political level. A retailer cannot be blamed for its commercial ambition, no more so than the owner of a gas station can be blamed for global warming.

Vignettes in marketing ethics

Marketing vignettes

1. A store brand ecological label

An example of an issue related to marketing that was discussed during a recent meeting of the ethics committee pertained to ecologically labeled store brand products. In general, Auchan is extremely careful with store brand products, for obvious reasons. If there is a problem with any item sold in your stores, that is not good for your reputation. If, however, the product is sold under the brand of the store, reputation damage is much worse.

Therefore, like all retailers, Auchan tries to realize a good quality/price ratio for store brand products. But the concern goes further than this. If Auchan takes care in general that, for example, Southeast Asian suppliers are audited on working conditions, priority of these audits is given to suppliers that produce store brand products.

Within the set of store brand products, Auchan has a special category of products which is labeled "mieux vivre," that could be translated as "a better life," which addresses the activist consumers, or at least consumers with an above average awareness of social and environmental issues. This general label is used in three varieties; an ecological one (Mieux vivre. Environnement), an organic one (Mieux vivre. Bio), and a range of fair trade products (Mieux vivre. Equitable).

In 2010 the marketing managers for the ecological Mieux vivre products raised the following problem with the ethics committee. Many of these ecologically labeled products turned out not to be 100% ecological, despite the very serious lists of criteria that are systematically taken into consideration on four levels: the product itself (non-renewable resources, the production process, the lifecycle of the product, energy consumption,...), the packaging (not biodegradable), the site of the production (social conditions), and transportation (airplane, train, truck, distance). There are several examples of products that troubled the buyers. The first one concerns shrimp raised in Madagascar, in ecologically and socially excellent conditions. However, a problem arises with packaging: there is no protective cap available that is at the same time satisfactory in terms of sanitary transportation conditions and satisfactory in terms of sustainability. Moreover, there is the very long transportation distance.

A second example concerns anti-insect spray for plants. The product is probably among the best, from an ecological viewpoint, on the market, but there is nevertheless an "N" sign (pictogram) on the package, the European sign for poisonous or harmful products, because of the presence of pyrethrin and copper sulfate. The marketing people mention that competitors, even well-known and famously "green" brands have the same substances in their products.

The marketing staff have done some benchmarking and observed that Auchan products are, from an environmental perspective, in general closer to the "best" competitors than to the average standards of other as "ecological" labeled products (they compared only with ecologically labeled products).

The marketing department has the impression that they are cheating the client. They ask if it would be possible to give precise guidelines or should Auchan stop carrying some of these products?

2. Indonesian paper

During the summer of 2010 Greenpeace militants organized a protest action in a Taiwanese store from the Auchan Group (local brandname: RT Mart Taiwan). Greenpeace France has written to the Auchan management in France and an appointment is planned. The reason for this controversy is that RT Mart sells paper made by pulp produced by Asia Pulp & Paper (APP), a subsidiary of Sinar Mas, a major Indonesian Company. A Greenpeace report has explained that APP is really catastrophic from an ecological viewpoint. APP is at the origin of massive deforestation, without replanting the forest. Even worse, if they replant, they plant palm trees for oil. And palm oil is as such problematic.[7] The Auchan buyer based in Indonesia explains that APP has all kinds of ecological certificates, but, since corruption is so widespread, he nevertheless admits that the Greenpeace people are basically right.

Auchan is accused together with other multinational retailers like Walmart, Tesco, and Carrefour. Carrefour and Tesco have announced that they committed themselves to stop all supply from APP.

In fact, Auchan has APP as a supplier for its Asian market. Few paper products of Indonesian APP origin are sold in France. On the Asian market, competition in terms of price is rather intense and other suppliers are more expensive than APP.

On the French market, Auchan sells cheap notebooks made on the basis of APP pulp. Every year there is a sharp competition between French retailers to present the cheapest schoolbag (list of mandatory school materials fixed by the French Ministry of Education). Mostly, Auchan as a family-friendly company is together with another major French competitor, the cheapest brand. Greenpeace has not publicly attacked this competitor, since they are a local player.

What should the ethics committee recommend?

3. Fair trade

Ten to 15 years ago, fair trade products were mostly sold in the old centers of big European cities, almost confidentially, to militant alternative consumers, in small shops where a banker in a suit with a tie would not dare to enter. Things changed radically when the big retailers entered into this market. Fair trade coffee, the most important commodity in fair trade, was until then about twice as expensive as "non-fair trade" equivalent coffee. While respecting the constraints of the same independent fair-trade labels (Fair-trade, Max Havelaar), and, as a consequence, the same guarantees for small coffee growers in developing countries, big retailers offered, on the basis of much better performing logistics, coffee that was equivalent in terms of quality that was barely 15–20% more expensive than "non-fair trade" coffee. The volume of fair trade coffee consumption exploded during the last decade. Max Havelaar's (the most important label) website indicates that, in France, in 2001 fair trade products were sold for an amount of €12 million, in 2009 the amount was €287 million (source: www.maxhavelaarfrance.org/En-chiffres).[8]

The ethical issue for Auchan and other retailers is: if consumers make a particular effort to pay a bit more for reasons of solidarity with relatively poor coffee growers, should retailers also make a special effort and apply smaller gross margins on these fair trade products? It should be mentioned that the higher volume of sold fair trade coffee is basically at the expense of the store brand "non-fair trade" coffee, on which profit margins are particularly high.

Should Auchan make an effort to promote more strongly fair trade coffee?

4. Toy guns

During one of the most recent sessions, the buyers who were preparing for the Christmas period, that is, the commercial peak season for toys, were troubled by the rather violent aspect of some toy guns. The question was about the limits of the toy weapons that can be sold in a responsible retailer. On two large tables dozens of weapons were spread out. The buyers explained that there was no doubt that the guns and pistols were toys since they all had a red piece of plastic at the very end of the barrel. We learned that this was in fact a US requirement but that all producers systematically applied it everywhere. "However, look," they said, and they demonstrated how easily you could take the plastic ring away. Some of the toy guns were made of metal, quite heavy, and looked very realistic. With some of them you could actually shoot plastic bullets. Others made much noise. Besides guns there were handcuffs, swords, knives, etc. Most of what was shown was not currently available in the Auchan shops. There were also "softer" products like water pistols.

A committee first asked themselves why on earth parents would give these things to their children. But then most people remembered their own children or, especially the males, their own childhood, and recalled how they played policeman catching bandits, fighting cowboys or soldiers, etc.

How would you advise the ethics committee about selling the guns?

Questions

1. How would you describe the corporate culture at Auchan? What are its ethical underpinnings?
2. What ethical theory or theories did Auchan apply in reacting to the five scenarios discussed in the Levels of Responsibility section?
3. How would you answer each of the questions posed in the four marketing vignettes above?

20 A young pharmacist's dilemma[1]

Barbora Kocanova
and Veronika Vosykova

It is a late Sunday afternoon. Anna, a 23-year-old pharmacist, sits at home thinking about her job. It has been three months since she started to work for the Sun Pharmacy and tomorrow is going to be the last day of her probation period. Tomorrow she has to decide whether she stays or quits. She has to admit she liked the job very much; it was everything she was imagining it to be during her studies. If only there wasn't the ethical dilemma she's had ever since she started working at the pharmacy. And tomorrow is the day when she has to decide between the job she likes so much and her own conscience.

The Sun Pharmacy

The Sun Pharmacy was one of the first private pharmacies to open in Bratislava after the fall of communism in former Czechoslovakia. The owner, Mr. Peter Kovac, soon realized the potential of the business and started to open new pharmacies across town and later even in other parts of the country. Sun Pharmacies s.r.o. (Ltd.) was formed in 1999 with Mr. Kovac and his wife as sole proprietors. In 2005, the company sold all of its pharmacies positioned outside of the capital city due to increasing managerial demand and currently owns the remaining six.

The Sun Pharmacies were the first pharmacies to be awarded the certificate of quality ISO 9001:2001. Each of the Sun Pharmacies passed all inspection by the Health Care Surveillance Bureau which is the control authority of the Ministry of Health in Slovakia. One of the branches received the Pharmacy of the Year Award in 2005 and another one in 2006. All of the Sun Pharmacies are very popular among the people in Bratislava. Customers value the service they receive. The employees seem to be always very willing to suggest the right medication for each health problem. Furthermore, even when the customer asks for a specific product, they often suggest he buy a different one that might suit him or her better. When a product is required that is not in stock, it is quickly found at one of the other five pharmacies and ready for pick-up in less than 24 hours. Immobile and regular customers have the possibility of getting their medication delivered to their home. As a special service to the customers, one of the six pharmacies is always open 24 hours to provide medication to those in urgent need.

The working environment is very pleasant, there is no pressure or competition among coworkers, and everyone is happy to help if the others need it. Mr. Kovac is highly valued among his employees. He pays a fair salary and is very generous when it comes to bonuses and company benefits. Employees' obligations outside of work, such as the care of small children, are always taken into account when scheduling shifts. Double salary is paid when working between 10pm and 7am, which is more than the law prescribes. Mr. Kovac is on first name terms with all employees, always seems to be concerned about their private lives and occasional problems, and frequently has a joke ready to tell. He is known as a person of integrity and good character even outside of his work place.

All together Sun Pharmacies s.r.o. employs over 60 people. There are six people working at the Sun Pharmacy—Old Town, the pharmacy where Anna is employed. Five of the employees (including Anna) are female; three of them have been working for Sun Pharmacies over 10 years. The sixth, a male employee named Juraj, has only started to work at the pharmacy six months ago and it's his first job after graduating from the university, just like Anna.

Anna at the Sun Pharmacy

Anna was very happy to get the job at Sun Pharmacy. She had been looking for a job for some time. After graduation she had taken some time off to travel across North America and was then in desperate need to earn some money and start working on her career. The offer to work at one of the Sun Pharmacies came at the right time. She was already thinking about giving up and taking a job as a sales person to at least be able to cover her bills when her father called her to tell her his old friend, Mr. Kovac, was looking to hire a pharmacist and would like to know if Anna was looking for a new job. She got hired after the first interview.

The first week at her new job, Anna felt like it was a dream come true. The pay was excellent, more than she would earn anywhere else as an inexperienced newcomer. The pharmacy was located in the old town, only a 10-minute walk away from Anna's new apartment. She knew she would get along with her co-workers very well the first day she met them. In addition, she soon found out that Juraj and she had taken some classes together back at the university and shared a lot of friends. At the beginning, she knew she made some mistakes, as this was her first real experience, yet the others were always very helpful and were never annoyed when they had to do some work that Anna hadn't mastered yet. Everything seemed too good to be true.

After a few days, Anna noticed that when customers asked for medication for certain problems they were always served certain brands. Even when they asked directly for a certain product, her co-workers would politely and indirectly suggest a different one, the same they would have sold to the customer had she or he not asked for any specific brand. She quickly realized the products usually offered to the customers were also strongly advertised in the pharmacy. There were a number of posters on the walls, the water dispenser was visibly branded, and even the cash tray was promoting a certain brand. A short time after she came to this realization, Mr. Kovac asked her to have coffee with him after work to talk a bit more about her new job. Anna was happy to go as she liked Mr. Kovac as an employer as well as a family friend and wanted to ask him about the things she noticed if she had the opportunity. Mr. Kovac's answer was nothing like she expected. After she initiated the subject, he told her in a very familiar yet patronizing way what was expected from her. He said that certain products were to be offered to the customers first. And even if the customer walked into the pharmacy already knowing which exact brand he wanted to buy, Anna should advise him to buy one of those that are "preferred." Mr. Kovac said he'd give her the list of preferred brands the next day. When he saw Anna's astonishment, he smiled kindly and assured her that was the way business was done at all pharmacies.

The next morning at work, Anna confided in Juraj, with whom she felt the closest. He confirmed what Mr. Kovac said before and added that there was nothing to it and that all other pharmacies would do the same. He explained to Anna that pharmaceutical companies try to support sales by providing certain benefits to pharmacies that "push" their products. He said that Mr. Kovac and his wife would twice a year go on a luxurious vacation paid for by the pharmaceuticals and covered up as a conference. Furthermore, the pharmacy would receive more products than they paid for. For example, there would be 130 packages of a painkiller in a delivery instead of the 100 that are on the invoice. The revenue from the sales of the remaining 30 packages would go entirely to the pharmacy. That was the way things were done everywhere else, he added. Yet Anna wondered how he knew. He's only been working in the industry for six months and this was his first job.

At first Anna decided to go along and see how things would evolve. It was easy for some time, because the preferred brands were among the highest quality products and in most cases it really didn't matter which brand the consumer would use. However, some of the products were more expensive than others. Every time she suggested a more expensive product to a customer she hoped that he would ask if there was a cheaper alternative. Then, by law, she would have to offer him the cheaper alternatives they had in stock. She felt especially uncomfortable when she saw that the customer was an elderly person or someone who clearly had no money to waste. Luckily she was able to ask one of her colleagues to switch at the counter when she saw such a person standing in the line, using the excuse that she wasn't sure about some prescription.

Only about a week before her probation period was over, a man came into the pharmacy. He stood at a different counter, but as he was the only customer there and Anna's colleague was in the back dealing with a supplier on the phone, she kindly asked him to come to her counter. The man was very polite, asked her how she was, smiled and then asked for a specific drug. Anna knew straight away that the drug was strictly to be sold on prescription only and told him accordingly. Yet the man just smiled, said he was a friend of Mr. Kovac, that he talked to him before and that Mr. Kovac was supposed to call the pharmacy and let them know he was coming to pick up the drug. Anna was just about to object when her colleague pushed her away and told the customer she had spoken to Mr. Kovac and that the drug was ready for him. Anna couldn't believe her ears. Back at the university her lecturers were very strict about teaching their students that they were under no circumstances allowed to sell prescription drugs without a prescription. Furthermore, she knew that such action was against the law and, should she get caught, she alone would be held responsible. After the man had left, she asked her colleague what was going on. Her colleague said that was common practice in the pharmacy. If a friend asked Mr. Kovac for a minor favor such as selling him a drug without having to go to the doctor to have it prescribed, he couldn't turn it down, of course. She also added that the man surely knew what drug to take and that his prescription probably just ran out or something. When she saw Anna's astonishment she said: "Don't worry darling, no one ever finds out. They pay the whole price. It's not like we charge it on the insurance company so they don't have a reason to come knocking on our door. And it doesn't happen more than once or twice a month so you're unlikely to be the one to serve them anyway."

The dilemma

Anna was sitting in her small apartment thinking about her new job and trying to decide what to do. She had to admit she liked the job very much. It was probably the best she could get with her experience. And the pay was great; she could afford her own place and could still save some money for the future. She realized that, unlike many other people, she liked going to work every morning. At least until her conscience came knocking. The things she was told to do were against her values. She could appease herself by believing she hasn't done anything wrong yet, but she knew that should she continue to work at the pharmacy, she would eventually be put in a compromising situation. She had to admit she was confused. Everyone believed Mr. Kovac to be a great man of high character and morals, even her father did. Yet he was asking people to do things that were clearly not right. Or were they? Anna remembered Juraj telling her that was the way things were done in all other pharmacies too. Anna wondered if that was really so or if Juraj just said that to calm her down. All the other employees seemed to be perfectly okay with what was happening.

Questions

1. What should Anna do?
2. Would she stand a chance if she tried to explain her position to them?
3. She knew she would do a lot to keep the job but where were her boundaries?

21 TOMS

One for One movement[1]

Alicja Spaulding, Stephanie Fernandez,
and Jennifer Sawayda

TOMS Shoes is a for-profit business with a philanthropic component. Its mission statement is simple: "To make life more comfortable." It seeks to do this by selling a fun product while helping those in need.[2] TOMS Shoes was started in 2006 after entrepreneur Blake Mycoskie witnessed the poverty among villagers in Argentina, poverty so extreme that the villagers could not even afford a pair of shoes. The 29-year-old Mycoskie returned to the US with 200 Argentinean shoes and a mission. He went from one retail store to another with a unique business proposal. He would start an organization that would provide a pair of shoes for a child in need for every pair of shoes purchased. Finally, a few Los Angeles boutiques agreed to sell the shoes. Mycoskie's idea was picked up by the *Los Angeles Times*, which ran an article on his business idea. To his surprise, that weekend garnered him $88,000 in orders. Two years after officially establishing TOMS Shoes, the business had $9.6 million in revenue.[3]

The TOMS business model is unusual. While many businesses engage in cause-related marketing, at TOMS the philanthropic component is just as important as the for-profit business. The cost of providing the shoes to children in need is built into the shoes' sales price. The customer is thereby turned into the benefactor, enabling TOMS to become a sustainable organization based on giving back to the world on a continuous basis. As long as people continue to purchase TOMS shoes, children in need will receive a pair in return. In the process, TOMS is also able to turn a profit, support itself, make the world a better place, and educate consumers on how they are helping children in need by providing them with a pair of shoes.

This case discusses Mycoskie's revolutionary business model and how it has achieved such success. It begins by analyzing the background and origins of the TOMS Shoes business concept. We then discuss TOMS' operational approach, including how the organization manages to carry out its central mission. We also examine the corporate culture—a necessity for the successful operation of TOMS shoes—and the marketing of TOMS. Next, we analyze how this business model has impacted both society and other organizations. Since no business is immune from ethical issues, the following section details some of the criticisms and risks of TOMS Shoes. We conclude by speculating about the future of this company.

Background history

Blake Mycoskie is the founder and Chief Shoe Giver of TOMS Shoes. Before founding TOMS Shoes, Mycoskie had started five companies that ranged from billboard advertising to laundry services.[4] His foray into the shoe industry, however, was almost accidental.

After participating in the 2002 Amazing Race reality television show, Mycoskie made a decision to return to all the countries he had visited during the show. One country on his stop was Argentina. Mycoskie traveled to Argentina in 2006 with no idea that the backwoods of Argentina would be his inspiration for a new company. Two incidents inspired Mycoskie to create TOMS. First, he noticed that many of the villagers could not even afford a pair of shoes for their children. Second, he discovered the alpargata, a type of shoe that local farmers wore. The alpargata is a flat slip-on shoe made from either canvas or fabric material. These two discoveries convinced Mycoskie to take action.[5]

Upon coming back home, Mycoskie sold his online driver education company for $500,000 and used that money to finance TOMS Shoes. TOMS was derived from "tomorrow," which was taken from the original company concept "shoes for tomorrow project." TOMS Shoes opened for business in May 2006.[6] TOMS also runs the non-profit subsidiary, Friends of TOMS. The for-profit and non-profit organizations work in conjunction in operating the enterprise. Since its founding, TOMS has been widely successful among regular individuals and celebrities. Scarlett Johansson and Keira Knightley were among the first to become celebrity fans of TOMS products.[7] The non-profit component is also achieving its objective of providing shoes for those in need. In 2010 TOMS Shoes distributed its one-millionth pair of shoes.[8]

The importance of shoes

TOMS decided to develop its product line and business model around shoes for several key reasons. First, many children in impoverished countries live in areas with unsafe terrains. Lack of paved roads and other hazards can cause injury for children walking barefoot. The second reason involves health concerns. Children can contract a range of soil-transmitted diseases from not wearing shoes.[9]

For example, soil-transmitted Helminthiasis, an infection developed from intestinal worms, is common in South Africa. The disease Podoconiasis is also an infection transmitted through the soil and occurs in places like southern Ethiopia. This illness causes the lymphatic system to break down and the feet to become swollen. A second unfortunate consequence of this disease is ostracism and ridicule imposed upon infected children in their communities. Many of these diseases can be prevented simply by wearing shoes.[10]

The third reason involves education. In many nations, shoes are required in order to attend school. Owning a pair of shoes provides a child with an opportunity to be educated, leading to higher school attendance. According to TOMS, this combination of education and health provides children the opportunity for a better tomorrow.[11]

TOMS movement: management and business model

Mycoskie's organization consists of two parts. TOMS Shoes is a for-profit company that manages the overall operations and logistics. Friends of TOMS, the company's non-profit subsidiary, is responsible for organizing volunteer activities and all shoe drops. Friends of TOMS is not a corporate-backed foundation that the company supports through donations; rather, it is a necessary part of TOMS' distinct business model, One for One™. The model is simple: for every pair of shoes that TOMS sells, it donates a pair of shoes to a child in need on behalf of the customer. Mycoskie dubs this business system "Philanthropic Capitalism" because the company makes a profit but incorporates philanthropy into its business strategy. The company's ultimate vision is to demonstrate the effect of how working together as a society can "create a better tomorrow by taking compassionate action today."[12]

The key for any organization, even non-profits, is to be sustainable. Non-profits that depend largely on donations struggle to remain in operation during economic downturns. By incorporating the non-profit component into the business model, TOMS mitigates this risk. The One to One model enables Friends of TOMS to remain in operation because the shoes sold cover the cost of the extra shoes and shoe drops. When developing the company, Mycoskie recognized that simply donating money to children would be a one-time deal. However, he felt that creating a sustainable business would create continual opportunities to provide shoes for those in need as long as the company remains in business. As long as people keep purchasing shoes, the non-profit will remain sustainable.[13]

It might appear that the non-profit subsidiary Friends of TOMS depends entirely on the for-profit business. In reality, however, the relationship between the two operations is interdependent. The philanthropic component of TOMS likely contributes to its widespread popularity among consumers. One consumer survey revealed that nearly half of respondents had purchased or would purchase items during a certain time period if part of the revenues supported charitable causes.[14] Cause-related marketing is growing, and businesses like TOMS Shoes—where philanthropy is embedded within the business model—are likely to attract the support of consumers who want to make a difference.

Already, TOMS has developed successful collaborations with recognizable brands such as Ralph Lauren and Element Skateboard. Ralph Lauren worked with TOMS to develop a co-branded Polo Rugby shoe, which maintained the One for One premise.[15] Element Skateboard joined forces with TOMS as well to fashion limited edition TOMS + Element shoes, donating a pair of shoes to a child in need for each pair sold. To further the One for One movement, Element Skateboard also promised that for every skateboard purchased, one would be donated to a child participating in the Indigo Skate Camp in Durban, South Africa.[16]

Finally, the TOMS Shoes business model does not support any form of traditional paid marketing or advertising. TOMS does not have a marketing budget. Instead, the company relies on word of mouth, viral marketing, and social networks for its marketing efforts.[17] Word-of-mouth is one of the most effective forms of marketing because many consumers believe it to be more trustworthy than corporate advertisements. The challenge for organizations is how to convince customers to talk about its products. For TOMS Shoes, many customers are excited that their purchase is going toward a good cause and are eager to discuss it with others. TOMS Shoes has taken proactive steps to encourage word-of-mouth communication. Each pair of TOMS Shoes comes with a blue-and-white TOMS' flag and a small card asking customers to take pictures of themselves wearing their new shoes and holding up the flag. The customers are then asked to upload those photos to the "HOW WE WEAR THEM" section on the company's website, in addition to other social networking websites such as Facebook and Twitter.[18] The photos of customers using TOMS products increases both awareness and the credibility of the brand. Consult the TOMS website at www.toms.com/ for pictures of the shoes.

TOMS' supply chain: getting the shoes where they need to be

Due to their lack of knowledge about the shoe industry, Mycoskie and his team initially faced supply chain management problems. Mycoskie was unaware how fast demand for TOMS shoes would escalate. Two weeks after Mycoskie began selling his products to retailers, a fashion reporter wrote an article about Mycoskie's business and mission in the *Los Angeles Times*. The TOMS website sold 2,200 pairs of shoes that same day—but Mycoskie had only 40 pairs available. The situation required him to hire interns to personally call customers and ask them to wait eight weeks for delivery. Mycoskie then flew back to Argentina where he had 40,000 shoes manufactured. All pairs in the batch were sold within the next few weeks.[19]

Since then TOMS has improved at managing its supply chain. It has opened up additional manufacturing factories in China, Argentina, and Ethiopia, and has plans for another location in Brazil.[20] These factories are audited by third parties to ensure that workers are being treated fairly. TOMS has its factory workers sign a code of conduct stating that they will follow all the stipulations. TOMS' productions staff visits each of the factories on a regular basis to verify that the factories are continuing to adhere to the code of conduct and other working standards. TOMS manufacturing standards are modeled after International Labor Organization compliance standards.[21]

Over 500 retailers around the world now carry TOMS shoe collections. In its first of couple of years in business, TOMS was able to secure distribution of its shoes with Nordstrom's, Bloomingdale's, Neiman Marcus, Whole Foods, and Urban Outfitters.[22] Now TOMS has also expanded to retailers that are independently owned small businesses. TOMS continuously seeks retailers that are passionate about TOMS' mission. Retailers are able to purchase their bulk of shoes at cost from TOMS and thus are able to turn a profit as well as support the One for One movement. All shoes that the retailers purchase are directly shipped to the retailers—TOMS does not operate on a consignment basis. TOMS shoes are sold in retail stores in the United States, the United Kingdom, Australia, Canada, Germany, and France. Consumers can also purchase TOMS' shoes on its website, www.toms.com.

Manufacturing the shoes and selling them to customers is only the first step of the process. Next, TOMS must distribute shoes to the children that need them. TOMS collaborates with nonprofits to identify children in need. These giving partners must be actively involved with the children in their communities and objectively evaluate where TOMS shoes can have the biggest impact on children's lives. The organizations TOMS chooses are ones in humanitarian, health, and education fields. For instance, TOMS has joined forces with Partners in Health to distribute shoes to children in Haiti and the health organization SANA Guatemala to distribute shoes to Guatemalan children.[23] In Argentina, TOMS works with an organization that provides Podoconiasis treatment programs, assisting children who are at a high risk of developing the disease. In Rwanda, TOMS is currently partnered with a nonprofit business to help with over 100,000 genocide orphans. TOMS also works with a Zimbabwean organization to provide shoes to children who make long walks to school in different weather conditions.

In order to become a giving partner, organizations must go through audits to ensure that they meet TOMS' specific criteria. These five criteria are detailed in Box 21.1. Through TOMS' giving partnerships, locations are identified to show where providing a pair of shoes to children in need contributes the most toward improving the standard of living for the community. When a customer purchases a pair of TOMS' shoes, a child in the chosen community will receive a pair of shoes approximately four to six months from the initial date of purchase. Currently, TOMS distributes shoes to children in need in 24 countries.[24]

When shoes are distributed to the communities, they are referred to as Shoe Drops. Its non-profit subsidiary Friends of TOMS helps coordinate the Shoe Drops. Every time a shoe drop occurs, TOMS seeks volunteers and individuals affiliated with TOMS to fly to the area for one week and work with their partners to distribute the shoes. Those involved in the Shoe Drop personally place the shoes on each child's feet.[25]

Even after the shoes have been delivered, TOMS continues to maintain relationships with its giving partners and the communities. TOMS constantly monitors its partners

---

Box 21.1 TOMS' criteria to become a giving partner

1. **Repeat giving**—The potential organization must have the capability to be active within the same communities on a regular basis throughout the years. This ensures that as the children grow they are continuously provided with a new pair of shoes.
2. **High impact**—The organization's mission and goals need to support health and education in a fashion that underlies the principle of giving a child an opportunity they normally would not have.
3. **Enhancing impact through partnerships**—TOMS strives to make an influential impact in communities where they donate. The potential partnering organization that TOMS strategically chooses needs to have their mission and goals founded on supporting health and education for children while giving children opportunities they normally would not have available to them. For example TOMS will partner with organizations that will not only help with Shoe Drops, but will also be involved in educating families and children on the importance of wearing shoes on a daily basis to prevent disease and infection.
4. **Considerate of local economy**—TOMS ensures that when partnering up with a local organization in a poverty-stricken country, that it does not negatively impact the local shoe-selling economy. The organizations TOMS selects need to have a thorough understanding of its community in the sense of knowing how to be socially correct in the distribution of shoes. It is an important goal of TOMS that the children who receive a pair of new shoes on a regular basis will not be harassed by others and placed in danger.
5. **Large volume shipments**—The potential partnering organization needs to be able to receive large shipments of TOMS Shoes.
6. **Health/education focused**—The potential partnering establishment needs to be comprehensively founded on health and education, so that the distribution of the new shoes not only supports TOMS' mission but runs parallel with the establishment's goals.

---

for accountability. Additionally, the organization recognizes that one pair of shoes is not going to last for the child's entire lifetime. Therefore, as the children grow out of their shoes—approximately every six months—TOMS provides replacement shoes to these same children on a regular basis. A schedule is set up with the identified community and local giving partner to maintain a regular Shoe Drop for the children. TOMS' believes that repeat giving allows it to understand the locale's needs more thoroughly.[26] TOMS also works to adapt its products to account for the region's terrain, weather, and education requirements.

TOMS' product line

TOMS' original product lines were derived from the Argentinean Alpargata shoe design worn by farmers in the region. Since its inception, TOMS has introduced different styles of shoes, including the Bota and the Cordones for both genders along with wrap boots and wedges for women. The Bota resembles an ankle boot with soft materials, while the Cordones are more of a traditional canvas style sneaker with laces. The children's line includes Velcro Alpargatas.[27]

TOMS has also created some new lines of shoes, Vegan TOMS and the wedding collection. Vegan TOMS are comprised of 70 percent recycled plastic bottles and 30 percent hemp. Hemp is an extremely sustainable product that outlasts organic cotton. TOMS is committed to creating more products that are better for the environment. Additionally, TOMS recently introduced comfortable shoes meant for weddings. Wearing comfortable slip-on shoes to a formal event may seem odd, but some young people have already worn their TOMS for prom.[28]

Aside from selling shoes, TOMS has expanded into selling apparel, including TOMS t-shirts, sweatshirts, and caps. Any of the apparel purchased also comes with the One for One movement guarantee, meaning that for every t-shirt purchased a pair of shoes will still be given to a child in need. TOMS has also started selling the TOMS flag, stickers, necklaces, and T-shirts. For each of these items, TOMS continues to use the One for One Model—it gives a pair of shoes to a child in need with every purchase. TOMS Shoes recently announced that it has expanded its one-to-one model into eyewear. TOMS will now be selling sunglasses, and for each product purchased, the company will donate glasses to someone in need who could otherwise not afford them.[29]

Not all the shoes that are available for purchase are actually donated to children. TOMS does not give the wedge or the wraparound boot to children. Primarily the shoe that the children receive is the canvas Alpargata with modifications to suit the local residents. With each new community that TOMS enters, research is conducted to learn about the environment and terrains. TOMS alters its shoes to fit the children's lives. For example, in some of the regions that experience monsoons, the shoes include more of a ridged thicker rubber sole. The shoes are typically black because that is the required shoe color to attend school in several countries. TOMS is in the process of developing a wider shoe as children living barefoot for the majority of their lives tend to have wider feet.[30]

TOMS corporate culture

Because TOMS does not engage in traditional advertising, it is important to have enthusiastic employees willing to spread the word about the organization. When the business first started, TOMS did not have a lot of money to pay individuals. The company instead focused on individuals who were passionate about its mission. Due to the lack of money, Mycoskie hired recent college graduates and even high school graduates. Despite their youth, the employees rose to their responsibilities.[31] Employees and interns not only know that their work is supporting a good cause, but many get to see the cause in action by participating in Shoe Drops.

TOMS soon realized that full-time employees were not the only ones willing to help the company achieve its mission. The company also relies upon interns and campus clubs to spread the word and support its endeavors.

Internships (summer interns and vagabonds)

TOMS dislikes the term "intern." It prefers the term Agents of Change who work to make a positive difference in the world. TOMS offers two types of internships: a traditional internship program and vagabonds. TOMS provides its traditional agents of change with a high degree of responsibility in the individual's chosen discipline, whether it's online marketing, retail marketing, operations, or something else. The number one criterion that TOMS looks for in the applicants are that the individuals truly believe and are enthusiastic about what TOMS stands for. According to TOMS, the company would not be where it is today if it were not for interns. The company started off with Blake and two interns, who managed to propel TOMS into a successful business. These initial interns have prompted TOMS to hire interns on a regular basis. TOMS offers paid internships in the Fall, Spring, and Summer.[32]

TOMS has also created a very unique and distinct type of internship opportunity known as the Vagabond internship. The Vagabonds' responsibility is brand awareness. Vagabonds are interns whose foremost responsibility is to spread the word about TOMS to colleges and high schools. They travel around the US and the world hosting screenings and parties to educate people about the company and its mission. Despite the demanding work, these internships are in high demand. In the summer of 2009, more than 1,000 individuals applied for only 15 summer internships.[33]

When an internship ends, a TOMS' intern coordinator works with the intern to strengthen his or her resume with an updated work summary of the experience gained at TOMS. The intern coordinator also provides guidance on future development career goals.[34]

Campus Clubs

TOMS Campus Clubs are groups of students at high schools and colleges who spread the message about TOMS Shoes and what it supports. These Campus Clubs are founded on the premise of helping children in need. Each semester TOMS Campus Clubs hold events to educate others about how important shoes are to children's lives. As a result of being involved in a TOMS Campus Club, students acquire practical business and leadership skills. TOMS greatly encourages Campus Clubs and will even help interested students start one at their schools. As a thank you for the students' contributions, TOMS sends out a letter of recognition highlighting the students' involvement. TOMS also features a Campus Club each month on their blog to recognize specific Campus Clubs for their dedication.[35]

Promotions

Like all businesses, TOMS must undertake promotional activities even if it does not have a marketing budget. As mentioned already, customers, employees, interns, and students engage in significant word-of-mouth advertising. However, TOMS also markets itself through events, DVD screenings, and social media.

One day without shoes

Perhaps the most popular event promoting TOMS is the One Day without Shoes campaign. This campaign was started in 2008 to raise public awareness about the impact a pair of shoes can have on a child's life. It asks the average individual to go one day without shoes. Going without shoes lets people see how it feels to be in these children's situations. The premise is to instill a sense of appreciation for what a difference a pair of shoes can make. Furthermore, the sight of a bunch of barefoot individuals walking around makes an impression on others. In both cases, TOMS' mission and its brand is spread to those that otherwise may not have known about it.

The success of this campaign was largely due to college students and Campus Clubs nationwide. In April 2011, individuals and companies in over 25 countries participated in

One Day without Shoes. Participants included Kris Ryan, Charlize Theron, the Dallas Cowboys Cheerleaders, Nordstrom, Microsoft, and AOL. This campaign continues to grow every year.[36]

Style your SOLE parties

Another event that TOMS Shoes encourages is Style Your SOLE Parties. These parties occur when individuals get together and decorate blank TOMS canvas shoes. The parties can be small or large and can range from baby showers to large community events. Everyone who participates in this event starts off with a blank canvas shoe and expresses his or her individuality by decorating the shoes. These parties not only appeal to the artistic individual, but it also introduces the brand to other party-goers who did not know about TOMS Shoes. When a party orders more than 25 pairs of shoes for this event, TOMS provides a 10 percent discount as an added incentive.[37]

TOMS DVD screenings

TOMS Shoes also developed a 35-minute documentary on how the company was founded, along with the importance of the One for One movement. The DVD is shipped free to those who are interested in organizing a screening. Screenings can be for large events in auditoriums or small imitate events in living rooms. Viewers are encouraged to discuss the documentary and come up with unique ideas to spread the word about TOMS. DVD screenings are a popular event for Campus Clubs to hold.[38]

Social media

As an alternative to traditional advertising, Mycoskie has chosen to use the inexpensive social media option. This method is less costly and creates a unity among the individuals that promote TOMS. TOMS has used viral videos, blogs, Facebook, and Twitter to spread the message about its cause.[39] Its approach has allowed TOMS to reach a vast audience worldwide. TOMS maintains its own blog to educate the public about current events in the company and its Shoe Drops. The company has also posted clips on YouTube. Additionally, many consumers create their own digital content regarding their experiences with TOMS Shoes. By encouraging events and word-of-mouth communication, TOMS is allowing consumers to do much of the marketing for the company.

TOMS impact

During its first year in business, TOMS donated 10,000 shoes to children living in Argentina.[40] Since then TOMS has expanded to distribute shoes to other regions of the world. As of September 2010, they have donated 1,000,000 pairs of new shoes worldwide.[41] TOMS now gives in 24 nations around the world including Argentina, Peru, Ethiopia, Rwanda, and South Africa.[42]

TOMS was honored in 2007 with the People's Design Award from the Cooper-Hewitt National Design Museum, Smithsonian Institution. TOMS was also awarded the 2009 ACE award given by Secretary of State Hillary Clinton. The Award for Corporate Excellence recognized TOMS for its "commitment to corporate social responsibility, innovation, exemplary practices, and democratic values worldwide."[43]

The One for One Movement is inspiring many social entrepreneurs to create their own organizations based on the model. However, Mycoskie's revolutionary idea might be difficult to replicate in other fields. First, the One for One concept must be embedded into the business strategy. The business must also be sustainable on its own; this is difficult to achieve for many non-profits that depend upon fundraising. The product and mission must be something that people will care about. Thus, for the movement to work effectively, the product should be tangible and identifiable. Product differentiation is an important component for success, as consumers appear less able to identify with commodity products.

Mycoskie offers additional advice to entrepreneurs who want to create businesses that will make a difference in the world. He advises businesses to look at their strengths and comprehend how those strengths can be used to help those who need them the most. For instance, TOMS Shoes and its Giving Partners study the communities before dropping off the shoes to ensure that the shoes will make a positive difference in children's lives. They pick out the communities that appear to have the most need for its products.[44] Additionally, according to Mycoskie, it is important that companies with a philanthropic focus allow their products to speak for themselves. The products should be able to impress consumers, prompting them to spread the word to others without constant marketing from the company.

Not many businesses have attempted to replicate the One for One movement in terms of incorporating it into their business models. Two companies that have created businesses around this concept include a bedding and mattress organization, which donates one bed to those in need for every product bought, and an apparel store, which will match customers' purchases by giving clothes to those in disadvantaged areas.[45] The difficulty is in creating a for-profit business with a strong philanthropic component. Time will tell whether these companies, and additional organizations, will succeed to the extent of TOMS Shoes.

Criticisms and ethical issues

Most people might find it hard to understand why anyone would criticize TOMS Shoes. As a successful philanthropic for-profit company, TOMS has been able to help children in need all over the world. However, criticisms about the company's model do exist, many of which come from other philanthropists. Probably the biggest criticism is that TOMS Shoes makes people in poor countries dependent upon the good will of others rather than creating opportunities for them to better themselves. Many social entrepreneurs and philanthropists of today believe that the best way to create sustainable change is through education and job creation. Only then will people be able to get themselves out of poverty and no longer require humanitarian aid.[46] Microfinance, which provides small loans to low-income individuals to start their own businesses, is based upon this idea.

Another criticism has been the fact that TOMS has manufacturing locations in China—a country that has received much scrutiny for factory abuse.[47] One could successfully argue that as a business, it is advantageous to manufacture products in countries where labor costs are lower in order to keep prices reasonable. Supporters also point out that TOMS' factories are creating jobs in disadvantaged countries like Ethiopia. As a for-profit business, TOMS Shoes will constantly have to balance the financial aspects of its for-profit business with the humanitarian elements of its philanthropic organization.

Since TOMS is for-profit, the company faces the same risks as other for-profit companies. Ethical lapses can occur just as easily in philanthropic organizations as they can in large corporations, particularly as it relates to the supply chain. It is necessary for TOMS to monitor business activities such as factory compliance, sustainability, finances, and even its

Shoe Drop operations in order to maintain appropriate business conduct. TOMS Shoes must never be complacent regarding these risks simply because it has built philanthropy into its business. The company must also innovate constantly. Although consumers tend to like purchasing from a philanthropic organization, they appear to be more financially supportive when they get something in return.[48] In the case of TOMS, it is a pair of unique shoes. However, with consumer tastes constantly changing, TOMS must remain vigilant regarding new designs and products. The risks of outdated styles and designs plague the fashion industry. Mycoskie himself has noted the importance of innovation to keep consumers' business. TOMS Shoes must remain proactive in managing these risks to maintain its current success rate.

The future of TOMS Shoes

The question in a business type atmosphere is: "Is the TOMS business model sustainable for the future?" A new emphasis on social entrepreneurship is sweeping the nation, supported by such high-profile individuals as President Barack Obama and former President Bill Clinton. Mycoskie has revolutionized this concept by introducing his One for One Movement. It is likely that many more organizations with a focus on social responsibility will try to replicate this movement. Mycoskie's invention may introduce an entirely new way of doing business.

Moving forward into the future, TOMS will need to keep an eye on risks that affect both for-profit and non-profit organizations. In a way, Mycoskie's combination of these two business models has limited certain industry-specific risks. For instance, the for-profit business supports the non-profit component, which means TOMS does not have to rely on donations. On the other hand, the model has also introduced additional risks. Non-profit organizations often sell very few products; thus, the risks that come with manufacturing are much lower. Because TOMS sells a tangible product, it requires a supply chain that must be constantly monitored for compliance. The company also must manage criticism of its philanthropic endeavors, an issue not as common among corporations where philanthropy is a secondary activity.

Despite these challenges, the future of TOMS Shoes looks bright. The excitement over the release of TOMS eyeware demonstrates that consumers remain enthusiastic about the One for One model. With careful risk management, its strong mission and values, and successful promotional campaigns, TOMS Shoes will likely remain a sustainable business for years to come.

Questions

1. Will the One for One movement be a sustainable model in the long run? Is it appropriate for any other businesses?
2. Who are TOMS most important stakeholders, and why?
3. Which of the ethical issues discussed at the end of the case is the most significant?

22 Cadbury's chocolate bars

Not such a sweet smell of success?[1]

Andrea Prothero

Cadbury is a world-renowned manufacturer of confectionary products (candy/sweets, biscuits/cookies and the famous Cadbury creme eggs) and was founded by a Quaker family in 1824 in the UK. The company acquired Schweppes line of tonic water and related products in the late 1960s. Cadbury Schweppes went on to acquire Sunkist, Canada Dry, Dr. Pepper, Snapple, and Royal Crown over the years. In March 2007, it was revealed that Cadbury Schweppes was planning to split its business into two separate entities: one focusing on its main chocolate and confectionery market; the other on its US drinks business. The demerger took effect on May 2, 2008, with the drinks business becoming Dr. Pepper Snapple Group, Inc. In 2010 Cadbury was acquired in a controversial hostile takeover by Kraft Foods. The acquisition of Cadbury faced widespread disapproval from the British public, as well as groups and organizations including trade union Unite, who fought against the acquisition of the company which, according to then Prime Minister Gordon Brown, was very important to the British economy.

Cadbury had a history of positive ethical practices over the years because of strong leadership from the Cadbury family. One of the last members of the founding family to hold the Chairman role was Sir Adrian Cadbury. In an interview with one of the editors of this book, he stated that product quality was very important to the firm and that his view was that nothing should be done to cheapen the products, even in lesser developed countries. He said, "my name is on the bar and we are not going to compromise quality anywhere in the world."

In the UK, on June 23, 2006 the company issued a product recall and food hazard warning for seven of its products, all of which were part of the successful Dairy Milk product line. At the same time the company temporarily suspended its sponsorship of the television soap *Coronation Street,* one of the most watched television shows in the UK, and also suspended its television advertising.[2] Over one million bars of chocolate[3] were recalled by the company and various reports estimate that the recall cost the company between £20–£30 million. Following a court case in 2007, at which the company pleaded guilty to serious offences, Cadbury's indicated that they had spent £20 million on changing their procedures to ensure such an event could not happen again. Following the recall then CEO, Todd Spitzer said,

> We have apologised to our consumers, customers and colleagues for any concerns caused and are implementing changes to our UK manufacturing and quality assurance processes so that this cannot happen again.[4]

At the same time a company spokesperson who sought to alleviate fears amongst the public said,

> The levels [of salmonella] are significantly below the standard that would be any health problem, but we are taking this measure as a precaution. If there are people who have eaten one of these chocolate bars today they should not worry, but they can get in touch with us if they are concerned for a full refund.[5]

In January 2006 the results of independent laboratory tests carried out on samples of chocolate crumbs from Cadbury's manufacturing facility in Marlbrook, Herefordshire showed minute traces of a rare strain of salmonella. The results of these tests indicated salmonella levels at 0.3 cells per 100g of chocolate crumb, and as these fell below the 10 cells alert level[6] the company did not report the findings to either the government watchdog the Health Protection Agency (HPA) or the Food Standards Agency (FSA). In fact, it was some five months later when the product recall was issued. During this time period the HPA had been investigating an unusual outbreak of salmonella in the UK, with 42 reported cases of the illness. The HPA highlighted that the outbreak was likely to have been between three and five times higher than the actual number of reported cases.[7] Symptoms of salmonella include vomiting and diarrhea, abdominal cramps, nausea, fever, chills and headaches, and can, on rare occasions, be fatal. Following investigations by both the FSA and the HPA, the cause of the salmonella was eventually traced to the Cadbury's plant at Marlbrook. The outbreak was the result of a leaking pipe at the plant which had allowed dirty water to contaminate one of the plant's conveyor belts.

The authorities in the UK were quick to condemn Cadbury and seriously questioned why it had taken so long for the outbreak to be publicized. One Environmental Health Officer pointed out,

> Cadbury had a zero salmonella policy but they did not comply with it and they did not liaise with us or with their home authority, Birmingham, even when they knew that there was a problem.[8]

In 2007 Cadbury pleaded guilty to nine charges filed against them by the FSA. They were fined £1 million and also ordered to pay court costs of £152,000. The judge in the case accused the company of "serious negligence," and this was reflected in the very high fines levied against the company. The fines included a £500,000 charge for selling unsafe chocolate, as well as fines for a failure to notify authorities about the positive salmonella tests and smaller fines for six breaches of food safety laws at the Marlbrook plant. Paul Burnley a food safety and product recall lawyer stressed, "This is an enormous amount of money to be fined. It shows that companies have to move fast when it comes to dealing with product recall issues."[9]

In addition to being found guilty of negligence by the British legal system for taking so long to remove the products from the shelves, the company was also criticized for the way in which the belated recall was handled. In the blogosphere, a number of bloggers stressed that the company had missed an opportunity to use social media to help in its interactions with consumers regarding the case. One blogger emphasized, "But they want total message control and NO feedback, which is, quite simply, an outdated way to handle the situation. There's no email on the site, no name of a human anywhere in the contact information, and no effort to engage the customer in an interactive conversation."[10] And went on to say,

> Cadbury has a great opportunity here to create the means for some two-way dialogue with consumers as part of their communication activity on what they need to do to allay consumer concerns about health risks as well as reinforce the values of their brand as being safe to consume. Blogs could have featured as part of that plan, but it's too late now—you need to have your social media in place as part of your crisis planning well before the crisis actually comes along.[11]

Cadbury did have a series of blogs set up for newly hired graduates to talk about their experiences as new employees. Those blogs are closed now. A pity, as that could have been an interesting and already established place for some discussion surrounding this issue.[12]

In the four weeks following the recall not only did the firm's BrandIndex score fall, sales of chocolate bars fell by 14% and independent research indicated that Cadbury's reputation was at an all time low.[13] Following a drop in the Cadbury grocery brands' rankings in 2007, the director of BrandForensics Jonathan Gabay indicated,

> In the old days, people would buy brands because of the size and stature behind the name. Today, it is not just about the size and stature behind the brand and the name. It is about the quality of the product. In terms of the consumer, there is no smoke without fire, and it sometimes takes even longer—even for a brand as large as Cadbury—to dispel such concerns.[14]

By the third quarter of 2007, however, Cadbury's was posting strong results in its confectionary markets and the company noted that despite a difficult year, following the product recall and the subsequent large fine, sales of its confectionary products were up by 10 percent. Following the recall the company embarked on a number of new marketing initiatives, including some very successful and innovative marketing communications campaigns.[15]

Questions

1. You work for a marketing communications company and have been contracted by Cadbury to write a report on the product recall in the UK. Consulting the product recall literature include in your report comments on the following issues:

    a. What were the key ethical problems with Cadbury's recall strategy?
    b. What alternative recall strategies would you have advised the company to consider and how would you have suggested they implement these?
    c. What are the advantages and disadvantages to companies in initiating product recalls?

2. In 2008 Cadbury's were forced to issue another major product recall for 11 of its products sold in Asia and the Pacific. The recall was a result of chocolate produced in its Chinese manufacturing plants being contaminated with the industrial chemical melamine. Find out as much as you can about this product recall and write a report on the

similarities/differences between this recall and the one in the UK in 2006. From your research what lessons did Cadbury's learn/not learn from the earlier incident in 2006? How would you advise the company on dealing with product recalls in the future?

3.   What are the marketing ethics lessons learned from this case study?

4.   Compare this situation with the Johnson & Johnson recalls in 2011 in the US (see David Voreacos, Alex Nussbaum and Greg Farrell, "Johnson & Johnson Fights to Clear its Once-Trusted Name," *Bloomberg Businessweek,* April 4–11, 2011, 64–71).

23 Caterpillar, Inc.[1]

Jennifer Sawayda, Ethan Fairy,
and Matt Yepez

Caterpillar, Inc. (CAT) is a leading global manufacturer of construction and mining equipment, machinery, and engines headquarted in Peoria, IL (USA). The company is best known for its machinery, including its crawler tractors, off-highway trucks, wheel dozers, and backhoe loaders. CAT is a global firm with more than 500 dealer and facility locations worldwide. In 2010, the company achieved global revenues of more than $42.5 billion, with $13.4 billion coming from exported products.[2] As a result, CAT faces the challenging tasks of managing a complex network of stakeholders. Despite some ethical lapses, CAT has made a name for itself not only for its quality products but also for its high ethical standards and corporate social responsibility (CSR). This case will emphasize CAT's ethical initiatives and CSR efforts. We start off by providing a brief background of CAT's history. We then examine CAT's progress in areas such as ethical conduct, stakeholder relations, and sustainability. The case will conclude by analyzing some ethical risks and issues that CAT has encountered and likely will continue to experience.

History of Caterpillar

Caterpillar Inc. had its origins during the early 1900s when inventor Benjamin Holt created the first crawler tractor. To sell his tractors, Holt created the Holt Manufacturing Company. For the first decade of the nineteenth century, Caterpillar machines were used in construction projects and disaster relief. However, once the First World War began, Caterpillar tractors became a part of the battlefront carrying supplies and artillery. In 1925 Holt Manufacturing Co. and its competitor, C.L. Best Gas Tractor, merged to become the Caterpillar Tractor Company. The Caterpillar name was coined as part of the brand name because the products crawled on the ground like the caterpillar insect. The newly formed company spent the next 15 years seeing its products used on several important construction projects, including the King Albert Canal in Belgium, the Hoover Dam, the Golden Gate Bridge, and the Grand Coulee Dam. Over the next several decades, Caterpillar Tractor Co. grew to become a multinational corporation. In 1986 the company was renamed Caterpillar Inc. Today, Caterpillar Inc. has customers in more than 180 countries and employs more than 100,000 people globally.[3]

Products

Over the years, Caterpillar has amassed a vast array of products under a number of different brand names. Its most famous brand is the CAT brand. Many of the large-scale machinery for which Caterpillar is known sport the familiar CAT logo with the yellow pyramid covering part of the "A." CAT products have been used in the agriculture, construction, forestry, demolition, waste, and mining industries, among many others. These products sport the yellow and black colors that have become associated with the company. Other brands that Caterpillar owns include CAT Financial, CAT Logistics, Progress Rail, Solar Turbines, and AsiaTrak.[4]

CAT sells more than 300 machines, along with parts, turbines, engines, and electronics. The company also provides a variety of services involving logistics, financing and insurance, and rental services. The breadth of products and services that CAT offers has made it the leading company in the construction industry. CAT's closest competitor in the agriculture industry is Deere & Co., home of the green John Deere brand. The company's closest competitor in the construction industry is Japanese company Komatsu Limited, the second largest construction manufacturing company in the world but with higher market share in places like China and Japan.[5]

Achievements and goals

In addition to its success as a multinational corporation, Caterpillar, Inc. has won many awards for its strong ethical conduct. The company was listed in Ethisphere's 2011 World's Most Ethical (WME) Companies under Industrial Manufacturing. It also ranked number 27 on *Fortune* magazine's 2011 "World's Most Admired Companies" and scored twelfth in *Women Engineer* magazine's "Top 50 Employers."[6] One reason why CAT has scored so highly in ethics likely results from its strong goals and strategies. For instance, CAT outlined a sustainability vision, mission statement, and strategy to express its commitment toward the environment, the economy, and the workforce. These three elements are outlined in Box 23.1.

Box 23.1 CAT's sustainability vision, mission, and strategy

Vision:
A world in which all people's basic requirements—such as shelter, clean water, sanitation, and reliable power—are fulfilled in a way that sustains our environment.

Mission:
To enable economic growth through infrastructure and energy development, and to provide solutions that protect people and preserve the planet.

Strategy
To provide work environments, products, services, and solutions that make efficient use of the world's natural resources and reduce unnecessary impacts on people, the environment and the economy. This means that they leverage resources including technology and innovation to

- Promote and protect individual safety and well-being
- Provide employment, education, and training
- Minimize the use of energy, materials, water, and land
- Maximize recycling
- Minimize emissions
- Optimize the use of renewable resources

CAT's mission and strategies emphasize a stakeholder orientation that considers the well-being of all its constituents. However, determining ethical strategies and successfully implementing them are two different things. The following sections will describe how CAT puts its vision and mission into practice through its comprehensive code of conduct and CSR initiatives.

Code of Conduct and Vision 2020 Strategy

CAT implemented its Worldwide Code of Conduct in 1974 to ensure consistent ethical standards among its networks across the world. Many ethical codes require updating to adapt to the constantly changing business environment, and CAT is no exception. The company updated its Worldwide Code of Conduct in 2010 for the fifth time after formulating its Vision 2020 Strategy. The Vision 2020 Strategy is a set of goals that describe the strategic direction the company wants to take in the next few years. CAT has set forth three strategic goals: achieve superior results, become a global leader, and have the best team—goals that directly involve its stockholders, employees, and customers. As part of its operating principles, CAT plans to become more customer-focused, hold itself more accountable for results, establish a strong dealer network, and more.[7]

CAT has identified four core values that will make its strategic goals a reality: integrity, excellence, teamwork, and commitment. The values also make up the framework for CAT's ethical code. CAT's Worldwide Code of Conduct expands upon these values to address the following ethical issues:

Integrity
- Act honestly and with integrity
- Avoid and manage conflicts and potential conflicts of interest
- Compete fairly
- Ensure accuracy and completeness of financial reports and accounting records
- Communicate openly, honestly, and fairly
- Handle "inside information" appropriately and lawfully
- Refuse to make improper payments

Excellence
- Accept nothing but the best quality in products and services
- Focus on delivering the highest value to customers, always with a sense of urgency
- Establish a work environment that supports excellence
- Select, place, and evaluate employees based on qualifications and performance
- Provide employees with opportunities to develop
- See risk as something to be managed *and* as a potential opportunity
- Take an "enterprise point of view"

Teamwork
- Treat others with respect and do not tolerate intimidation or harassment
- Treat people fairly and prohibit discrimination

- Foster an inclusive environment
- Conduct business worldwide with consistent global standards
- Collaborate with key entities and organizations outside the company
- Build outstanding relationships with dealers and distribution channel members
- View suppliers as business allies

Commitment
- Protect the health and safety of others and ourselves
- Support environmental responsibility through sustainable development
- Take personal responsibility
- Protect hard assets, brands, and other intellectual property
- Safeguard confidential information
- Use electronic communications technology responsibly and professionally
- Recognize and respect personal privacy
- Be proactive members of communities
- Make responsible ownership and investment decisions
- Participate in public matters in an appropriate manner

Adapted from *Our Values in Action: Caterpillar's Worldwide Code of Conduct*, www.caterpillar.com/cda/files/2500099/7/English_OVIA_v05.pdf (accessed May 24, 2011).

CAT's Worldwide Code of Conduct describes its commitment and responsibilities to its customers, employees, suppliers and distributors, and communities. Although stockholders are not mentioned specifically in these key points, the code describes how being an ethical company and following these ethical guidelines will increase stockholder value. (More information on CAT's Worldwide Code of Conduct can be found at www.caterpillar.com/cda/files/2500099/7/English_OVIA_v05.pdf.)

CAT's stakeholder relationships

CAT recognizes that its operations will not only affect its stockholders but also its customers and employees. The company has therefore taken steps to create mutually beneficial relationships with these two primary stakeholder groups.

Customer relations

CAT tries to meet the needs of its customers through quality products based upon environmental and safety considerations. The company offers many services to customers that go beyond selling, from financing to providing safety information and videos. Above all, CAT views high quality products as one of the most important aspects of a successful customer relationship. Thus, the company strives to create new innovative products as well as improve the quality of its existing ones. Much of this improvement comes through the manufacturing process. CAT has developed the Guiding Principles of the Caterpillar Production System (CPS) to ensure that certain steps are followed in manufacturing, such as reducing waste and stopping to fix defective products before they go further down the production process.

CAT also strives to improve its operations using Six Sigma, a method used to manage process variations that can lead to product defects. By ensuring that its equipment is of high quality, CAT is able to establish good relationships with customers while simultaneously reducing the risk of liabilities from faulty products.[8]

As a manufacturer, many of CAT's direct customers are independent dealers. The company sells its products to dealers, who then sell to end users. However, there are many end users of CAT products that span across industries, from government to mining to railroads. This creates customer relationships that CAT must manage. To show its commitment toward customers, current Caterpillar Inc. CEO Douglas Oberhelman has adopted the practice of personally meeting with one customer each week. By gaining an understanding of what customers think of the company, Oberhelman can use this feedback to help improve operations. CAT also expresses its commitment toward customer safety. Since improper use of CAT products can result in injury or even death, CAT has created the website SAFETY.CAT.com to educate consumers about how to use its equipment safely. CAT also releases a newsletter every quarter informing subscribers of news, safety information, and tips.[9]

Employee relations

CAT's relationships with its employees have not always run smoothly. For example, in the 1980s and 1990s, CAT imposed cost-cutting devices during times of economic hardship that negatively impacted employees, such as freezing wages and cutting benefits. In response the United Auto Workers (UAW) union led two major strikes against the company. In the early 1990s, CAT locked out thousands of UAW union employees in response to strikes and threatened to hire replacement workers. Large scale strikes occurred once again in 1994 over the firing of UAW workers. In 1998, the company and the UAW agreed upon a six-year contract. The contract gave CAT more power in certain areas but also compelled it to rehire 160 union workers.[10]

Since then CAT has worked to emphasize its commitment toward employees. CAT supports diversity through several employee affinity groups and networks, including its African American Network, Armed Forces Support Network, Chinese Affinity Group, Korean Affinity Group, Lambda Network, Women's Initiative Network, and Young Professionals of Caterpillar. These groups provide networking, service, and leadership opportunities for members while also educating the entire CAT work force about diversity. CAT's strides in diversity have earned it recognition from different institutions. For instance, CAT won the Greater Lafayette (Indiana) Commerce Diversity Roundtable's Workforce Diversity Best Practice Award and was named as a Top Supporter of Historically Black Colleges and Universities of 2010.[11]

CAT also recognizes its responsibilities to employees regarding safety. CAT's goal is for every employee to be careful and incident free. To keep track of its progress in working toward zero incidents, CAT compiles data on the number of injuries per 20,000 hours worked and monitors how much time is lost due to injuries per 20,000 hours worked. These data allow CAT to establish benchmarks and goals for improvement. By acting upon the information it has collected, CAT has been able to decrease its injuries over the past seven years. In 2010, CAT recorded 1.18 injuries per 20,000 hours worked and 0.35 in lost time per 20,000 hours worked due to injuries. This is a significant decrease from its 6.06 injuries and 2.90 in time lost recorded in 2003.[12]

CAT's corporate social responsibility

Corporate social responsibility (CSR) is defined as an organization's responsibility to maximize its positive impact on its different stakeholders while minimizing its negative impact on society. As a multinational company, CAT is expected to undertake CSR initiatives by giving back to the communities in which they do business. Rather than being a burden on businesses, these voluntary responsibilities can help them to demonstrate their commitment to people, communities, and the environment.[13] CAT has adopted many philanthropic practices to show its dedication to community stakeholders, including its creation of The Caterpillar Foundation, its matching gifts program, and its involvement with the United Way.

The Caterpillar Foundation

The Caterpillar Foundation is the vehicle that the firm uses to direct money, aid, and resources to the public. Founded in 1952, the Caterpillar Foundation has donated over $300 million toward such areas as education, the environment and other philanthropic causes. Disaster relief is also a core focus of the Caterpillar Foundation. Following the 2011 Japanese tsunami, the Caterpillar Foundation announced a $1 million grant to the American Red Cross for relief efforts to the region; agreed to match employee, retiree, and dealer employee contributions up to $500,000; and allowed the Japanese government to use its machinery and generators. The Caterpillar Foundation has also committed resources to disaster relief in Brazil, New Zealand, and Australia.[14]

The Caterpillar Foundation is highly committed to international causes. It donated $2 million to the Susan G. Komen for the Cure Program that were directed toward the Central America region to increase breast cancer awareness. Approximately 41 percent of the Foundation's investments in philanthropic projects occurred outside the United States.[15] This demonstrates that CAT is becoming more of a global company headquartered in the US than a US company with a global presence.

Matching gifts program

The Caterpillar Foundation also has a matching gifts program that is designed to align employee and retiree donors with specific areas of the community. CAT will match up to $2,000 of each individual's donation to certain charitable causes. Eligible organizations for matching include cultural, environmental, art organizations, and colleges/universities. The matching gifts program is beneficial to CAT's stakeholders because it gives employees/retirees the ability to leverage CAT's funds in donating to a worthy cause. The stakeholders who receive the donated funds also benefit, as does CAT's reputation.[16]

United Way

The Foundation is also involved with the United Way, which is a coalition of charitable organizations in the US. CEUWA (Caterpillar Employees United Way Appeal) is a program in which the firm solicits donations from its employees. In turn, CAT will match these donations and distribute them to the local United Way of the employee's choice. Since CEUWA was created 100 percent of employee contributions have been dispersed to the United Way. CAT was a top donor to United Way in 2010 with $250,000 in employee donations.[17]

Environmental stakeholders: CAT's Sustainability Initiatives

Sustainability has become a core tenet of CAT's corporate strategy, so much so that the company releases an annual Sustainability Report in seven languages to inform stakeholders about its progress. As the world becomes more concerned about the environment, CAT sees sustainability as a necessary component for its future success. One of CAT's older sustainability programs still in use today is "Certified Rebuild." This program was designed to prevent older machines from being discarded by rebuilding them instead. In 2010, the program celebrated its 5,000th rebuilt machine. The program makes financial sense for CAT as it can reuse the parts from its old machines rather than having to buy new components. It is also highly beneficial to the environment; since much of the material from the original machine is reused, CAT estimates that rebuilding the machine uses approximately 50 to 60 percent less energy. Through its Certified Rebuild program, CAT promotes sustainability by reducing waste in the manufacturing process.[18]

Similar to Certified Rebuild are CAT's remanufacturing and reconditioning programs. Progress Rail Services, a business acquired by Caterpillar Inc. in 2006, uses reconditioning for locomotives. The company takes the reusable parts of old locomotives and uses them to build reconditioned ones. Those parts that are not used by Progress Rail's Locomotive and Railcar Division or the Engineering and Track Division are used in Caterpillar's steel mills. Thus, the life cycle of these components is extended considerably.

CAT has reduced waste in other areas as well. Over the years CAT has increased the amount of waste it recycles to 87 percent. Cat Logistics in the United Kingdom was able to achieve zero-waste for the first time. Since 2006 the firm has also reduced its water usage by nearly 20 percent. Yet CAT plans to take its sustainability goals even further. For example, the firm plans on holding water consumption flat through the year 2020. It plans to increase its own energy efficiency by 25 percent during the same time. Finally, CAT is setting an example of sustainability through its corporate headquarters. This facility is LEED (Leadership in Energy and Environmental Design) Gold certified and has reduced its overall energy consumption and greenhouse gas emissions by 48 percent and 44 percent respectively. CAT plans to use its headquarters as a benchmark for its other buildings.[19]

In addition to being sustainable in its own business practices, CAT aids its customers in being sustainable. The EHL (Extended High Lift) is a feature available on certain loaders that CAT sells. This feature increases the lift height of the loaders. After conducting loading tests using the EHL, CAT concluded that the feature decreased cycle time, thus increasing productivity. It also reduces emissions. Additionally, CAT provides numerous retrofits to existing products. Retrofits are used to upgrade existing machines without having to replace them. The purpose of these retrofits is to increase efficiency, extend the machine's life cycle, and use fewer materials than it would take to replace the machine. Another example of how the firm provides methods for its customers to be environmentally sustainable can be found—surprisingly—in its products used for demolition. Zurich-based Eberhard Co., a customer of CAT, demolished an airport with CAT products but was able to recycle 80 percent of the debris.[20]

Ethical issues

Despite CAT's achievements, the firm has confronted several ethical issues that it must address. Some of these issues deal more with the nature of the company's products than with anything the company itself has done. However, CAT has also experienced some ethical challenges stemming from its own operations.

One ethical challenge CAT continues to face concerns its unionized employees. Although there have not been strikes in recent years, the union and CAT periodically undergo intense negotiations over issues such as wages and benefits. The newest six-year contract will provide some additional benefits to union workers but will not give any wage increases to those who were hired at CAT over six years ago. Although both sides indicated approval with the contract, the UAW indicated that the original proposal from CAT was filled with harsh cutbacks, such as the elimination of certain benefits and reductions in pay. Although the economic downturn has required cutbacks for most businesses, CAT must strive to treat its employees fairly and work with the union to ensure smoother relationships with workers.[21]

CAT has also been accused of violating environmental laws. In August 2000, the Clean Air Trust named CAT the "Clean Air Villain of the Month." The company had violated the Clean Air Act after it sold defective diesel engines that emitted nearly three times the allowed limit of nitrogen oxides (which creates smog). Other companies were found to have similar defects. It is estimated that in 1998 these defective engines were responsible for emitting pollution comparable to more than 60 million cars. CAT was required to pay over $128 million in penalties.[22]

To restore its reputation, CAT began releasing more environmentally-friendly products that meet or exceed Environmental Protection Agency standards. In 2004, CAT introduced Advanced Combustion Emissions Reduction Technology (ACERT) engines. These engines exceeded federal emissions guidelines. However, meeting emissions requirements continues to be a challenge for CAT. Because it is a global company, CAT is encountering even more stringent emissions laws in places such as the European Union. These laws, along with new regulations from the US called Tier 4 standards, required CAT to undergo an extensive research and development program to reengineer its off-road products. These reengineered products would have to meet standards calling for almost zero emissions of particulates and nitrogen oxides—the same gases that got CAT in trouble years before. To meet these new requirements, CAT partnered with Tenneco, Inc. to create the Clean Emissions Module (CME). This module will be installed in its ACERT™ engines.[23]

Another ethical issue touched upon earlier is the safety implications of CAT's products. While CAT might not be able to control how its customers use its products, it can limit to whom it sells. Caterpillar has been criticized for the fact that the Israeli Defense Forces (IDF) has been using CAT's bulldozers to destroy Palestinian homes, along with other violent acts. In 2003 a young American activist was crushed to death by a Caterpillar tractor operated by the IDF. In spite of the controversy over whether the death was accidental or intentional, the fact that CAT's products are being used in this manner creates an ethical dilemma. Critics argue that CAT's complacency is aiding human rights abuses. CAT claims that its bulldozers were sold to the US government, which then sent them to Israel through the US Foreign Military Sales Program. Critics, however, are not accepting CAT's reasoning; rather, they feel CAT should not participate in this program if its bulldozers end up being used for violence. The question over how much responsibility CAT should have over its products is not an easy one to answer.[24]

Finally, the nature of CAT products and its extensive network of suppliers and dealers create a number of risks that CAT must manage to avoid ethical conflicts. Because CAT sells heavy equipment such as tractors and wheel dozers, the chances of injury can be high if safety precautions are not followed. This is likely the reason why CAT provides so many safety resources for its employees and customers. Still, some consumers have used CAT products in ways not anticipated or approved of by the company. This can create liability issues for the company if stakeholders believe that CAT knew or should have known that the product might be used in such a way—even if the product was being improperly used. CAT must be diligent in anticipating foreseeable problems and taking appropriate precautions to protect itself should injuries occur.

CAT also sells its products to independently owned dealers and contracts much of its local parts production to outside parties. Both situations require CAT to exert proper oversight in ensuring that suppliers and dealers are following appropriate compliance procedures. Because quality is such an important part of the CAT brand, the company must carefully monitor its suppliers to ensure that the parts meet its standards. In terms of dealers, one might assume that CAT does not have to worry about oversight as these dealers are independently owned. However, serious misconduct on the part of CAT dealers could jeopardize the brand name. These risks involving third parties become harder to manage as CAT's network of suppliers and dealers grows. CAT must have effective controls in place to monitor these risks and take corrective action when necessary to prevent future misconduct.

Conclusion

CAT has made impressive achievements in the ethics and corporate social responsibility area. Its shared values, strong stakeholder relationships, and extensive sustainability initiatives have earned it recognition from a variety of sources. CAT's persistence in obtaining a more sustainable future is an important step in light of today's current social concerns. Its inclusion as a World's Most Ethical (WME) Company demonstrates the admiration stakeholders feel for the firm. However, CAT will likely encounter obstacles in the future.

Questions

1. What is one ethical issue that Caterpillar is facing?
2. What evidence can you provide that CAT lives its values and code?
3. Which of CAT's stakeholder relationships do you believe are the strongest? Weakest?
4. How much responsibility does a company like Caterpillar have for the misuse of its products?

Notes

1 Foundational perspectives for ethical and socially responsible marketing decisions

1 D. Voreacos, A. Nussbaum and G. Farrell, 'Johnson & Johnson fights to clear its once-trusted name', *Bloomberg Businessweek*, April 4–10, 2011, pp. 64–71.
2 G. Laczniak and P. Murphy, *Ethical Marketing Decisions: The Higher Road*, Boston: Allyn & Bacon, 1993.
3 This section of the chapter is adapted from G. Laczniak and P. Murphy, 'Normative perspectives for ethical and socially responsible marketing', *Journal of Macromarketing*, 26 (2), 2006, pp. 154–77.
4 I. Kant, *Grounding for the Metaphysics of Morals*, Indianapolis, IN: Hackett Publishing. 1785/1981.
5 K. Davis, W. Frederick, and R. Blomstrom, *Business and Society: Concepts and Policy Issues*, New York: McGraw-Hill, 1980.
6 G. Katz and J. Crandall, 'Foreign Corrupt Practices Act: what every contractor should know', *Construction Accounting & Taxation,* 20 (2), 2010, pp. 5–14.
7 T. Dunfee, C. Smith, and W. Ross, 'Social contracts and marketing ethics', *Journal of Marketing* 63 (2), 1999, pp. 14–32.
8 T. Garrett, *Business Ethics*, Englewood Cliffs, NJ: Prentice Hall, 1966.
9 P. Werhane, *Moral Imagination and Management Decision Making*,' New York: Oxford University Press, 1999; M. Drumright and P. Murphy, 'How advertising practitioners view ethics: moral muteness, moral myopia, and moral imagination', *Journal of Advertising*, 33 (2), 2004, pp. 7–24.
10 L. Kohlberg, 'Stage and sequence: the cognitive developmental approach to socialization', in D. Goslin, *Handbook of Socialization Theory and Research*, Chicago, IL: Rand McNally, 1969, pp. 347–480.
11 M. Jennings, *Business Ethics: Case Studies and Selected Readings*, sixth ed., Mason, OH: Southwestern, 2009.
12 G. Laczniak and P. Murphy, 'Ethical leadership for improved corporate governance and better business education', in R. Peterson and O. Ferrell, eds., *Business Ethics: New Challenges for Business Schools and Corporate Leaders*, Armonk, NY: M.E. Sharpe, 2005, pp. 175–95.
13 G. Cavanagh, *American Business Values with International Perspectives*, Upper Saddle River, NJ: Prentice Hall, 2010, p. 232.
14 Laczniak and Murphy, 2005, op. cit.
15 B. George with P. Sims, *True North: Discover Your Authentic Leadership*, San Francisco: Jossey-Bass, 2007.
16 L. Paine, *Value Shift*, New York: McGraw-Hill, 2003.

2 Advanced perspectives for ethical and socially responsible marketing decisions

1 J. Bentham, *An Introduction to the Principles of Morals and Legislation*, New York: Hafner Publishing, 1984; J. Mill, *Utilitarianism*, Indianapolis, IN: Hackett Publishing, 1979.

2 G. Laczniak and P. Murphy, 'Ethical leadership for improved corporate governance and better business education', in R. Peterson and O. Ferrell, eds., *Business Ethics: New Challenges for Business Schools and Corporate Leaders*, Armonk, NY: M.E. Sharpe, 2005, p. 186.

3 I. Kant, *Grounding for the Metaphysics of Morals,* Indianapolis, IN: Hackett Publishing. 1785/1981.

4 N. Bowie, *Business Ethics: A Kantian Perspective,* Malden, MA: Blackwell Publishers, 1999. See also S. Reynolds and N. Bowie, 'A Kantian perspective on the characteristics of ethics programs', *Business Ethics Quarterly*, 14 (2), 275–92.

5 T. Donaldson and T. Dunfee, *Ties That Bind: A Social Contracts Approach to Business Ethics,* Boston, MA: Harvard Business School Press, 1999.

6 J. Rawls, *A Theory of Justice,* Cambridge, MA: Harvard University Press, 1971.

7 A. MacIntyre, *After Virtue,* 2nd ed., Notre Dame, IN: University of Notre Dame Press, 1984.

8 Aristotle, *Nicomachean Ethics*, New York: MacMillan Publishing, 1962.

9 Aristotle, *Ethics,* London, UK: Penguin Books, 1976, 94.

10 P. Murphy, 'Character and virtue ethics in international marketing: An agenda for managers, researchers and educators', *Journal of Business Ethics* 18, 1999, 107–24.

11 'Economic Justice for All: Catholic Social Teaching and the U.S. Economy', *Origins,* 16:4, November 27, 1986.

12 T. Klein and G. Laczniak, 'Applying Catholic social teaching to ethical issues in marketing', *Journal of Macromarketing*, 29 (3), 2009, pp. 233–43.

13 National Conference of Catholic Bishops, 'A Catholic framework for economic life', *U.S. Catholic Conference*, 1997.

14 Pope Pius XI, *Quadragesimo Anno* (*On Reconstructing the Social Order*), Vatican City, 1931.

15 National Conference of Catholic Bishops, op. cit.

16 National Conference of Catholic Bishops, op. cit.

17 Pontifical Council for Justice and Peace, *Compendium of the Social Doctrine of the Church*, Rome: Pontifical Council, 2005.

18 R. Freeman, *Strategic Management: A Stakeholder Approach*, Boston: Pitman, 1984.

19 N. Santos and G. Laczniak, 'Marketing to the poor: an integrative justice model for engaging impoverished market segments', *Journal of Public Policy & Marketing*, 28 (1), pp. 3–15.

20 P. Werhane, *Moral Imagination and Management Decision Making*, New York: Oxford, 1999.

21 American Marketing Association (2011), AMA Definition of Marketing, www.marketingpower. com/AboutAMA/Pages/DefinitionofMarketing.aspx, accessed 5 May 2011.

22 P. Kotler and K. Keller, *Marketing Management*, 14th edition, Upper Saddle River, NJ: Prentice Hall, 2011.

3-1 Decision model, sample case (L'Oréal), analysis and the rest of the story

1 This case was prepared by Marie-Theres Riegler under the direction of Professor Patrick E. Murphy for classroom discussion rather than to illustrate either effective or ineffective handling of an ethical or legal decision.

2 www.loreal.com

3 www.loreal.com/_en_ww/html/our-company/diversity-is-a-priority.aspx

4 www.loreal.com/_en/_ww/html/our-company/our-teams.aspx?

5 http://business.timesonline.co.uk/tol/business/industry_sectors/consumer_goods/articles6572173.ece

6 http://business.timesonline.co.uk/tol/business/industry_sectors/consumer_goods/article6572173.ece

7 www.telegraph.co.uk/news/worldnews/europe/france/5635825/LOreal.

3-2 Decision model, sample case (L'Oréal), analysis and the rest of the story

1 This summary of the outcome of the L'Oréal case was written by Stephanie Piszczor under the direction of Professor Patrick E. Murphy.

2   www.telegraph.co.uk/news/worldnews/europe/france/5635825/LOreal-fined-for-race-discrimination.
    html
3   http://business.timesonline.co.uk/tol/business/industry_sectors/consumer_goods/article6572173.ece
4   http://business.timesonline.co.uk/tol/business/industry_sectors/consumer_goods/article6572173.ece
5   www.insee.fr/fr/themes/detail.asp?ref_id=bilan-demo&page=donnees-detaillees/bilan-demo/
    pop_age2.htm
6   http://business.timesonline.co.uk/tol/business/industry_sectors/consumer_goods/article6572173.ece
7   www.guardian.co.uk/lifeandstyle/2008/aug/09/fashion.race
8   http://business.timesonline.co.uk/tol/business/industry_sectors/consumer_goods/article6572173.ece
9   http://business.timesonline.co.uk/tol/business/industry_sectors/consumer_goods/article6572173.ece
10 www.loreal-finance.com/_docs/us/rapport-2009/LOreal_Rapport_Annuel-Tome_2_va.pdf
11 www.loreal.com/_en/_ww/html/our-company/diversity-is-a-priority.aspx

4 Going along to get along

1   This fictional case was prepared by the late Professor Raymond F. Keyes of Boston College for
    classroom discussion rather than to illustrate either effective or ineffective handling of an adminis-
    trative, ethical, or legal decision by individuals or management.

5 Hunky Dory

1   This case was prepared by Professor Andrea Prothero of University College Dublin for classroom
    discussion rather than to illustrate either effective or ineffective handling of an administrative,
    ethical, or legal decision by individuals or management.
2   McBride C., 2010, 'We'll take legal action over crisps Ad–IRFU', *The Herald*, April 28th, www.
    herald.ie/national-news/well-take-legal-action-over-crisps-ad-irfu-2155526.html (accessed May
    19, 2011).
3   Craig J., 2010, 'Racy Crisps ads not so hunky dory, say rugby chiefs', *The Irish Independent*,
    April 28th, www.independent.ie/sport/rugby/racy-crisps-ads-not-so-hunky-dory-say-rugby-chiefs-
    2155138.html (accessed May 19, 2011).
4   *The Irish Independent*, 2010, 'Saucy Crisps ads see sales soar', June 4, www.independent.ie/
    business/irish/saucy-crisp-ads-see-sales-soar-2207436.html (accessed May 19, 2011).
5   O'Leary Analytics, 2010, 'Is everything hunky dory? Examining the social media response to a
    crisp campaign', http://olearyanalytics.com/634/is-everything-hunky-dory-examining-the-social-
    media-response/ (accessed May 19, 2011).
6   Boards.ie, 2010, 'Hunky Dory's Ad', www.boards.ie/vbulletin/showthread.php?p=65674590
    (accessed May 19, 2011).
7   Advertising Standards Authority for Ireland (ASAI), 2010, Complaint: Largo Foods, Bulletin
    10(3), www.asai.ie/complaint_view.asp?CID = 726&BID = 36 (accessed May 19, 2011).
8   ASAI, 2010, ibid.
9   Power E., 2010, 'Advertising's Bottom Line', *The Irish Independent*, April 29, www.independent.
    ie/lifestyle/advertisings-bottom-line-2156839.html (accessed May 19, 2011).
10 McNeilly C., 2010, 'Model shocked by reaction to racy crisps ad', *The Irish Independent*, www.
    independent.ie/national-news/model-shocked-by-reaction-to-racy-crisps-ad-2159681.html
    (accessed May 19, 2011).
11 ASAI, 2010, ibid.

6 Tracking down counterfeits on eBay: whose responsibility is it?

1   This case was prepared by Professor Barbara Stöttinger, Institute for International Marketing
    Management, Vienna University of Economics and Business. The author would like to extend
    special thanks to Ms. Zora Asef, Ms. Julia Pichler, and Mr. Christoph Uferer for their support in
    collecting background information on this case. This case study was developed for classroom

discussion rather than to illustrate either effective or ineffective handling of an administrative, ethical, or legal decision. The people mentioned in the case text are purely fictitious characters.

2 The Anti-Counterfeiting Group (2010). Retrieved August 3, 2010, from www.a-cg.org/guest/index.php.

3 Anti-Counterfeiting Group (2008). "What is product counterfeiting." Retrieved October 12, 2010, from www.a-cg.org/guest/pdf/what_is_product_counterfeiting.pdf.

4 International Chamber of Commerce (2010). "Counterfeiting Intelligence Bureau." Retrieved December 23, 2010, from www.icc-ccs.org/home/cib.

5 bpCouncil (2008). "Made in France: Can Luxury Brands Counterfeiting Really Be Stopped?". Retrieved November 2, 2010, from www.bpcouncil.com/viewArticle.aspx?articleID=410

6 Passariello, C. (2004). Luxury-goods firms hunt copycats as Web market expands. *The Wall Street Journal*. New York, 244, D3, 26.8.2004.

7 Ibid.

8 Corcoran, C. T. (2007). Brands Fight Online Deluge of Counterfeit Goods. *Women's Wear Daily*. 193: 10.

9 eBay (2010). "Replicas, counterfeit items, and unauthorized copies policy." Retrieved August 3, 2010, from http://pages.ebay.com/help/policies/replica-counterfeit.html.

10 eBay (2010). "What is eBay doing about counterfeits?". Retrieved August 3, 2010, from http://web.ebay.co.uk/safetycentre/againstcounterfeits/.

11 eBay (2010). "eBay Against Counterfeits." Retrieved August 3, 2010, from http://pages.ebay.com/againstcounterfeits/.

12 Chao, L. (2006). What happens when an eBay steal is a fake. *The Wall Street Journal*, New York.

13 Ibid.

14 Lynch, M. (2008). Luxe Brand Smackdown: Tiffany loses to eBay in fight over fake goods. *Women's Wear Daily*. 196: 3.

15 Passariello, C. (2004). "Luxury-Goods Firms Hunt Copycats as Web Market Expands." *The Wall Street Journal* – Eastern Edition 244(40): D3, 26.8.2004.

16 Mengisen, A. (2008). 'Did eBay Start a Counterfeit Crackdown? Freakonomics – The Hidden Side of Everything'. *New York Times*, New York; 2010.

17 Chao, L. (2006). 'What happens when an eBay steal is a fake'. *The Wall Street Journal*, New York.

18 Passariello, C. (2004). 'Luxury-Goods Firms Hunt Copycats as Web Market Expands'. *The Wall Street Journal* – Eastern Edition 244(40): D3.

19 Simpson, L. (2006). 'Watchdogs on the Internet – Protecting Consumers against Online Fraud'. *Advances in Consumer Research* 33(1): 303–4.

20 VERO (2010), 'Verified Rights Owner Programme: Fighting Fakes with eBay' (accessed 20 August 2010), retrieved from http://pages.ebay.co.uk/vero/fighting_fakes_with_vero.pdf.

7 Casas Bahia

1 This case was prepared by Urvashi Mathur and revised by Professor Patrick E. Murphy for class-room discussion purposes rather than to illustrate either effective or ineffective handling of an administrative, ethical, or legal decision by individuals or management.

2 Marcelino, Francisco; Fontana, Camila. (2009-12-04). 'Pao De Acucar Agrees to Buy Casas Bahia; Shares Jump'. www.bloomberg.com/apps/news?pid=20601086&sid=aRn2WP20kfow. Bloomberg.

3 Halasz, Robert, 'International Directory of Company Histories', Volume 75 (2004).

4 Halasz, Robert, 'International Directory of Company Histories', Volume 75 (2004).

5 Halasz, Robert, 'International Directory of Company Histories', Volume 75 (2004).

6 The CIA World Factbook, www.cia.gov/library/publications/the-world-factbook/geos/br.html.

7 Price Waterhouse Coopers, '2006/2007 From Sao Paulo to Shanghai, New consumer dynamics: the impact on modern retailing', www.pwc.com/en_GX/gx/retail-consumer/pdf/brazil.pdf.

8 Prahalad, CK, *The Fortune at the Bottom of The Pyramid* (2006), Wharton School Publishing, p. 18.
9 Jordan, Miriam, 'A retailer in Brazil has become rich by courting poor', *The Wall Street Journal*, June 11, 2002.
10 Halasz, Robert, 'International Directory of Company Histories', Volume 75 (2004).
11 Prahalad, CK, op. cit, p. 161.

8 Toys from China and the new Yum Burger Kids' Meal

1 This case was prepared by Marie Derdzinski, Jacob Bagha and Professor Gene Laczniak for classroom discussion rather than to illustrate either effective or ineffective handling of an administrative, ethical, or legal decision by individuals or management. The case is fictional, but it draws on an amalgam of real world events.

9 Koodo in the Canadian cell phone market

1 This case was prepared by Nyla Obaid under the direction of Professor Patrick E. Murphy for the purpose of classroom discussion rather than to illustrate either the effective or ineffective handling of an administrative, ethical, or legal decision.
2 Tara Kimuri, "Early-termination fees: Taking the bit out of consumers' bark," CBC News: September 8, 2002.
3 For ad images, see: www.marccizravi.com/2009/customer-service-koodo/. www.flickr.com/photos/26027428@N03/2519140635.
4 For YouTube video of this ad, see: www.youtube.com/watch?v=7NN1-GG-7p8.
5 Paul Jay, "Marketing discontent: Koodo taps into consumer frustration," CBC News: December 1, 2008.
6 Ibid.
7 Paul Jay, "Marketing Discontent: Koodo taps into consumer frustration," CBC News: December 1, 2008.
8 TELUS Ethics Policy, "Integrity: Personal and Corporate Integrity," TELUS Inc, February 2010.
9 Paul Jay, "Marketing Discontent: Koodo taps into consumer frustration," CBC News: December 1, 2008.
10 Peter Nowak, "New cellphone carrier launching in 2nd half of 2009," CBC News: September 4, 2008.
11 Kate O'Brien, "BBB gives Canada's cellphone companies an "F"," CBC News: June 17, 2010.

10 PETA

1 This case was prepared by Karin Besenbaeck and revised by Professor Patrick E. Murphy for classroom discussion rather than to illustrate either effective or ineffective handling of an administrative, ethical or legal decision.
2 www.peta.org/annual-review-2009.
3 www.peta.org.
4 Freeman, Carrie. *"Who's Harming Who? A PR Ethical Case Study of PETA's Holocaust on Your Plate Campaign"*, International Communication Association – 2007 Annual Meeting (accessed via EBSCO).
5 "Animal Rights and the Holocaust," Wikipedia, section entitled "PETA and the use of Holocaust imagery." www.wikipedia.org (accessed June 22, 2011).
6 www.ingridnewkirk.com.
7 www.obesityaction.org.
8 www.who.int.
9 www.peta.org/mc/.

10 www.feministezine.com.
11 www.motherjones.com.

11 Drug testing in India

1 This fictional case was prepared by Nicholas J.C. Santos, S.J. of Santa Clara University and Jacob Bagha of Marquette University for classroom discussion rather than to illustrate either effective or ineffective handling of an administrative, ethical, or legal decision by individuals or management.
2 Department of Health, Government of India, 2005. The Drugs and Cosmetic Act 1940 and the Drugs and Cosmetic Rules 1945 (as amended up to June 30, 2005). Available at http://cdsco.nic.in/index.html (accessed November 2, 2010).
3 The name of the company and other statistics has been altered so as to provide anonymity.
4 Government of India, Ministry of Home Affairs. 2003. Census data 2001. Available at www.censusindia.gov.in/Census_Data_2001/National_Summary/National_Summary_DataPage.aspx (accessed November 2, 2010).
5 Alkire, Sabina and Maria Emma Santos. 2010. India Country Briefing. Oxford Poverty & Human Development Initiative (OPHI) Multidimensional Poverty Index Country Briefing Series. Available at: www.ophi.org.uk/policy/multidimensional-poverty-index/mpi-country-briefings/ (accessed November 2, 2010).
6 India. 2010. CIA – The World Factbook. Available at: https://www.cia.gov/library/publications/the-world-factbook/geos/in.html (accessed December 6, 2010).
7 India. 2010. CIA-World Factbook.
8 Healthcare in India. 2010. Available at: http://en.wikipedia.org/wiki/Healthcare_in_India (accessed on December 6, 2010).
9 The World's Billionaires. 2010. Forbes. Available at: www.forbes.com/2010/03/10/worlds-richest-people-slim-gates-buffett-billionaires-2010_land.html [accessed on December 6, 2010].

Additional sources used: (but not footnoted).
   Carney, Scott. 2005. "Testing Drugs on India's Poor." *Wired.* Available from: www.wired.com/medtech/drugs/news/2005/12/69595 (accessed October 5, 2010).
   Kahn, Jennifer. 2006. "A Nation of Guinea Pigs." *Wired.* Available from: www.wired.com/wired/archive/14.03/indiadrug.html (accessed October 4, 2010).
   O'Meara, Alex. 2009. *Chasing Medical Miracles: The Promise and Perils of Clinical Trials.* New York: Walker & Company.
   Hundley, Kris. 2008. "The latest industry being outsourced to India: clinical drug trials." *St. Petersburg Times*, December 14. Available from: www.tampabay.com/news/business/article934677.ece (accessed November 2, 2010).

12 Tough decisions: something to snack on

1 This case was prepared by Brendan D. Murphy and Patrick E. Murphy for classroom discussion rather than to illustrate either effective or ineffective handling of an administrative, ethical or legal decision. The authors want to thank Michael J. Etzel and Gene Laczniak for their helpful comments on the case.
2 Plan-o-gram (POG) = a diagram of fixtures and products that illustrates how and where retail products should be displayed, usually on a store shelf in order to increase customer purchases.
3 SKU = stock-keeping unit. Used to represent one particular product, or UPC. For example: 18-ounce bag of Breston's Original Potato Chips.
4 Facing = Dimension on a POG given to each SKU and distributed proportionately for how quickly that item might sell through. For example, a retailer would give an Original Potato Chip four facings, while giving Salt & Vinegar one facing, because Original is likely to sell four times as many before a new shipment of product is delivered.
5 Reset = Rearrangement of POG in order to reallocate facings in favor SKUs with the greatest sales.

13 Honest Tea and Coke: an unlikely couple

1 This case was prepared by Mark Vander Heiden under the direction of Professor Patrick E. Murphy for classroom discussion rather than to illustrate effective or ineffective handling of an administrative, ethical or legal decision.

2 *HONEST TEA – NATURE GOT IT RIGHT. WE PUT IT IN A BOTTLE.* Web. December 13, 2010. http://honesttea.com/community/sustainability/2009missionreport/.

3 *HONEST TEA – NATURE GOT IT RIGHT. WE PUT IT IN A BOTTLE.* Web. December 13, 2010. http://honesttea.com/.

4 *HONEST TEA – NATURE GOT IT RIGHT. WE PUT IT IN A BOTTLE.* Web. December 13, 2010. http://honesttea.com/community/sustainability/2009missionreport/.

5 *HONEST TEA – NATURE GOT IT RIGHT. WE PUT IT IN A BOTTLE.* Web. December 13, 2010. http://honesttea.com/community/sustainability/2009missionreport/.

6 Murphy, Patrick E., Gene R. Laczniak, Norman E. Bowie, and Thomas A. Klein. *Ethical Marketing.* Upper Saddle River, NJ: Pearson Prentice Hall; 2005. Print.

7 Pressler, Margaret Webb. "Shelf Game: When Stores Force Makers to Pay Them Fees, You Lose," *Washington Post,* January 18, 2004, F5.

8 Pressler, Margaret Webb. "Shelf Game: When Stores Force Makers to Pay Them Fees, You Lose," *Washington Post,* January 18, 2004, F5.

9 Jed, Emily. "Coca-Cola Acquires Honest Tea." *Vending Times* March 2011. www.vendingtimes.com/Vending Times. March 8, 2011. March 25, 2011. www.vendingtimes.com/ME2/dirmod.asp?sid=EB79A487112B48A296B38C81345C8C7F&nm=Vending+Features&type=Publishing&mod=Publications%3A%3AArticle&mid=8F3A7027421841978F18BE895F87F791&tier=4&id=283C6C48C3F04676BF40E07BC6B1154B.

10 *Coca-Cola History: Coca-Cola Heritage Timeline.* The Coca-Cola Company. Web. December 13, 2010. http://heritage.coca-cola.com/.

11 The Coca-Cola Company. *2010 10-K Report.* The Coca-Cola Company, 2011. Web. April 18, 2011.

12 *Coca-Cola History: Coca-Cola Heritage Timeline.* The Coca-Cola Company. Web. December 13, 2010. http://heritage.coca-cola.com/.

13 Fromartz, Samuel. "Seth, Why'd You Sell Honest Tea to Freakin' Coke?" *Chews Wise.* February 5, 2008. April 18, 2011. www.chewswise.com/chews/2008/02/seth-whyd-you-s.html.

14 Gunther, Marc. "Coke Swallows Honest Tea." *Marc Gunther – A blog about business and sustainability.* February 5, 2008. April 10, 2011. www.marcgunther.com/2008/02/05/coke-swallows-honest-tea/.

15 Gunther, Marc. "Coke Swallows Honest Tea." *Marc Gunther – A blog about business and sustainability.* February 5, 2008. April 10, 2011. www.marcgunther.com/2008/02/05/coke-swallows-honest-tea/.

16 Walker, Andrea K. "Drink Maker Finds Coke its Cup of Tea" *Baltimore Sun.* Timothy E. Ryan, April 16, 2008. Web. December 10, 2010. www.baltimoresun.com/features/green/sns-honest-tea-coke-green,0,4779978.story.

17 Gunther, Marc. "Coke Swallows Honest Tea." *Marc Gunther – A blog about business and sustainability.* February 5, 2008. April 10, 2011. www.marcgunther.com/2008/02/05/coke-swallows-honest-tea/.

18 Olson, Elizabeth. "Case Study: Can Honest Tea Say No to Its Biggest Investor (Coke)?" *The New York Times.* Arthur Sulzberger Jr., July 7, 2010. Web. December 10, 2010. www.nytimes.com/2010/07/08/business/smallbusiness/08sbiz.html.

14 Another day in paradise?

1 This case was written by Gerald Benson and Rachel Fisher under the direction of Professor Patrick E. Murphy for classroom discussion rather than to illustrate either effective or ineffective handling of an administrative, ethical or legal decision. The authors contributed equally to the case and are listed in alphabetical order.

2 www.buzzle.com/articles/unique-corporate-gift-giving-experience-in-the-japan.html.

3 www.1worldglobalgifts.com/japangiftgivingetiquette.htm

4 http://library.thinkquest.org/05aug/00723/indexfiles/Page357.htm

5 http://nudehiker.wordpress.com/2004/10/17/the-japanese-culture-of-gift-giving/

6 www. I worldglobalgifts.com/japangiftgivingetiquette.htm

7 http://hubpages.com/hub/art-of-japanese-gift-wrap

8 www.1worldglobalgifts.com/japangiftgivingetiquette.htm

9 www.motivationnetwork.com/article9

10 www.conocophillips.com

11 According to *IRS.gov*, "expenses for entertaining clients, customers or employees may be deducted if they are both ordinary and necessary and meet a 'Directly-related test'…[where] the main purpose of the entertainment activity is the conduct of business, business was actually conducted during the activity and the taxpayer had more than a general expectation of getting income or some other specific business benefit at some future time, or an 'Associated test'…[where] the entertainment was associated with the active conduct of the taxpayer's trade or business and occurred directly before or after a substantial business discussion." Generally, tax deductions on gifts are limited to $25 per recipient per year.

12 www.emilypost.com/everyday/corporate_gift_giving.htm

13 www.emilypost.com/everyday/corporate_gift_giving.htm

14 http://walmartstores.com/Suppliers/248.aspx

15 http://solutions.3m.com/wps/portal/3M/en_US/businessconduct/bcmain/policy/policies/protect3m/giftsentertain/

16 www.chevron.com/documents/pdf/chevronbusinessconductethicscode.pdf

17 http://corporate.ford.com/doc/corporate_conduct_standards.pdf

15 Montenegro Electronics, Ltd.

1 An earlier version of this case was prepared by Professors Raymond Keyes (deceased) and Joseph Gannon, Carroll School of Management, Boston College, as a basis for class discussion. It was substantially revised by Jacob Bagha and Professor Gene Laczniak of Marquette University. The situation in the case is based on an actual business experience. However, the situation, names, and facts have been disguised and any similarity to real world evens or persons is unintentional.

2 Literally Serbian for "commission."

3 The Foreign Corrupt Practices Act of 1977, and its later amendment.

16 Arctic Desert

1 This case was prepared by Katie Hesemann and Rachel Mellard under the direction of Professor Patrick E. Murphy for classroom discussion purposes rather than to illustrate either effective or ineffective handling of an administrative, ethical, or legal decision by individuals or management

17 Superior Services: should short skirts sell software?

1 This case was prepared by Lori Lepp Corbett and revised by Professors Patrick E. Murphy and Gene Laczniak for classroom discussion purposes rather than to illustrate either effective or ineffective handling of an administrative, ethical, or legal decision by individuals or management. The case is an amalgam of "real world" events reported by former students but the story and characters presented are purely fictional.

18 Facebook

1 This case was prepared by Urvashi Mathur and Ryan Mack under the direction of Professor Patrick E. Murphy for classroom discussion rather than to illustrate either effective or ineffective handling of an administrative, ethical or legal decision.

2 Boutin, Paul, "Status Update: Megasuccessful," *The Wall Street Journal*, June 8, 2010.

3 "Goldman Offering Clients a Chance to Invest in Facebook," *New York Times Deal Book*, January 2, 2011.
4 "The World's Billionaires #52 Mark Zuckerberg," *Forbes*, March 1, 2011.
5 "Connecting with an Application or Website," www.facebook.com/policy, April 27, 2011.
6 "Pre-Approved Third Party Websites and Applications," www.facebook.com/policy, April 27, 2011.
7 www.facebook.com/advertising/?campaign_id = 194417723019&placement = exact&creative = 5811896912&keyword = facebook+ads&extra_1 = 75d9f1f7–45e3–0ec9-c347–0000345e181c
8 "Facebook Privacy Breach," *The Wall Street Journal*, December 18, 2010.
9 Facebook Privacy Changes Have Nothing To Do With Advertising," *Business Insider*, May 26, 2010.
10 "Facebook Marketers Can Glean Private Data," *New York Times*, October 23, 2010.
11 "Adults and Social Network Websites," Pew Internet, January 14, 2009.
12 "Facebook Seeking Friends in Beltway," *The Wall Street Journal*, April 20, 2011.
13 "Facebook Seeking Friends in Beltway," *The Wall Street Journal*, April 20, 2011.

19 Auchan (France)

1 This case was prepared by Professor Geert Demuijnck for classroom discussion rather than to illustrate either effective or ineffective handling of an administrative, ethical, or legal decision. This case on Auchan is based partially on my "From an Implicit Christian Corporate Culture to a Structured Conception of Corporate Ethical Responsibility in a Retail Company: A Case-Study in Hermeneutic Ethics," in *Journal of Business Ethics* 84: 387–404.
2 Detailed information about financial results are to be found on www.groupe-auchan.com. The website also provides detailed information about Auchan's CSR and environmental policies. The yearly social and environmental report of the company is downloadable. For details about the shareholder family, one may consult Gobin and d'Herblin (2007).
3 Source: L'Expansion.com -06/02/2009; www.lexpansion.com/economie/les-supermarches-hard-discount-grignotent-des-parts-de-marche_174170.html.
4 For a detailed analysis of Catholic social teaching on wealth, income, and their distribution, see Alford e.a. (2006). Chapter 4 of this reader, written by Francis Hannafey, focuses on "Entrepreneurship in Papal Thought" and is the most relevant for the issues at stake here. It discusses excerpts of the encyclicals which are essential for the responsibilities of the owners of capital.
5 The Employee savings law, LOI n° 2001–2152 du 19 février 2001 sur l'épargne salariale. See Balligand J-P. and de Foucauld J-B. (2000), *L'épargne salariale au cœur du contrat social*, La documentation française.
6 Since then, a much stricter set of European regulations have made things easier for retailers.
7 www.greenpeace.org/belgium/fr/actualites-blogs/actualites/deforestation-en-indonesie/. Moreover, the region Bukit Tigapuluh, where APP massively cuts the wood, is one of the last places on earth where there are Sumatra tigers and orang-utans. For general objections against palm tree plantations see www.greenpeace.org.uk/forests/faq-palm-oil-forests-and-climate-change.
8 For a description of the evolution of fair trade business in France from a marketing perspective see Nil Ozcaglar-Toulouse, N., A. Béji-Bécheur and P. Murphy: 2010, "Fair trade in France: from individual innovators to contemporary networks," *Journal of Business Ethics*, 90 (4), 2009, 589–606.

20 A young pharmacist's dilemma

1 This case was prepared by Barbora Kocanova and Veronika Vosykova and revised by Professor Patrick E. Murphy for classroom discussion purposes rather than to illustrate either effective or ineffective handling of an administrative, ethical, or legal decision by individuals or management. The case is an amalgam of "real world" events reported by former students but the story and characters presented here are purely fictional.

21 TOMS: One for One movement

1 This case was prepared by Alicja Spaulding, Stephanie Fernandez, and Jennifer Sawayda for and under the direction of Professors Patrick Murphy, O.C. Ferrell, and Linda Ferrell. It was prepared for classroom discussion rather than to illustrate either effective or ineffective handling of an administrative, ethical, or legal decision by management. All sources used for this case were obtained through publicly available material.

2 "TOMS Shoes," Zappos!, www.zappos.com/toms-shoes (accessed June 17, 2011).

3 Craig Sharkton, "Toms Shoes – Philanthropy as a Business Model," sufac.com, August 23, 2008, http://sufac.com/2008/08/toms-shoes-philanthropy-as-a-business-model/ (accessed June 3, 2011).

4 Stacy Perman, "Making a Do-Gooder's Business Model Work," *Bloomberg Businessweek*, January 23, 2009, www.businessweek.com/smallbiz/content/jan2009/sb20090123_264702.htm (accessed June 3, 2011).

5 Mike Zimmerman, "The Business of Giving: TOMS Shoes," *Success Magazine,* September 30, 2009, www.successmagazine.com/the-business-of-giving/PARAMS/article/852 (accessed June 3, 2011).

6 Linda Miller, "Shoes offer a better tomorrow," NewsOK, April 5, 2009, http://newsok.com/shoes-offer-a-better-tomorrow/article/3358735 (accessed June 3, 2011).

7 Athima Chansanchai, "Happy feet: Buy a pair of TOMS shoes and a pair will be donated to a poor child abroad," *Seattle Pi,* June 11, 2007, www.seattlepi.com/default/article/Happy-feet-Buy-a-pair-of-TOMS-shoes-and-a-pair-1240201.php (accessed June 3, 2011).

8 Patrick Cole, "Toms Free Shoe Plan, Boosted by Clinton, Reaches Million Mark," *Bloomberg,* September 15, 2010, www.bloomberg.com/news/2010-09-16/toms-shoe-giveaway-for-kids-boosted-by-bill-clinton-reaches-million-mark.html (accessed June 2, 2011).

9 *TOMS One for One Giving Report,* http://images.toms.com/media/content/images/giving-report/TOMS-Giving-Report-2010.pdf (accessed June 3, 2011).

10 *TOMS One for One Giving Report,* http://images.toms.com/media/content/images/giving-report/TOMS-Giving-Report-2010.pdf (accessed June 3, 2011); World Health Organization and UNICE, *Prevention and control of schistosomiasis and soil-transmitted helminthiasis,* 2004; Stacy Perman, "Making a Do-Gooder's Business Model Work," *Bloomberg Businessweek*, January 23, 2009, www.businessweek.com/smallbiz/content/jan2009/sb20090123_264702.htm (accessed June 3, 2011).

11 *TOMS One for One Giving Report,* http://images.toms.com/media/content/images/giving-report/TOMS-Giving-Report-2010.pdf (accessed June 3, 2011).

12 "One for One," TOMS, www.toms.com/our-movement/movement-one-for-one (accessed June 3, 2011); "About – TOMS Campus Clubs," TOMS Campus Clubs, www.tomscampusclubs.com/page/about-1 (accessed June 2, 2011); Mike Zimmerman, "The Business of Giving: TOMS Shoes," *Success Magazine,* September 30, 2009, www.successmagazine.com/the-business-of-giving/PARAMS/article/852 (accessed June 3, 2011); Erin Alberts, "COLUMN: TOMS' business model a self-sustaining charity," The Volante, April 12, 2011, www.volanteonline.com/opinion/column-toms-business-model-a-self-sustaining-charity-1.2540233 (accessed June 3, 2011).

13 Mike Zimmerman, "The Business of Giving: TOMS Shoes," *Success Magazine,* September 30, 2009, www.successmagazine.com/the-business-of-giving/PARAMS/article/852 (accessed June 3, 2011).

14 Erin Kutz, "Consumers like it when their purchases help charities," *USA Today*, December 23, 2010, www.usatoday.com/money/industries/retail/2010-12-23-retailcharity23_ST_N.htm (accessed June 2, 2011).

15 "Our Social Action Initiatives," Rugby Ralph Lauren, www.rugby.com/social_action/default.aspx (accessed June 3, 2011).

16 "One for One: TOMS + Element Collaboration," Element, www.elementeden.com/TOMS/ (accessed June 3, 2011).

17 Emily Lerman, "PhiLAnthropist Interview: TOMS Shoes Founder Blake Mycoskie Plans to Give Away 300,000 Pairs in 2009," Laist, April 15, 2009, http://laist.com/2009/04/15/what_happens_when_you_travel.php (accessed June 3, 2011).

18 "How We Wear Them," TOMS, www.toms.com/how-we-wear-them/ (accessed June 3, 2011).

19 "Solid Ground," APICS eXTRA, September 14, 2008, www.apics.org/APICSXtra/img/sunday_solidground.html (accessed June 3, 2011).

20 M.J. Prest, "The Other Shoe Drops," Ethical Style, March 26, 2009, http://ethicalstyle.com/issue-12/the-other-shoe-drops/ (accessed June 3, 2011).

21 "TOMS Manufacturing Practices," TOMS, www.toms.com/manufacturing-practices (accessed June 3, 2011); "TOMS Company Overview," TOMS, www.toms.com/corporate-info/ (accessed June 3, 2011).

22 Stacy Perman, "Making a Do-Gooder's Business Model Work," *Bloomberg Businessweek*, January 23, 2009, www.businessweek.com/smallbiz/content/jan2009/sb20090123_264702.htm (accessed June 3, 2011).

23 "Our Movement: Giving Partners," TOMS, www.toms.com/our-movement-giving-partners (accessed June 3, 2011); "Get to Know Our Giving Partners: Guatemala SANA," TOMS Blog, http://toms.com/blog/node/901. www.toms.com/blog/hqupdates (accessed June 3, 2011); "TOMS Helps Haiti," TOMS Blog, January 10, 2010, www.tomsshoesblog.com/http:/www.tomsshoesblog.com/toms-helps-haiti (accessed June 3, 2011).

24 Patrick Cole, "Toms Free Shoe Plan, Boosted by Clinton, Reaches Million Mark," *Bloomberg*, September 15, 2010, www.bloomberg.com/news/2010-09-16/toms-shoe-giveaway-for-kids-boosted-by-bill-clinton-reaches-million-mark.html (accessed June 2, 2011); *TOMS One for One Giving Report*, http://images.toms.com/media/content/images/giving-report/TOMS-Giving-Report-2010.pdf (accessed June 3, 2011).

25 "Our Movement: Shoe Drop*s*," TOMS, www.toms.com/our-movement-shoe-drops (accessed June 3, 2011).

26 "How We Give," TOMS, www.toms.com/how-we-give (accessed June 3, 2011).

27 TOMS Webpage, www.toms.com/ (accessed June 3, 2011).

28 Emily Lerman, "PhiLAnthropist Interview: TOMS Shoes Founder Blake Mycoskie Plans to Give Away 300,000 Pairs in 2009," Laist, April 15, 2009, http://laist.com/2009/04/15/what_happens_when_you_travel.php (accessed June 3, 2011); TOMS Webpage, www.toms.com/ (accessed June 3, 2011).

29 TOMS Webpage, www.toms.com/ (accessed June 9, 2011).

30 *TOMS One for One Giving Report*, http://images.toms.com/media/content/images/giving-report/TOMS-Giving-Report-2010.pdf (accessed June 3, 2011).

31 Emily Lerman, "PhiLAnthropist Interview: TOMS Shoes Founder Blake Mycoskie Plans to Give Away 300,000 Pairs in 2009," Laist, April 15, 2009, http://laist.com/2009/04/15/what_happens_when_you_travel.php (accessed June 3, 2011).

32 Emily Lerman, "PhiLAnthropist Interview: TOMS Shoes Founder Blake Mycoskie Plans to Give Away 300,000 Pairs in 2009," Laist, April 15, 2009, http://laist.com/2009/04/15/what_happens_when_you_travel.php (accessed June 3, 2011); "Don't Be An Intern At TOMS," TOMS, www.toms.com/our-movement/intern (accessed June 9, 2011).

33 Booth Moore, "Toms Shoes' model is sell a pair, give a pair away," *Los Angeles Times*, April 19, 2009, http://www.latimes.com/features/image/la-ig-greentoms19–2009apr19,0,3694310.story (accessed June 9, 2011); Emily Lerman, "PhiLAnthropist Interview: TOMS Shoes Founder Blake Mycoskie Plans to Give Away 300,000 Pairs in 2009," Laist, April 15, 2009, http://laist.com/2009/04/15/what_happens_when_you_travel.php (accessed June 3, 2011).

34 "Don't Be An Intern At TOMS," TOMS, http://www.toms.com/our-movement/intern (accessed June 9, 2011).

35 "About – TOMS Campus Clubs," TOMS Campus Clubs, www.tomscampusclubs.com/page/about-1 (accessed June 2, 2011); *TOMS Campus Club Program*, http://images.toms.com/media/content/images/campus-clubs-assets/TOMSCampushandbook_082510_International_final.pdf (accessed June 2, 2011).

36 "One Day Without Shoes," TOMS, www.onedaywithoutshoes.com/ (accessed June 3, 2011).

37 "Have Your Own Style Your Sole Party with TOMS," TOMS, www.toms.com/style-your-sole (accessed June 2, 2011).

38 *TOMS Campus Club Program*, http://images.toms.com/media/content/images/campus-clubs-assets/TOMSCampushandbook_082510_International_final.pdf (accessed June 2, 2011).

39 Emily Lerman, "PhiLAnthropist Interview: TOMS Shoes Founder Blake Mycoskie Plans to Give Away 300,000 Pairs in 2009," Laist, April 15, 2009, http://laist.com/2009/04/15/what_happens_when_you_travel.php (accessed June 3, 2011).

40 M.J. Prest, "The Other Shoe Drops," *Ethical Style*, March 26, 2009, http://ethicalstyle.com/issue-12/the-other-shoe-drops/ (accessed June 3, 2011).

41 Patrick Cole, "Toms Free Shoe Plan, Boosted by Clinton, Reaches Million Mark," *Bloomberg*, September 15, 2010, www.bloomberg.com/news/2010-09-16/toms-shoe-giveaway-for-kids-boosted-by-bill-clinton-reaches-million-mark.html (accessed June 2, 2011).

42 Patrick Cole, "Toms Free Shoe Plan, Boosted by Clinton, Reaches Million Mark," *Bloomberg*, September 15, 2010, www.bloomberg.com/news/2010-09-16/toms-shoe-giveaway-for-kids-boosted-by-bill-clinton-reaches-million-mark.html (accessed June 2, 2011).

43 Cathleen McGuigan, "Designed to Help: A Pair for You, A Pair for the Needy," *Newsweek*, October 19, 2007, (accessed June 3, 2011). www.newsweek.com/2007/10/18/toms-shoes-wins-design-award.html (accessed June 9, 2011); Stacy Perman, "Making a Do-Gooder's Business Model Work," *Bloomberg Businessweek*, January 23, 2009, http://www.businessweek.com/smallbiz/content/jan2009/sb20090123_264702.htm (accessed June 3, 2011).

44 "How We Give," TOMS, www.toms.com/how-we-give (accessed June 3, 2011).

45 World Clothes Line Website, www.worldclothesline.com/ (accessed June 3, 2011); Gretchen Fogelstrom, "Another Business Giving One for One!" Global Endeavors, April 13, 2011, http://global-endeavors.com/2011/04/13/another-business-going-one-for-one/ (accessed June 3, 2011).

46 Kelsey Timmerman, "The problem with TOMS shoes & its critics," http://whereamiwearing.com/2011/04/06/toms-shoes/ (accessed June 3, 2011).

47 M.J. Prest, "The Other Shoe Drops," Ethical Style, March 26, 2009, http://ethicalstyle.com/issue-12/the-other-shoe-drops/ (accessed June 3, 2011).

48 Jeff Rosenthal, "Products with Purpose Will Change the World," *Huffington Post*, January 27, 2010, www.huffingtonpost.com/jeff-rosenthal/products-with-purpose-wil_b_437917.html (accessed June 3, 2011).

22 Cadbury's chocolate bars: not such a sweet smell of success?

1 This case was prepared by Professor Andrea Prothero of University College Dublin for classroom discussion rather than to illustrate either effective or ineffective handling of an administrative, ethical, or legal decision by individuals or management.

2 The sponsorship deal of £5 million was the highest for a television show outside the USA. By the end of 2006 the company had terminated its sponsorship of Coronation Street (LAB, 2009, "Cadbury's Social Media Success Story (Part 1), www.mrlukeabbott.com/marketing/cadburys-social-media-success-story-part-1/ (accessed online May 19, 2011).

3 The affected products accounted for less than one-half percent of total group sales for Cadbury's Schweppes.

4 Walsh F., 2006, "Product Recall Costs Cadbury £20m", *The Guardian*, August 2, www.guardian.co.uk/business/2006/aug/02/food.foodanddrink (accessed online May 19, 2011).

5 Naughton, P., 2006, "Cadbury's Recalls 1m Chocolate Bars in Salmonella Alert", *Times Online*, June 23, http://business.timesonline.co.uk/tol/business/industry_sectors/consumer_goods/article1083755.ece (accessed May 19, 2011).

6 Derbyshire D., 2006, "Salmonella Scare Hits Cadbury's Chocolate", *The Telegraph*, June 30, www.telegraph.co.uk/news/uknews/1522153/Salmonella-scare-hits-Cadburys-chocolate.html (accessed online May 19, 2011).

7 Hickman, M. (2007), "Cadbury Fined £1m After Last Summer's Salmonella Outbreak", July 17, *The Independent*, www.independent.co.uk/news/business/news/cadbury-fined-1631m-after-last-summers-salmonella-outbreak-457599.html (accessed online May 19, 2011).

8 Environmental Health News 2008, "Cadbury 'Slow on Salmonella'", June 27, www.cieh.org/ehn/ehn3.aspx?id=12730 (accessed online May 19, 2011).

9 Herman M. and D. Jordan (2007), "Cadbury Fined £1m Over Salmonella Outbreak", *The TimesOnline*, July 16, http://business.timesonline.co.uk/tol/business/industry_sectors/consumer_goods/article2083030.ece (accessed online May 19, 2011).

10 Ochman B.L., 2006, "Cadbury's Goes For Total Message Control in Product Recall, June 23, www.whatsnextblog.com/2006/06/cadbury_goes_for_total_message_control_in_product_recall/ (accessed online May 19, 2011).

11 Hobson N., 2006, "Cadbury Product Recall Needs Two-Way Dialogue", June 24, www.nevillehobson.com/2006/06/24/cadbury-product-recall-needs-two-way-dialogue/ (accessed online May 19, 2011).

12 Hobson N., 2006, ibid.

13 R. Murray-West and C. Muspratt 2006, "Salmonella Scare to Cost Cadbury £20m", August 3, www.telegraph.co.uk/news/uknews/1525448/Salmonella-scare-to-cost-Cadbury-20m.html (accessed online May 19, 2011).

14 *Birmingham Post*, 2007, "Cadbury's Prestige Rank Soured By Salmonella Outbreak", October 22, http://asq.org/qualitynews/qnt/execute/displaySetup?newsID=2307 (accessed online May 19, 2011).

15 Cadbury's *Glass and A Half Full* marketing communications campaign was launched in 2007.

23 Caterpillar, Inc.

1 This case was prepared by Jennifer Sawayda, Ethan Fairy, and Matt Yepez for and under the direction of Professors Patrick Murphy, O.C. Ferrell, and Linda Ferrell. It was prepared for classroom discussion rather than to illustrate either effective or ineffective handling of an administrative, ethical, or legal decision by management. All sources used for this case were obtained through publicly available material.

2 *Caterpillar / 2010 Year In Review*, www.caterpillar.com/cda/files/2616640/7/images/FullReport.pdf (accessed May 25, 2011); "Products," CAT, www.cat.com/products/ (accessed May 25, 2011). "Offices & Facilities," Caterpillar, www.caterpillar.com/company/offices-and-facilities (accessed May 25, 2011).

3 "History," Caterpillar, www.caterpillar.com/company/history (accessed May 24, 2011); "Caterpillar Inc. (CAT)," Yahoo! Finance, http://finance.yahoo.com/q/pr?s=CAT+Profile (accessed May 24, 2011); "Caterpillar Inc." Funding Universe, www.fundinguniverse.com/company-histories/Caterpillar-Inc-Company-History.html (accessed April 23, 2011); "Caterpillar," Business Insider, www.businessinsider.com/blackboard/caterpillar (accessed May 24, 2011); "CATERPILLAR INC (CAT: New York)," *Bloomberg Businessweek,* http://investing.businessweek.com/research/stocks/snapshot/snapshot.asp?ticker=CAT:US (accessed May 24, 2011).

4 "CAT," Caterpillar, www.caterpillar.com/brands/cat (accessed May 25, 2011).

5 "Caterpillar Inc.," Morningstar, http://financials.morningstar.com/competitors/industry-peer.action?t=CAT&region=USA&culture=en_US (accessed May 27, 2011); "Deere to Build $50M Equipment Plant in China," Manufacturing.net, December 15, 2010, www.manufacturing.net/News/2010/12/Facilities-Operations-Deere-To-Build – 50M-Equipment-Plant-In-China/ (accessed May 27, 2011); "Equipment," CAT, http://www.cat.com/equipment (accessed May 24, 2011).; Adam Fleck, "Japanese Disaster Could Offer an Opening for U.S. Construction Equipment Firms," thestar.com, March 18, 2011, http://torontostar.morningstar.ca/globalhome/industry/news.asp?articleid=374231 (accessed May 27, 2011).

6 "The 2011 World's Most Ethical Companies," *Ethisphere*, Q1 2011, 37–43; "Awards and Recognition," Caterpillar, www.caterpillar.com/careers/why-caterpillar/diversity/awards-and-recognition (accessed May 24, 2011).

7 "Enterprise Strategy," Caterpillar, www.caterpillar.com/cda/files/2530634/7/2010%2BCorp.%2BStrategy%2Bhandout_AEXQ0534_English.pdf (accessed May 24, 2011).

8 "Caterpillar Production Systems (CPS)," Caterpillar Marine Power Systems, http://marine.cat.com/cda/components/fullArticle?m=233421&x=7&id=966559 (accessed May 24, 2011).

9 "Caterpillar Safety," SAFETY.CAT.COM, http://safety.cat.com/ (accessed April 23, 2011).

10 Associated Press, "In Bid to Resume Talks, Caterpillar Stages Lockout," *Los Angeles Times,* November 8, 1991, http://articles.latimes.com/1991-11-08/business/fi-939_1_caterpillar-management (accessed May 24, 2011); "U.A.W. Members Back Contract With Caterpillar, First Since '91," *The New York Times*, March 23, 1998, www.nytimes.com/1998/03/23/us/uaw-members-back-contract-with-caterpillar-first-since-91.html (accessed May 24, 2011); Jonathon P. Hicks, "Union Agrees To End Strike At Caterpillar," *The New York Times,* April 15, 1992, www.nytimes.com/1992/04/15/us/union-agrees-to-end-strike-at-caterpillar.html (accessed May 24, 2011).

11 "Awards and Recognition," Caterpillar, www.caterpillar.com/careers/why-caterpillar/diversity/awards-and-recognition (accessed May 24, 2011); "Employee Affinity Groups," Caterpillar, www.caterpillar.com/careers/why-caterpillar/diversity/employee-affinity-groups (accessed May 24, 2011).

12 Caterpillar, *2010 Sustainability Report*, www.caterpillar.com/cda/files/2646184/7/2010SustainabilityReport.pdf (accessed April 30, 2011).

13 O.C. Ferrell, John Fraedrich, and Linda Ferrell, *Business Ethics: Ethical Decision Making and Cases*, 8th ed. (Mason, OH: South-Western Cengage Learning, 2011), 38, 248.

14 "Success Stories," *Caterpillar Foundation*, www.caterpillar.com/sustainability/caterpillar-foundation/success-stories (accessed April 23, 2011); "Caterpillar Update on Impact of Crisis in Japan," WGGB abc40/Fox 6," March 18, 2011, www.wggb.com/Global/story.asp?S=14277180&clienttype=printable (accessed May 24, 2011); America's Most Generous Corporate Foundations," *Bloomberg Businessweek,* http://images.businessweek.com/ss/10/01/0114_most_generous_corporate_foundations/20.htm (accessed April 23, 2011).

15 Paul Gordon, "Caterpillar tops Komen's donor list," pjstar.com, March 9, 2011, www.pjstar.com/business/x698035485/Caterpillar-pledges-2M-to-fight-breast-cancer (accessed May 24, 2011).

16 "Matching Gifts Program," *Caterpillar Foundation*, www.caterpillar.com/sustainability/caterpillar-foundation/matching-gifts-program (accessed April 23, 2011).

17 Stephanie Lulay, "'Superheroes' honored at United Way breakfast," *The Beacon-News*, May 21, 2011, http://beaconnews.suntimes.com/5468684-417/superheroes-honored-at-united-way-breakfast.html (accessed May 24, 2011).

18 "Certified Rebuild," *2010 Sustainability Report*, www.caterpillar.com/cda/layout?m=389975&x=7&ids=2646281 (accessed April 23, 2011).

19 Caterpillar, *2010 Sustainability Report*, www.caterpillar.com/cda/files/2646184/7/2010SustainabilityReport.pdf (accessed April 30, 2011).

20 Ibid.

21 Paul Gordon, "UAW ratifies new six-year contract with Caterpillar Inc.," pjstar.com, March 6, 2011, www.pjstar.com/business/x1512121718/UAW-voting-on-contract-with-Caterpillar-leader-support-ratification (accessed June 7, 2011).

22 "Clean Air Villain of the Month," Clean Air Trust, www.cleanairtrust.org/villain.0800.html (accessed April 23, 2011).

23 "Parts and Catalogs / Caterpillar Parts / Caterpillar Construction Machinery Parts," AGA Truck Parts, www.aga-parts.com/caterpillar-parts.shtml (accessed May 24, 2011); *Caterpillar | 2010 Year In Review*, www.caterpillar.com/cda/files/2616640/7/images/FullReport.pdf (accessed May 25, 2011).

24 "Caterpillar and Human Rights in Israel," University of Wisconsin, www.wisconsin.edu/tfunds/Caterpillar2004.htm (accessed May 27, 2011). "Caterpillar Should Suspend Bulldozer Sales," Human Rights Watch, www.hrw.org/en/news/2004/11/21/israel-caterpillar-should-suspend-bulldozer-sales (accessed April 23, 2011).

Index